These study notes take us to the heart of the meaning of this Gospel.

Canon John Chapman, Sydney

The art of simplification is not an easy one, but here it is at its best, and put to excellent use. This book is designed to help serious readers come to terms with what John's Gospel actually says, even though they have no background in reading the Bible. While encouraging readers to follow the line of thought in this Gospel, above all it encourages them to think clearly about who Jesus is. I strongly recommend it.

Professor Don Carson,
Trinity Evangelical Divinity School, Deerfield, Illinois

Read Mark Learn has taught hundreds of us over the years to know our Bibles and our God better. I am delighted that this paperback will open up John's Gospel for many more.

Rev. Hugh Palmer,
All Souls, Langham Place, London

Dear Reader,

The Lord used this book, & most importantly his Word to bring me back to Himself when my life became darkest. I pray the Lord also brings you, too.

Grace & Peace,

L. B.

Read Mark Learn

John's Gospel

St Helen's Church, Bishopsgate

ST HELEN'S
MEDIA

CHRISTIAN
FOCUS

© 1999 St Helen's Church, Bishopsgate

ISBN 978-1-84550-361-1

First published in Great Britain in 1999
by Marshall Pickering
Republished in 2008 and 2010
by
Christian Focus Publications Ltd.,
Geanies House, Fearn, Tain Ross-shire,
Scotland IV20 1TW, UK

www.christianfocus.com

Cover design by Paul Lewis
Printed by Norhaven A/S, Denmark

Contents

Foreword

The Read Mark Learn Bible studies at St Helen's have for very many years been central to our training programme for young Christians. I regard RML, as it is called, as one of the most significant initiatives ever taken in our church life together.

From the beginning, with the Mark studies, and now with these John notes prepared by my able successor, William Taylor, this material for group work has proved itself in the equipping of countless men and women for effective Christian witness.

I remain full of admiration for the staff and leaders who have made this course what it is by their labour, and I am profoundly grateful that, for many hundreds of people, attendance at RML has been the start of a growing love for the accurate study and the businesslike application of God's holy word.

Dick Lucas
Rector Emeritus of St Helen's

Introducing
'Read Mark Learn'

Blessed Lord, who has caused all holy Scriptures to be written for our learning: Grant that we may in such wise hear them, read, mark, learn, and inwardly digest them, that by patience and comfort of thy holy Word, we may embrace and ever hold fast the blessed hope of everlasting life, which thou hast given us in our Saviour Jesus Christ. Amen.

(Collect for the Second Sunday in Advent
in the Book of Common Prayer)

BEGINNINGS

Read Mark Learn is the title of a collection of small group Bible studies which has been developed, over a number of years, at St Helen's Church, Bishopsgate, in the City of London.

The original studies, undertaken for the first time in 1976, covered the whole of Mark's Gospel in one year. In subsequent years, studies in Paul's letter to the Romans were devised for those who had previously studied Mark; the aim was to provide a thorough training in Christian doctrine. Finally, a third-year study was established, consisting of a complete overview of the Bible. Thus, over three years, members of the church have the opportunity of gaining a firm grasp of how to read and understand the Bible. They are firmly grounded in Christian doctrine and practice from the scriptures, and so they are equipped for a lifetime in the service of Christ.

After some years it was felt that a change was needed, and so material for studies in John's Gospel was written. As with Mark and Romans, this material was written primarily for the leaders of small groups, to help them prepare, but it may, of course, be useful to any individual undertaking a study of John.

In all the Read Mark Learn studies there is a commitment to consecutive Bible study, with Bible passages being studied within the context of the scriptural whole. This is based on the conviction that when God's word is studied *in context*, God's voice is heard as His Holy Spirit speaks.

PRESENT ARRANGEMENTS

The format that we have found to work well is to have a pair of leaders for each small group, with eight to ten members in the group. The leaders are responsible for all the teaching over a period of three terms, each term running for about nine weeks.

Every member is expected to prepare for a study by reading the text carefully – there is no substitute for close and careful study of the text – and considering the discussion questions that have been handed out in advance. The leaders will do this preparation both individually and as a group, meeting together a week or so in advance of the study and using the study notes in this book. With the help of the suggested discussion questions, we study the passage that we will later teach. A key aspect of the leaders' preparation group is the time set aside for praying for each other and for the members of our groups.

TRAINING FOR LEADERS

We have found this preparation group to be a very helpful way of providing training for leaders, of supporting them in their ministry of leadership, and also, of course, of developing our understanding of the overall message of the book we are working on. In addition, there has been the long-term value of training people to lead house groups in the future.

The strength of Read Mark Learn depends, in human terms, upon the calibre of the leaders. Without the leaders' considerable degree of commitment – as indicated above – the whole enterprise would fail. And so a high priority is given to training and encouraging leaders on a continuing basis. Information on RML Leaders' Training Material may be found at the back of this book.

Introducing the Study Notes

These notes were written during the first three years of our studying John's Gospel as an RML study. They are the result of our studying the passages in groups, feeding back, and together correcting and revising our understanding. (This process of sharpening our understanding and our application of the message of John's Gospel is a continuous one, and we anticipate considerable revision following publication of this first set of notes!)

The notes are not intended to be a formal commentary on the Gospel; rather, the aim is to provide useful pointers to the main themes of each passage, and to show how these themes fit in with John's wider purpose in writing his Gospel. For more detailed comment we have found Don Carson's commentary *The Gospel According to John* to be the most helpful source.

STUDY PASSAGES

It will be noted that some of the earlier studies are quite long. The study divisions were made in accordance with Carson's helpful advice in the chapter on 'Preaching from the fourth Gospel' (pp. 100–103). Carson makes the useful point that since John's vision is more narrowly focused than that of the Synoptic writers, the preacher should 'proceed at a good pace through the text' to pick up the main points and to focus on Jesus Christ, thus avoiding both 'vain repetition' and a 'man-centred' interpretation.

John will frequently deal with just one main subject in an extended narrative passage. In studying these longer narrative passages we have found ourselves disciplined into concentrating on the one main point, rather than seeking to read significance into the details of the narrative which may, or may not, have been intended.

Bible study leaders, however, may feel that some of the studies are too long for their groups. If this is the case there are two possibilities. One is simply to split the study – but beware the temptation to speculate on the narrative details, which may simply be matters of historical record without any intended deeper significance. The other is to select the core part of the passage and summarise the surrounding material. (Some of our RML leaders do this to good effect.)

Section notes

John's Gospel has three major sections, each with a distinct point to make. Like all the NT (New Testament) writers, John has carefully structured his material in order to drive home his main points. In the notes each section is given a summary, and then there are notes on the main themes covered in that section.

Study notes

Each study has the following headings:

Context: How the passage being studied fits in with the wider context of the whole Gospel.

Structure: How the text of the passage may be broken down into smaller parts. The main point of each part is stated and from the titles it should be apparent how each part relates to the overall main point of the passage.

Old Testament background: John's Gospel, written against the backdrop of the Old Testament, contains many Old Testament ideas and concepts that John assumes we will understand. Here the most important ones are introduced.

Text notes: A brief commentary on the passage. More difficult verses are touched on, but the main aim is to see how John develops the main ideas.

Key themes: A succinct summary of the key ideas raised in the passage. The ideas are grouped by theme, and are not necessarily in the order in which they occur in the passage.

Application: One of the greatest errors in application is to apply the passage to ourselves immediately, without first thinking about the application that was intended for its first readers. The aim here is to identify the intended application then before driving that application through to the reader now.

Aim: The main point of the passage is taken as the aim of the study. The Bible study leader should enter the study itself with a clear aim and this aim ought to correspond to the main thrust of the passage.

Suggested questions: Suggested questions for leaders to use in the group study. They are only suggestions. They have been tried and tested on RML groups, but Bible study leaders will need to adapt them to suit their own groups. In addition to these questions, which leaders use to help them lead, there are preparation questions to help all members study the passage before coming to the group, and these may be found at the back of the book.

Introducing John's Gospel

THE AIM OF THIS STUDY

Almost at the end of his account of the life, death and resurrection of Jesus, John presents his readers with his aim:

> Jesus did many other miraculous signs in the presence of his disciples, which are not recorded in this book. But these are written that you may believe that Jesus is the Christ, the Son of God, and that by believing you may have life in his name.
>
> John 20:30, 31

Everything that John has recorded contributes to his purpose, that of convincing his readers about the identity of Jesus Christ, and about the necessity of a right response to Him in order to have life. As we read the Gospel, therefore, it is important to keep asking three main questions:

- ✤ How does this passage enable us to believe that Jesus is the Christ, the Son of God?
- ✤ What does it mean to 'have life' in His name?
- ✤ What does a right response of belief in Him look like?

Each passage should be approached in this manner, with questions such as the following: What does this teach about Christ? What sort of 'Christ' is He? What does it mean to have life? What is a genuine and right response to this Christ?

AN OVERVIEW

The best way to get started in John's Gospel is to read it! Set aside some time when you can read the whole book at one sitting. Read fairly rapidly, trying to get a feel for the book as a whole: the main themes, the structure, the language. The point of this exercise is to take in the big picture, so don't worry about understanding all the details at this stage. At the end, note down your first impressions. If you struggle to make mental notes, jot down a few very brief comments with references as you read, but don't lose your momentum.

THE STRUCTURE

In chapter 16 verse 28 Jesus makes an astonishing statement: 'I came from the Father and entered the world; now I am leaving the world and going back to the Father.' This statement summarises the two halves of the Gospel. In part one (chs. 1–10) Jesus describes Himself as the Christ and the Son who has come from His Father in heaven to reveal His Father. In part two (chs. 11–21) Jesus describes Himself as the Son who is returning to His Father in heaven to open the way to His Father. Elements of the main subject material of each part may also be found in the other part of the Gospel, but this division into two parts provides a useful structure.

This two-part division is further underlined by John's arrangement of his material around the 'signs'. As stated in chapter 20 verse 31, John deliberately selects a number of key 'signs' or 'miracles'. The signs are significant events – each one has a teaching point or meaning – and the sign's significance is pointed out by Jesus in the teaching that comes either just before a sign or just after it. So, the significance of changing the water into wine (ch. 2) is explained to us in verse 11 and also in the narrative of chapters 2–4; and the significance of the healing of the lame man (ch. 5) is made evident in the words of Jesus to the Jews later in the chapter.

John uses these signs in the Gospel to structure his material. The signs act as brackets, both introducing and concluding sections of teaching material; the material in between the signs expands on the themes that the signs introduce and also sum up.

The structure of the Gospel, therefore, may be summarised as follows:

PART ONE CHAPTERS 1–10

Jesus is the Son who has come down from heaven to reveal His Father

Chapter 1

Introduction: the everlasting Word, the long-awaited King

Chapters 2:1–4:54

Jesus is the Christ, come from His Father to His people to bring life (the two signs at Cana bracket this material)

Chapters 5:1–10:42

Jesus is the Son, come from His Father, who is rejected by His people but who continues to offer life (the two healings on the Sabbath bracket this material)

PART TWO CHAPTERS 11–21

Jesus the Son and Christ is returning to heaven to open the way to His Father

Chapters 11:1–20:31

What Jesus' death has achieved: Life! (the two resurrection signs bracket this material)

Chapter 21

Conclusion: 'Feed My sheep!' (the unpaired sign leaves the book open and the reader looking forward)

John 1:1–18 God on earth!

CONTEXT

John states plainly the overall purpose of his Gospel in 20:31: 'these [things] are written that you may believe that Jesus is the Christ, the Son of God, and that by believing you may have life in His name.' The key themes of this Gospel, therefore, are these:

- ✤ An explanation of who Jesus is.
- ✤ An appeal to respond to Him.
- ✤ A description of the benefits of belonging to Him.

The first eighteen verses, known as 'The Prologue', act rather like an overture, introducing these themes and raising many of the other major recurring ideas. And so the context of the Prologue, it could be said, is provided by the next twenty-one chapters!

STRUCTURE

1:1–4 The nature of the Word.
1:5–13 The work of the Father:
   5–11   Revelation.
   11–13   Regeneration.
1:14–18 The achievement of the Word: God made known!

OLD TESTAMENT BACKGROUND

The Word: Old Testament background teaches us that God creates and rules by His word, reveals Himself by His word, and rescues and delivers by His word (Gen. 1; Deut. 5:24; Ps. 107:20). 'In short, God's "Word" in the Old Testament is His powerful self-expression in creation, revelation and salvation, and the personification of the "Word" makes it suitable for John to apply it as a title to God's ultimate self-disclosure, the person of His own Son.' (See Carson pp. 115–16.)

Life: Ever since Adam and Eve were banished from the Garden and from the Tree of Life at the Fall, the issue of life and death has been a major Old Testament theme. Isaiah speaks of the 'shroud (of death) that enfolds all people' (Isa. 25:6ff) and looks forward to a day when death will be swallowed up forever.

Dwelling: The literal translation of this word 'dwelling' is 'tabernacled' or 'pitched His tent'. Prior to the building of the temple, God 'dwelt among His people' in the tabernacle in the wilderness. Exodus 29:45–6 is a key Old Testament passage expressing a key Old Testament idea. God dwelling among His people was a fulfilment of His promise to Abraham in Genesis 17. What was said of the tabernacle in the wilderness became true of the temple in Jerusalem: God dwelt with His people as their Ruler and Rescuer. But the expectations and hopes of the Old Testament all met with disappointment, as the temple was overrun and the exile took place. Now, says John, the Word has 'made His dwelling among us'. The Old Testament promise has become a reality as the 'Word became flesh' (v. 14).

Glory: When Moses asks to see God's glory (Exod. 33:18) God passes in front of Moses and proclaims Himself to be compassionate and gracious, and also just and righteous (Exod. 34:4–7). In claiming to have 'seen his glory, the glory of the One and Only ... full of grace and truth', John is claiming to have seen what Moses saw, but more! He has seen the compassion and the justice of God in human flesh.

TEXT NOTES

1–4 THE NATURE OF THE WORD

The first five verses introduce the Word to us, telling us who He is and where He came from. He is divine (v. 1), He is eternal (v. 2), He is the Creator of all things, the source of our being (v. 3), and He is the source of spiritual life (v. 4).

This 'life' is the spiritual life that God gave to humankind at creation. On a second reading of the whole Gospel, the reader realises that this claim to be the source of life has deeper meaning: the Word is able to provide the life that, throughout the Old Testament, people had been seeking; ever since the Fall they had been crying out for it.

Many of these themes will be picked up and enlarged upon later. However, for now, we need to note that the Word is *part* of the Godhead – He is eternal, the Creator, the life-giver, in intimate union with God. He was God, and yet was *with* God; the Word by Himself does not make the Godhead. The relationship between God the Father and God the Son will be dealt with later (see ch. 5).

For now it is enough that we allow the full impact of the Word's identity to sink in to our minds.

5–13 THE WORK OF THE FATHER

5–11 Revelation. The theme of revelation and response is introduced with a shattering and shocking negative. In spite of the nature of the Word, who has been shining since the creation of the world, the dark world has failed to understand Him. This explains why John needs to write his Gospel. Quite remarkably, the Light who came to bring life was unrecognised and so was rejected by His very own (referring to the Jews).

But humankind's rejection of the Light is seen in the context of God's grace, His grace in making the Light known (vv. 5–9) and His grace in bringing people into His family (vv. 12, 13). The sentence structure of verses 5–9 also serves to emphasise God's grace: verses 5 and 9 make a pair, as do verses 6 and 8, so that verse 7, which states God's purpose in sending the Baptist, is central. The Baptist had been sent to testify to the Light so that we might believe. This statement of God's merciful revelation makes the rejection all the more shocking.

The world failed to recognise Him and even 'His own' refused to receive (literally 'take hold of') Him. 'World' here, as in the rest of John, refers to God's created order – especially human beings in rebellion against the Creator. Again, this is explained in far greater depth later in chapter 3 and beyond. For now, the scandal of the world's rejection of its Creator, ruler and sustainer should make an impact upon us. The shock is that the world has rejected the true Light, who alone is able to bring life and therefore 'light' (see verse 5) to its darkness.

By telling the reader about people's response to the Word, John prepares us for the shock of Jesus' rejection. However, the fact that 'the world' and 'His own' reject Him should not deter us from belief, for God's purpose in sending the Word is regeneration.

12–13 Regeneration. With the arresting word 'yet' John now focuses our attention on God's purpose in sending the Word, and in doing so further highlights God's grace and mercy.

The Greek word for 'right' is a very strong word which implies absolute power and certainty. Those who believe and receive, therefore, are given the immediate and absolute right to belong to God. This is not something that happens naturally, for naturally we do not understand the light; rather it is by God's action. Membership of God's family is not by genetic inheritance, nor by an individual working it out, not even by parents deciding. This fact is both an encouragement to those who are not 'His own' (i.e. non-Jews), since membership of God's family is dependent upon His action and not upon racial descent, and also a warning to those who *are* 'His own', that they should not take their membership of God's family for granted. God's initiative and God's grace are pre-eminent in this paragraph.

14–18 THE ACHIEVEMENT OF THE WORD: GOD MADE KNOWN!

There is a strong theme of witness in these verses, which emphasises the major issue of what the Word has achieved. He has become flesh and thus made God known. This 'making God known' is the fulfilment of all that the Old Testament pointed to.

Verse 14 is a bombshell verse! This Word has 'tabernacled' amongst us: the promises made in Genesis 17 have been realised in a person (see Old Testament notes), and God's glory has been seen in a human.

The nature of this Word made flesh is that He is full of grace and truth. This means that the apostle has witnessed the glory, grace and truth of God that Moses only glimpsed. And so from the fullness of Jesus' grace (v. 16) the apostles have received blessing that even exceeds the blessing given to Moses, for the grace and truth that the law pointed to has arrived in Jesus Christ (v. 17). The Baptist's witness, 'He was before me' (v. 15), emphasises this fulfilment theme by reminding us of the Word's eternal nature (cf. vv. 1–5).

The passage reaches its conclusion in verse 18 where John draws the threads together and explains that, for the first time in the history of the universe, God has been fully revealed by the One who is in intimate union with Him. Note the negative. No-one has ever seen God – there is no claim to have seen God face to face in any other religion (see Exod. 33:19–23). Now He is knowable through 'the One and Only who ... has made Him known.'

Key themes

The central point that John wants to get across, as he explains his reasons for writing, is that God has now made Himself known by the entry of Jesus Christ, His eternal Word, into the world. His purpose is to bring life to men and women, but their natural response is to reject Him.

- ✤ *The nature of the Word:* Jesus is both God and man. As God He is distinguishable as a separate part of the Godhead. He is the One who is eternal, who made us and now sustains us, and who enables us to see divine reality. As man He is fully human – 'He became flesh'.
- ✤ *The nature of human response:*
  - ↘ Since God has mercifully and graciously provided clear testimony as to who Jesus is, through the Baptist and the apostles, Jesus should be listened to!

↘ Yet, despite His nature and His ability to give the 'life' that the Old Testament cries out for, the 'Word' has largely been rejected by the world, and even by His own people, the Jews.

↘ A positive response to Jesus is possible only through divine action, but it leads to membership of God's family and the receiving of grace, truth and the blessings of eternal life.

APPLICATION

Many of us still secretly carry around mental images of Jesus as 'gentle Jesus meek and mild' – the young man holding a lamb in his arms, with a dove on his shoulder and standing in a field of flowers – Jesus the New Age Traveller!

This passage should make us *aware* of how awesome He is; *shocked* that He is largely rejected by His creation; *conscious* of our own inability to recognise Him and of our natural rebelliousness against Him; *alert* to the eternal effect of our decisions regarding Him; *humbled* in the knowledge that it is God's work to bring us to recognise Him; *confident* that what we read in John about Jesus is reliable, and *hungry* to know this God who has revealed Himself in human flesh in human history.

THE AIM OF THIS STUDY

To see that, as promised, God has made Himself known in the divine person of His Son, with the express purpose of calling together His children.

SUGGESTED QUESTIONS

1–4 THE NATURE OF THE WORD

Fill out the following CV for the character introduced by John: name, date of birth, title, address, previous work experience, strengths ... any other headings.

↘ How does the sentence structure of verses 1–2 work to force John's point home?

↘ Why doesn't John just say, 'Jesus is God'?

↘ What does John achieve by including the negative in verse 3?

✤ Christians often call Jesus their 'friend'. How does such a statement sit alongside these verses? How do these verses alone change the way *you* think about Jesus?

5–13 THE WORK OF THE FATHER

✤ What is the main subject of these verses?

✤ What different things do these verses tell us about what God has done?

↘ If you had to draw up a character reference for God and for humanity from these verses, what would you want to say?

↘ How do these verses change the way you think about God, and the way you think about men and women?

↘ verses 12–13 are often used to encourage Christians to be confident, humble, and excited. How do they achieve these three things?

✤ Why do you think John included this paragraph in the introduction to his Gospel?

14–18 THE ACHIEVEMENT OF THE WORD: GOD MADE KNOWN!

✤ verse 18 contains both a negative and a positive. How do they challenge modern understanding of God and man?

✤ In what ways do verses 14–17 show Jesus Christ achieving what the Old Testament pointed towards? (*Take a sheet of paper and divide it into two columns, one containing Old Testament ideas and the other showing their fulfilment in Jesus. You may need to explain the significance of 'glory', 'dwelling', 'grace' and 'truth'. Use a simple summary such as in 'Old Testament background'.*)

✤ So why do you think John included verses 14–17 in his Prologue?

✤ How does the Prologue serve John's aim in 20:31?

APPLICATION

✤ The subject of these first eighteen verses is clearly Jesus. But what have these verses taught us about God the Father? How might this affect the way we relate to Him?

✤ There are at least seven negatives in the first eighteen verses. How do they help us in our understanding both of ourselves and of our apathetic or anti-Christian friends?

    ↘ What implications does this passage have for our evangelism?

✤ The aim of John's Gospel is that 'we might believe that Jesus is the Christ and so have life in His name.' How has this passage helped you in this way?

✤ What single most important thing have you learned in today's study?

    ↘ How will it affect you this year? Write it down and take it away to pray about this week.

S T U D Y 2

John 1:19–51

'We have found the Messiah!'

CONTEXT

The claim in John's Prologue, that 'the One and Only has made Him known', leaves the reader thinking, 'Can this really be so? Show me!' In this passage we see Jesus coming to a waiting people as the Messiah promised in the Old Testament. The links to the pre-existent Word are unmistakable – 'the Word became flesh'.

STRUCTURE

1:19–34 'I have seen! Look!' The Baptist prepares the way.
1:35–51 'We have found!' The disciples begin to follow ... but much more awaits.

OLD TESTAMENT BACKGROUND

The Old Testament background is more than usually important in this passage, where John's aim is to show Jesus arriving as the long-awaited Messiah.

'Make straight the way for the Lord': Chapters 40–66 of Isaiah are full of promises to the exiled people of God that their period of exile will not go on for ever. There will be a time of rescue when God will come and lead His people home. God the Rescuer will come in the form of a triumphant conqueror who is also a suffering servant.

29

When He comes His glory will be revealed and He will establish a great new Jerusalem at the centre of a new heaven and a new earth. This glorious future, promised to God's people by Isaiah, had never been fully realised. When John the Baptist comes and announces himself as 'the voice calling in the desert', he is heralding the fulfilment of God's rescue plan through the arrival of God's Rescuer.

The Lamb of God: There are a number of suggestions as to precisely which Old Testament idea this phrase refers to. The most likely answer is that John the Baptist has in mind both the Passover lamb of Exodus 12 and the 'Servant' of Isaiah 53.

The Passover lamb was a substitutionary sacrifice which averted the judgment of God from His people on the night when they were redeemed from slavery in Egypt: the blood of the slaughtered lamb was to be put on the door-frame of the Israelites' houses, so that as the Lord went through the land to strike down the Egyptian first-born, He would see the blood and 'pass over' those houses.

The 'Servant' of Isaiah 53 is described as dying an atoning death 'like a lamb' (v. 7). His death is a 'guilt offering' (v. 10). He takes the punishment on behalf of guilty sinners in order to deal with the problem of sin. His death brings peace (between sinners and an utterly holy God), healing (from sin), and the removal of iniquity (vv. 5–6). Jesus is identified by the Baptist as the one who will deal once and for all with the problem of sin.

The Spirit came down: In the book of Judges and the two books of Samuel there are descriptions of God's Spirit coming down on Israel's judges and kings (Judg. 3:9–10; 6:34; 11:29; 1 Sam. 10:6; 16:13). The difference with this king, Jesus, is that the Spirit *remains* on Him (v. 32). In Isaiah 42:1 we see that God's Servant will also have the Spirit 'resting on Him'. Thus the coming of the Spirit on Jesus points to the fulfilment of these two great Old Testament themes: He is the King who will rule forever and the Servant who will die for sin.

He will baptise with the Holy Spirit. The prophets promised a time when God's people would have their sin dealt with and would be moved to follow His decrees. At this time they would be able to be

God's people with God in their midst – the covenant people of God. The coming of God's Spirit would make this possible (Ezek. 6:27).

Christ/Messiah/Son of God: These are titles for God's anointed ruler and king, whose coming is foretold in the Old Testament. He is the one through whom God will rule His people forever. (See 2 Sam. 7:11b-16; Isa. 9:6–7.)

The one Moses wrote about/The Prophet: Through Moses God had promised to send His people another 'prophet like you' (Moses). 'The Prophet' in verse 21 refers to this expected figure. (See Deut. 18:18–20.)

Jacob's dream: With the words 'and the angels of God ascending and descending', Jesus' hearers would have been reminded of the account in Genesis 28:12 of Jacob's dream. God's covenant with Jacob, in that dream, marked him as the one through whom, and through whose offspring, 'all peoples on earth will be blessed'. In making a parallel between Jacob and Himself, Jesus is claiming to be the Messiah, the One through whom God will bless all peoples on earth.

The Son of Man: This is an Old Testament title that Jesus uses to refer to Himself. In the Old Testament the Son of Man is the one who will be God's everlasting ruler after the final judgment (Dan. 7:13–14).

Text notes

19-34 'I HAVE SEEN! LOOK!'

The Baptist's witness is summarised in verse 34. He is here to identify the Son of God for us.

19–23 He is the coming one. John caused quite a stir, and a special delegation of priests and Levites was sent from Jerusalem to find out who he was. This is important to us because it shows us both that the Baptist was recognised as someone special and that the Jewish rulers themselves were expecting a messianic figure. They are concerned about the Baptist's identity. In reply he quotes Isaiah 40:3, preparing them, and us, for the arrival of one far greater.

24–28 He is here! He is greater. A second interview takes place, this time with some Pharisees – again, a special delegation who had 'been sent'. They are concerned about the meaning of John's baptism.

John doesn't answer the question immediately but again points away from himself to one far greater who 'is here' already.

29–34 This is God's Son. The Baptist points to Jesus, identifying Him and also explaining what He will do: Jesus is the sacrificial Lamb who will solve the problem of sin (see Old Testament notes). The whole purpose of the Baptist's ministry is to reveal God's pre-existent Lamb. The divine word and the divine sign (v. 33) enable the Baptist to appreciate just who Jesus is (see Old Testament notes), the Son of God. The Baptist's repeated statement 'I myself did not know him ...' reminds us of God's determination to make Himself known, and also assures us that this really is God's Son because God Himself witnesses to Him. The Spirit has come on Jesus both as Servant and as King, and so He will fulfil all that is anticipated by these two Old Testament 'types' as He deals with His people's sin.

To understand what is meant by Jesus baptising with the Holy Spirit, it is essential to understand the Old Testament context. Later in the Gospel (14:16,26) John records Jesus' promise that the Holy Spirit will come to His disciples, the promise that was fulfilled on the day of Pentecost (Acts 2).

35–51 'WE HAVE FOUND!'

The point of this passage is to take us from the witness of John to the call of Jesus. Jesus is the one John promised.

35–42 Look at Him! You must follow! A second time the Baptist announces Jesus by pointing to His sacrificial ministry. Andrew listens to the Baptist and follows Jesus. His response is to announce the discovery of the Messiah. In coming to Jesus Peter finds one whose ministry supersedes the Baptist's ministry, for Jesus' divine knowledge enables Him to know Peter so thoroughly that He knows what he will become.

43–50 Follow me! You will see! Jesus now takes centre stage. Once again the focus is on His identity. He is 'the one Moses wrote about in the Law, and about whom the prophets also wrote'; He is 'the Son of God ... the King of Israel', and the 'stairway' to heaven (v. 51 refers to Jacob's dream, in Gen. 28:12; see Old Testament notes). The point is that the disciples are now able to identify Him for themselves when He calls them. They are then able to pass on the invitation: 'Come and see' and 'We have found.' The Baptist has now faded from view and Jesus is prominent.

The striking difference between Jesus and the Baptist is again evident in Jesus' call to Philip – 'Follow me!' – and His knowledge of Nathanael. Jesus knows him through and through, and knows exactly what Nathanael was doing. Nathanael is convinced by Philip's witness and Jesus' divine knowledge. He is a true Israelite, recognising the true King of Israel – 1:12,31. The Baptist's function (1:6–8) has now been achieved.

Verse 51. This verse provides us with a link into the rest of the book. The 'you' is plural, so it is the disciples who are promised the sight of 'greater things'. When Jacob had his dream (see Gen. 28:12) the substance of the revelation was that God's covenant with Abraham was now being made with Jacob also. God had promised Abraham that He would reverse the effects of the Fall through Abraham's offspring. All peoples would be blessed through him, God would be with him and would establish him and his people in the land.

For Jacob it was only a dream! Now the disciples are being told that they will see the reality for themselves. Instead of the angels ascending and descending on a stairway to Jacob, they are to ascend and descend on Jesus. He (the Son of Man) will supersede Jacob as the centre and source of God's purposes for His covenant people. As we move into chapters 2 and 3 we shall see Jesus saying that *He* is the 'house of God', whereas Jacob had said '*this* is the house of God', and Jesus claiming that *He* is the way to heaven, whereas Jacob had said '*this* is the gateway to heaven'. Our response should be the same as Jacob's, but instead of 'How awesome is this *place*' we should say, 'How awesome is this *person*'.

KEY THEMES

There is just one central issue in this passage: the coming of Jesus, the fulfilment of all God's promises to rescue and draw together a people who will be His very own. Jesus has arrived! John, in his narrative, loses no time in presenting his readers with key facts about Jesus.

✤ He is the long-awaited Lamb who will deal with sin once and for all.

✤ He is the long-promised King/Christ/Son who will rule God's people forever.

✤ He is the central and enabling figure in the fulfilment of God's promise to pour out His Spirit, so that God's people may remain His people forever.

✤ He is identified to the Baptist by God and to the disciples by the Baptist. The Baptist prepares the disciples who recognise Him and turn to follow Him.

✤ He demonstrates His divinity by displaying complete knowledge of the disciples He calls.

✤ He promises far greater things for those who follow Him, which suggests that all God's Old Testament promises will find their fulfilment in Him.

APPLICATION

To them then: The Baptist's words about Jesus persuaded the disciples that Jesus really was the long-awaited Messiah, and also convinced them that Jesus' central purpose in 'becoming flesh' was to be the Lamb of God. The Baptist was an authentic spokesman who authentically identified the Messiah using a whole range of Old Testament criteria. Jesus' call to the disciples assured them that the Baptist's witness was true. They are convinced by Jesus' divine knowledge and turn to follow the One for whom the whole Jewish race had been waiting. They are left with a promise of far greater things to come, for those who follow Him.

To us now: The application to us must follow the same lines as to 'them'. We should listen to the Baptist and open our eyes to see the identity and purpose of this long-awaited Messiah. We should see the disciples responding to Jesus' call and learn from them that the Baptist's witness is valid, that the Messiah really has arrived. The application of the passage is not to learn a lesson in personal evangelism but to come to the same conclusion as the disciples did on first encountering Jesus. Jesus' promise that they would see 'greater things' concerning Himself should make us eager to read on.

The aim of this study

That we should acknowledge the coming of God to His world, as He promised He would do, and understand His purpose of opening the way to heaven through His sacrificial ministry. We will then be eager to see what 'greater things' about Jesus will be shown in the rest of the book.

Suggested questions

> ✤ If you had to write a job description for John the Baptist from 1:1–18, what would it be?

OVERVIEW OF TODAY'S PASSAGE:

> ✤ In what different ways do we see the Baptist fulfilling his job description in this passage? (*Use a large piece of paper to record the different ways he does it.*)

> ✤ As we have seen, the passage is loaded with Old Testament references. What is the main point of the passage?

> ✤ How does this tie in with John's purpose statement in 20:30-31?

19–34 'I HAVE SEEN! LOOK!' THE BAPTIST PREPARES THE WAY

> What do the events of these two days tell us about Jesus, the Baptist and the Jewish authorities? (Use a piece of paper with three columns to record the answers.)

>> ↘ In what ways is Jesus' ministry going to be greater than the Baptist's? (*Look up 1 Sam. 16:13 and Isa. 42:1 to establish the significance of the Spirit coming down ... and explain the meaning of baptising with the Holy Spirit.*)

>> ↘ Look carefully at verses 26, 31 and 33. What does the Baptist have in common with the religious authorities? What does this tell us about Jesus' ministry?

> ✤ How does the action of day two answer the questions that were left unanswered at the end of day one? Summarise what the Baptist has achieved by the end of verse 34.

35–51 'WE HAVE FOUND!' THE DISCIPLES BEGIN TO FOLLOW
... BUT MUCH MORE AWAITS

- ✤ Why do you think John includes these accounts of the first
  disciples being called by Jesus and following Him? How
  does this tie in with what you think is the main point of the
  passage?

  - ↘ How do the reactions of the first disciples to Jesus, and
    the titles they give Him, show that they have understood
    the Baptist's message?

- ✤ Jesus' promise in verses 50–51 sets us up for the rest of the
  Gospel. Look up Genesis 28:10–19. How did Jacob respond
  to the things God promised him?

- ✤ How does Jacob's response help us understand what Jesus is
  promising His followers in 1:50–51?

- ✤ If you had to write a job description and title for Jesus from
  this passage, what would they be? Why do you think John
  included this after 1:18?

Application

- ✤ In 1:7 John identifies the Baptist's ministry as being that of
  enabling 'all men' to believe. How has his ministry achieved
  this for you?

- ✤ In what ways has your understanding of who Jesus is, and
  what God is doing, been stretched and expanded? What
  challenge does this hold for you, and what encouragement?

This passage is not intended to be a lesson in one-to-one personal
evangelism. But how might we benefit from the lessons John has
taught us, about Jesus and about God, if we were trying to persuade
a friend to take Jesus seriously?

Section Notes: John 2:1–4:54

The first two signs recorded in the Gospel, in 2:1–11 and 4:43–54, act as a pair of brackets, one at the beginning and one at the end of this section of material; they indicate that everything within the section hangs together. John structures the whole Gospel in this way, recording two further pairs of signs which, as here, introduce and conclude a section of material. Therefore, as we read each section we should be on the look-out for the major themes that will be introduced by the first sign and summed up by the second.

Closer study of the two miracles confirms that they *are* like brackets: both take place in Cana in Galilee, as John points out (4:46), and they are carefully numbered (2:11 and 4:54). Then, the two miracles have a similar feature – in one Jesus holds back His mother, in the other He rebukes the official; and also a similar outcome – at the wedding Jesus' disciples put their faith in Him, and at the official's house, the whole household believes. Finally, the purpose of the signs appears to be similar: the first sign shows that the Messiah really has come, and the second is proof that the Samaritans were correct in recognising Jesus as the Messiah.

Having established that John did intend to provide this structure, we now need to find out how the selected material fits into the section.

The following incidents and explanations occur in these three chapters:

2:1–11   Jesus in Cana in Galilee: Sign 1 – The Messiah is here!
2:12–25   Jesus in Jerusalem: clearing the temple – an uncomfortable but genuine Messiah. How will you respond?

3:1–21   How is it possible to enter the kingdom of God? Through faith in the work of God's Messiah who has come down to earth.

3:22–36   Jesus in Judea: the Baptist authenticates Jesus' claims and ministry.

4:1–42   Jesus in Samaria: the gift of the Messiah is offered to all people; He really is the Messiah who will unite Jew and Samaritan as promised.

4:43–54   Jesus in Cana in Galilee: Sign 2 – The Messiah is here! How will we respond?

The themes of the chapters are as follows:

Chapter 2   The Messiah is here!
Chapter 3   How does anyone enter the kingdom of God? Through belief in the Messiah's work.
Chapter 4   Who enters the kingdom of God? Anyone who believes in the Messiah.

RECURRING THEMES

- The arrival and authentication of the long-awaited Messiah. Jesus fulfils the prophecies about wine flowing in abundance and the cleansing of the temple. He is the One who has come down from heaven and who, through the Spirit, makes regeneration possible. He is the Lord of the harvest who unites Jew and Samaritan.

- The need for a response of genuine faith that accepts both the Father's word in scripture and Jesus' word as He teaches. Such genuine faith grows and develops through hearing and trusting Jesus' word. Jesus is not the comfortable Messiah the Jews were expecting. But this response of genuine faith in Him is necessary to new birth and entry into the kingdom. This response, rather than nationality or respectability, is the key to membership.

Both these themes appear in the accounts of the signs and are further developed within the section.

APPLICATION

Having established the themes and purpose of the section, it is important that our application is in line with John's intention. He wants to expand and deepen our understanding of what it means to recognise Jesus as the Christ. We should therefore find ourselves responding as Jacob did, when he saw heaven opened:'How awesome is this place!' (cf. 1:51). And we should be asking ourselves whether our response of faith is genuine or somehow inadequate, like the Jews' (2:24). Jesus is the 'place' where heaven is opened – have we entered?

SIGNS IN JOHN

The purpose of the signs is explained well by Carson (p. 175):'signs [are] significant displays of power that point beyond themselves to the deeper realities that could be perceived with the eyes of faith'. They are never 'simply naked displays of power, still less neat conjuring tricks to impress the masses'. The intention is that the reader of the Gospel should see the sign and listen to the explanatory words of Jesus, and so come to genuine faith.

John 2:1–25
God's king is here. Glory! Judgment!

CONTEXT

The verses at the end of the last passage, 1:50–51, gave us the promise of 'greater things' to be revealed. The Son of Man is to be the centre and fulfilment of God's covenant promises to His people. He is to be the new focus of Jacob's response, 'This is none other than the house of God, and this is the gate of heaven.' (Gen. 8:17). In the next part of John's narrative, chapter 3:1–26, we shall see how someone may enter into God's kingdom – Jesus is the gateway to heaven. But first, this passage shows us what it means to say that Jesus is the long-awaited Messiah (see 20:30–31) – He is the 'house of God!' This is not as comfortable as it might sound, and for the first time we are given a hint that the Christ for whom the authorities in Jerusalem were obviously waiting (1:19ff) will not conform to their expectations. The chapter shows us two possible responses to this Messiah.

STRUCTURE

The messianic age is here!

2:1–11   Glory! A credible Messiah! (The first sign: water turned into wine.)

2:12–25   Judgment! A revolutionary Messiah!

Old Testament background

Wine in abundance: The prophets who spoke to the people of Israel in exile held out to them a vision. They described a day in the future when God would bring His people back from captivity and restore them to the land He had given to their forefathers. At this time God's people would be gathered together, God Himself would dwell with them, and they would live in joyful obedience to Him in a land filled with peace and plenty. 'That day', as the prophets referred to it, was to be the messianic age (see Amos 9:13–15 and Jer. 31:1ff), and one of the marks of abundance would be new wine dripping from the mountains and flowing from all the hills (Isa. 25:6–8; Amos 9:13; see also Joel 2:24). As with Isaiah's promises that we looked at in the last study (Isa. 40–66), these promises of a messianic age had clearly not yet been fulfilled. The water changed into wine at Cana gives a glimpse of the arrival of 'that day'.

The temple: The purpose of the temple was to symbolise God's dwelling with His people. The temple also symbolised His inaccessibility to His people, and the sacrificial system was a constant reminder of this. Sacrifices spoke of the need for the atonement of sin if God were to dwell among His people. In addition the temple was the focal point for all God's people, both as the place of sacrifice – there was no other – and as the prime centre for teaching. At national festivals such as the Passover the whole Jewish nation was supposed to come up to Jerusalem and to the temple (Deut. 2).

All that the temple was meant to symbolise, however, had been turned into a hypocritical sham by the priests who served at the temple. They were notorious. But there was nothing new in this. The prophets, centuries before, had constantly criticised the priests for their repetitive ritual that lacked any real repentance. In contrast to this desperate situation, the prophets looked forward to a day when the 'messenger of the covenant' would come to His temple and cleanse it, in an act of judgment that would restore real worship (see Mal. 3:1–5).

Psalm 69: This psalm is important in John's Gospel; three of its verses (4, 9 and 21) are picked up by John as being fulfilled by Jesus.

The psalm sees King David as a figure who is opposed and rejected by his enemies on account of his zeal for God's house. This zeal finds its expression in true worship, defined as the honouring of God's name rather than the mere sacrifice of animals. The enemies referred to in Psalm 69 have as their counterpart, in this passage, the Jews who are presently in Jerusalem, celebrating the Passover and recalling God's judgment and rescue: the fact that they are at the same time opposing Jesus, God's rescuer, adds a striking irony to this passage (see text notes).

Resurrection: 2 Samuel 7:13 and Psalm 16:10 both tell us that God's anointed king, the Messiah, will reign on His throne forever. Resurrection is key to this. So Jesus' prediction of His own resurrection is a further claim to be that anointed king.

TEXT NOTES

1–11 THE MESSIANIC AGE IS HERE! THE GLORY OF A CREDIBLE MESSIAH! (*The first sign: water turned into wine.*) It is all too easy to focus on the minor details of this passage and, in so doing, allow ourselves to be drawn into many classic traps of interpretation. The commentaries are full of possible 'meanings' for the 'stone water jars used for ceremonial washing', the fact that they were 'filled to the brim', and so on. These details may be interesting but, if we read the text carefully, it is clear (v. 11) that Jesus has one major purpose in performing this sign: 'He thus revealed His glory, and the disciples put their faith in Him.' There is no comment on the significance of the jars; they may be significant, they may not. The central, most important questions we should be asking are 'How does this sign reveal Jesus' glory?' and 'How does this sign generate faith?'

The sign reveals Jesus' glory in two ways. First, there is the obvious and plain *fact* of the sign: no-one but God could do something like this! Secondly, there is the *nature* of the sign, the miraculous abundance of wine that speaks of the messianic age. The previous chapter has certainly heightened our expectation: the titles given to Jesus encourage us to look for evidence that He is the Messiah, and at the end of the chapter there is the promise to the disciples that they would see 'greater things'. This sign cries out to anyone with an understanding of the Old Testament that the messianic age is now here ... wine is here in abundance (see Old Testament notes).

But in another sense the messianic age is not here. A brief scan of the Old Testament promises concerning this age makes it clear that they predict a world we do not yet experience. Verse 4 encourages us to ask the question as to why this is so, and also helps us find the answer: Jesus performs a sign which suggests that this age has arrived, but there is a sense in which, as He says, His 'hour' has *not* yet come. Throughout the Gospel we shall find references to Jesus' 'hour'. They point to Jesus' death on the cross as His 'hour' (12:23), or else beyond His death and resurrection to an 'hour' way off in the future (5:28, NIV 'time' means 'hour'). Coming back to this passage with such references in mind, we see how the 'hour' has arrived and yet is still to come. This should prevent us from being disappointed that we do not now experience the messianic age completely; it should also keep us looking forward to the arrival of that 'hour'.

12–25 THE MESSIANIC AGE IS HERE! JUDGMENT BY A REVOLUTION-ARY MESSIAH!

In these verses Jesus cleanses the temple and then, in dialogue with the Jews, promises to rise from the dead. The violent action and the amazing promise are both fulfilments of scriptures that relate to God's Messiah-King (see Old Testament notes). The disciples recognise the first fulfilment at the time (v. 17) and the second at a much later stage (v. 22). With these two verses John provides the 'interpretative key' for understanding Jesus' action in the temple: Jesus is the Messiah, who cleanses and who will rise again. The 'scripture' referred to in verse 22 must be Old Testament references to the Messiah living forever, such as Psalm 16:10. It cannot mean the temple being replaced by the Messiah – there are no Old Testament scriptures that point to that, and in any case John tells us that 'the temple He had spoken of was His body'.

12–17. The Messiah is seen judging and cleansing the establishment that was central in the old era, but which was patently failing to achieve the purpose for which it existed. This action in itself showed that Jesus was the expected Messiah (v. 17), though His arrival proved uncomfortable and challenging.

18–22. Instead of responding to the Messiah's judgment in humble repentance, the Jews demand a sign. Jesus promises that they will get *the sign* given in scripture, namely His resurrection (v. 19), for He is the everlasting king (see last Old Testament note). The disciples recognise this, John tells us, after the resurrection has happened (v. 22). This passage, therefore, is primarily about who Jesus is: He is the judging eternal Messiah. However, verses 18–22 contain deep irony and further challenge. The Jews fail to respond in repentance to the arrival of the Messiah, with the result, eventually, that they put Him to death. The irony is that their judgment on Him guarantees His final judgment on them, on their failed temple, and on their abuses of its sacrificial systems. Jesus' sacrifice of Himself – totally effective, and made once for all – makes their cherished temple obsolete in the new messianic age. The *timing* of this action enhances the irony: it is the time of the Passover (v. 13), when Jerusalem and the temple would have been full of Jews recalling God's judgment on His enemies and His rescue of His people. Far from judging His enemies, however, this uncomfortable Messiah has come in judgment on His own people!

Response. Two types of response to this uncomfortable Messiah are seen in this passage. First, that of the disciples, whose faith is shown to be growing and developing as they observe Jesus (1:50; 2:11) and believe the Old Testament scriptures about Him. Secondly, that of the Jews whose faith is inadequate (2:23–25). The comment that Jesus 'knew what was in a man' suggests that their faith was inadequate because, though they saw the miracles, they were not ready to respond in repentance to the challenge of the judging Messiah (vv. 18,20).

KEY THEMES

↹ The long-awaited messianic age really is here. The water changed into wine shows that this totally new era has begun. Jesus is the longed-for Messiah who demonstrates His complete control over His creation.

↹ Jesus, the Messiah foretold by the prophets, is here as judge of His people. His judgment will eventually result in His replacing the temple and its system of worship, which lay at the heart of the old era, with His own person, which lies at the heart of the new era.

♄ Responses to this Messiah: the Jews begin to react against this revolutionary Messiah who challenges and judges – He is altogether too threatening but the disciples respond with a growing and developing faith.

Application

To them then: The application of verses 1–11 is shown in the disciples' response of growing faith in verse 11. As Jesus revealed His glory, so the claims of 1:34, 49 and 51 became credible. The transformation of water into wine is a staggering event which only God could bring about! The disciples put their faith in God's king who has come to usher in a whole new era. They begin to see Him as the culmination of all God's planning. But Jesus does not fulfil the promises of the Old Testament in quite the comfortable way that the Jews were expecting. His coming means challenge to the status quo and judgment on the Jews' corrupted worship. Eventually this judgment will lead to the temple being replaced by Jesus: *He* will become the 'place' of effective sacrifice and of meeting with God. He is at the very centre of the new era. There are only two possible responses to this uncomfortable king.

To us now: Our application must be along the lines mentioned above. First, we should discover who Jesus is and what He has come to do. He is not just some personalised god who comes to provide for my own felt needs. He is the king who has come to usher in a whole new era for God's people. But, secondly, His Messiahship is challenging. He does not fit comfortably with the Jews' expectations and will not fit comfortably with ours. The questions for us are as follows: will we continue to grow in faith as we learn from this uncomfortable Messiah? And, are we prepared to repent under His exposure – He knows what is in us – and recognise Him as the central figure in this new age?

STUDY 3

THE AIM OF THIS STUDY

To see that in Jesus, God's promised messianic age really has come. It is a time of glory, but also of judgment and challenge. How do we respond?

SUGGESTED QUESTIONS

What were the different titles given to Jesus in chapter 1? What has John been telling us about Jesus' identity and mission?

1–11 GLORY! A CREDIBLE KING!

- ✤ What impact does this first sign have on Jesus' disciples? And why? (*Amos 9:13–15 helps to explain the disciples' reaction.*)
  - ↘ How do the details of verses 6–10 help to make the point?
- ✤ As the Gospel unfolds it soon becomes very clear that the messianic age has not yet come in the wonderful way promised by the prophets. How does verse 4 help to explain this? (It may be useful to look up 5:28).
- ✤ How does the first sign throw light on the lessons we learned in chapter 1?

12–25 JUDGMENT BY A REVOLUTIONARY KING!

- ✤ This passage records two major events in Jesus' ministry. What are they?
  - ↘ *Explain the purpose of the temple in Israel's history.*
- ✤ Look up and read Psalm 69:7–11 and 30–31. How does King David show himself to be zealous for God's house in Psalm 69?
- ✤ How does Jesus show Himself to be zealous for God's house?
  - ↘ So why do you think John records the temple cleansing here?
  - ↘ What themes does this pick up from chapter 1? And how does it tie in with 2:1–11?
- ✤ The Jews demand a sign to show that Jesus has authentic authority to cleanse their temple. How does Jesus' answer authenticate His action?

↘ *Explain the Old Testament references to the true Messiah living forever.*

↘ So how do the disciples of verse 17 differ from the Jews of verse 18?

✤ What do verses 12–25 tell us about Jesus' place and function in the messianic age? In what ways do these things make Him a 'revolutionary Messiah'?

↘ How does the disciples' response in verses 1–22 differ from the response recorded in verses 23–25? What does this tell us about a genuine response to the Messiah?

✤ Imagine that you have a Christian friend whose primary reason for following Jesus appears to be the expectation that He will provide personal fulfilment for his or her life, that He brings answers to prayers for personal safety, health and happiness, and that He gives people a sense of belonging and worth. In what ways would you want this passage to expand and challenge his or her understanding of who Jesus is and what He has really come to do?

✤ These verses tell us a great deal about genuine 'worship' and genuine 'faith' now that the Messiah has come. How do these lessons challenge and unsettle our views of what worship and faith are all about?

John 2:23–3:36
Entry into the kingdom of God

CONTEXT

In 1:51 Jesus promised His disciples that they would see heaven opened and angels ascending and descending on the Son of Man. This clearly implied that Jesus was the long-awaited Messiah (see notes on Jacob's dream on p. 31). He was, in a figurative sense, none other than 'the house of God ... the gate of heaven'.

2:1–25 presented the arrival of the messianic age and the Messiah: Jesus claimed that He would be the new 'house of God'. But chapter 2 left two questions unanswered: 'How does one enter the messianic age?' (or the kingdom of God, as Jesus describes it in 3:3), and, 'Who gets in?' This chapter gives the answer as to the 'how': it is only by God's action, as He regenerates people through His Spirit, that they come to believe in His Son, the 'gate' to heaven. Chapter 4 gives the answer as to the 'who'.

STRUCTURE

The structure of the first half of the study (2:23–3:15) is dictated by the three questions, each beginning 'How…?', with their three replies, each beginning 'I tell you the truth…'.

2:23–3:3   Rebirth is essential for entry into the kingdom of God.
3:4–8   Rebirth is God's work by His Spirit – He regenerates.

3:9–15   Rebirth is possible only through God's Son – we must believe in Him to have life.

3:16–21   Explanatory comment:

      16–18   Why faith in God's Son is necessary.

      19–21   Why people reject God's Son.

3:22–36   The Baptist authenticates Jesus' message.

OLD TESTAMENT BACKGROUND

Kingdom of God: This is another way of referring to the messianic age that we were looking at in the previous study (see Isa. 9:1–7; 11:1–2). The prophets saw it coming at the end of history, presided over by David's Son. '"to see the kingdom of God" was to participate in the kingdom at the end of the age, to experience eternal, resurrection life' (Carson, p. 188).

Regeneration: By the time of the exile the prophets had begun to teach that it was impossible to be one of God's people if the problem of one's sin had not been dealt with. Here, in verse 5, Jesus refers to Ezekiel 36 which teaches that sin is the problem facing God's people. Their problem will only be solved when sin is dealt with. The solution, in Ezekiel 36, comes when past sin is cleansed away by the sprinkling of water and, for the future, when God puts His Spirit in people's hearts, giving them a new desire to obey Him (Ezek. 36:25–27). Ezekiel is quite clear that God is the only one able to do all this, and also that He is doing it for His glory (36:32). In chapter 37 he goes on to prophesy that God will do it through regenerating His people.

The snake in the desert: Deliverance from God's wrath was brought about through faith in God's miraculous and merciful intervention (Num. 21:8–9).

The Son of Man: This is one of Jesus' most common descriptions of Himself. The Old Testament depicts the Son of Man as the glorious heavenly figure who will rule forever (Dan. 7:13–14). Jesus adds to this, describing the Son of Man as the revealer of God (3:13) and as the crucified one (3:14).

The bridegroom: The future restoration of God's people is pictured as a wedding banquet with God as the bridegroom, betrothing Himself to His bride and rejoicing over her (Isa. 54:4–8; Hosea 2:19).

Text notes

2:23–3:3 REBIRTH IS ESSENTIAL FOR ENTRY INTO THE KINGDOM OF GOD

Nicodemus has seen the signs and now comes to question Jesus. We are not told whether Nicodemus' attitude towards Jesus is positive or negative – it obviously doesn't matter. By telling Nicodemus how a person may enter the kingdom of God, Jesus immediately identifies the issue that is central to this passage, i.e. how does anyone enter God's kingdom? The negative, in Jesus' words in verse 5, stresses the failure of sinful human beings to reach God's kingdom on their own. The whole of Israel's history has illustrated this failure and the prophets had finally prophesied a solution to it: God would eventually deal with sin. The reference to rebirth is a clear reference to Ezekiel 37 (see Old Testament notes).

4–8 REBIRTH IS GOD'S WORK BY HIS SPIRIT – HE REGENERATES

Nicodemus is confused, he doesn't understand. Jesus replies that participation is only possible through God's regenerative work. This is a clear principle established in the writings of the Old Testament prophets (see Old Testament notes). Spiritual life and membership of God's kingdom requires sin to be dealt with, by washing and by the indwelling of God's Spirit. Nicodemus should know that sinful human flesh can only give birth to flesh, and that the work of God is essential for dealing with the problem of sin in human beings. He should know what Jesus teaches in verse 8, that rebirth is entirely a matter of God acting through His Spirit.

9–15 REBIRTH IS POSSIBLE ONLY THROUGH GOD'S SON – WE MUST BELIEVE IN HIM TO HAVE LIFE

Nicodemus is still confused as to how a person can be washed and given life. Jesus rebukes him and asserts His authority as the true teacher of Israel: Jesus has authority as the Son of Man who alone has come from heaven. He is an eye-witness of what He is talking about. As He teaches He answers Nicodemus' question:

this washing and rebirth is only possible through the Son of Man coming from heaven and being 'lifted up' on the cross.

'Lifted up', in John's writing, always combines two meanings, the physical lifting up of Jesus on the cross and His exaltation (see Carson, p. 201). To give Nicodemus a parallel to His own 'lifting up', Jesus refers to an incident in Israel's desert history, in Numbers 21:8-9. Just as the dying Israelites had needed simply to look at the bronze snake set up by Moses, as the only way of accepting God's solution to their plight, and so survive, so now all people need to accept God's solution to the problem of sin, by believing in the Son of Man lifted up on the cross. Only in this way will they have eternal life. Jesus is already anticipating His death; He is the gateway to heaven.

16–21 EXPLANATION FROM JESUS: THE NECESSITY OF FAITH AND THE REASON FOR REJECTION

16–18 Why faith in God's Son is necessary. Jesus has just told Nicodemus that believing in the Son of Man is the key into God's kingdom. This passage begins with the word 'for', indicating that the verses will explain why faith in God's solution is necessary. The subject of verses 16–17 is God, so we are being told that faith is necessary because of what God has done: He has acted out of love in order to rescue a world in rebellion against Himself.

The focal point of His action is His Son. Without His Son's intervention the 'world' is destined to perish under His just condemnation. With His Son's intervention there is the possibility of rescue. ('World', in John's writing, refers to rebellious humankind under God's judgment – see Carson, pp. 122–23, on 1:9.) The kind of faith that Jesus has been talking about in verses 9–15 is a trust in this specific and objective act of rescue by God. It is not some subjective inner feeling, but a real trust in the real work of a real person which has real consequences.

19–22 Why people reject God's Son. Given that God has acted in this way, it sounds preposterous that people should reject His offer of life. But John forces us to face the fact that we do do this; he contrasts the love of God for a rebellious world in need of salvation (v. 16) with the love of humans for darkness and flight (vv. 19ff).

Our natural human response to God is to run from Him, and from His light, because we know that we are rebels and *we want* to *remain* rebellious. Rejection of the gospel, therefore, is not a matter of belonging to the wrong race or culture. It is a matter of not wanting God to rule over our lives. Verse 21 makes it clear that those who *do* accept the gospel do so only by God's merciful intervention, which takes us back to the truth of verses 1–8.

22–36 THE BAPTIST AUTHENTICATES JESUS' MESSAGE AND MOVES US ON…

Exactly what the argument is about in verse 25 doesn't really matter – we are not told. The reason the Baptist appears again is to answer the question 'Is it right that people are going to Jesus?' Jesus has been making radical claims. The Baptist once more fulfils the function of providing authentication. He confirms Jesus' identity – yes, Jesus is the bridegroom – and then, in verses 30–36, he gives us reasons why we should take seriously what Jesus says. Jesus is the Son, He really has come from God. Entry into God's kingdom is dependent upon one's belief in Him. Therefore, *whoever* believes in Jesus has life, and *whoever* rejects Him stands under God's wrath (cf. the Baptist's role 1:6–8). These verses contain John's authentication of Jesus' teaching and, at the same time, summarise the major themes of the chapter.

KEY THEMES

The key question is: How does a person enter into God's eternal kingdom?

- ✤ God's action:
    - ↘ Jesus declares that no-one can enter unless they are born again.
    - ↘ Rebirth is a spiritual phenomenon and is only possible through God's initiative and God's regenerative action.
    - ↘ God's action involves sin being dealt with.
    - ↘ God's initiative is focused in His giving up His Son to be 'lifted up' on the cross.
- ✤ Rebirth alone gives entry into the kingdom of God; people cannot force their way in. No matter how well-qualified they may be, religiously, rebirth is always necessary.

ᛒ Humanity's response:
  ↘ The only legitimate response is one of simple trust in what God has done on our behalf.
  ↘ The reason people reject God's action is because human beings are deeply rebellious and wish to remain that way.
ᛒ This is mind-blowing, but is it really true? Yes, because Jesus says so: He came from heaven, He is Israel's true teacher. Therefore, a really good Jew, who does everything the Law tells him, will come to Jesus for eternal life.

APPLICATION

To them then: Never mind that Nicodemus is high up in the Jewish religious establishment: he too is a moral being who has rebelled against God, and he too needs to depend absolutely on God's loving rescue plan, centred as it is on the death of Jesus. Throughout the chapter there are reasons for accepting that what Jesus is saying really is true. It ties in with the lessons that the Israelites learned in the desert, and it is validated by John the Baptist. In addition there is Jesus' claim to be the true teacher of Israel, the Son of Man who has come from heaven.

To us now: No matter how 'religious' we are, our membership of God's kingdom, our possession of eternal life, depends entirely upon God's loving action in sending Jesus to die on the cross. We are no different from anyone else, we are rebels who need to be cleansed and indwelt by God's Holy Spirit. Rebirth is essential, and we need to trust in the Son of Man lifted up. If we have realised this, it is entirely due to God's work, through His Spirit, in opening our eyes to spiritual realities.

There is no Christian alive who does not have the Holy Spirit, for his or her regeneration has been 'done through God' (v. 21) and because of God's love. This should both humble us and focus our faith on God's loving rescue. Those who reject Jesus (however religious, intellectual or apathetic their reasons) do so because they are rebels. Jesus, and faith in Him, is the fulcrum on which balances the eternal destiny of every single person.

STUDY 4

THE AIM OF THIS STUDY

To see that Jesus is the gateway to heaven. Entry into God's eternal kingdom is possible only on the basis of faith in Jesus, who will deal with the problem of sin. God's Spirit generates this faith.

SUGGESTED QUESTIONS

Evangelism is hard! Begin by discussing this question:

  ✤ If you were to conduct a studio discussion, what answers do you think would be given to the question 'Why do you think people won't accept Jesus' message today?'

2:23–3:15 ENTRY INTO THE KINGDOM OF GOD REQUIRES REBIRTH, THROUGH THE SPIRIT OF GOD GENERATING FAITH IN GOD

  ✤ How does 3:1–3 begin to address the question raised by 2:23–25?

   ↘ How does the phrase 'kingdom of God' pick up on 2:1–22?

  ✤ Look up Ezekiel 36:24–29. What do these verses tell us about humanity's natural condition? What does God promise to do in order to create a special people belonging to Himself? How do these verses help to explain Jesus' response to Nicodemus in verses 4–8?

  ✤ In what ways is Jesus shown to be a better qualified 'teacher of Israel' than Nicodemus?

   ↘ Why is it important that Jesus makes *these* points to Nicodemus at *this* stage of the Gospel?

  ✤ Jesus, the true teacher of Israel, explains to Nicodemus that certain things need to happen before anyone may enter into the kingdom. What are these things and how do they come about? (*Take a sheet of paper with two columns, for 'God's action' and 'Humanity's response'.*)

16–21 JESUS EXPLAINS THE GOSPEL

  ✤ What do these verses tell us about God, Jesus, believers and unbelievers?

  ✤ How should this chapter change the answers given to the question in the studio discussion?

✤ Why do you think John includes these verses here at this stage of chapter 3? How does your answer tie in with John's purpose statement in chapter 20?

22–36 JESUS' TEACHING AUTHENTICATED BY THE BAPTIST

✤ The teaching of verses 1–21 is hard to accept. According to verses 31–36, why should we accept it?

✤ The incident of verses 22–30 seems an odd one for John to include. What does he achieve by putting it in his Gospel? How does your answer tie in with 1:6–8?

APPLICATION

✤ The lessons we have been learning today are deeply offensive to religious people, who think that they can make their own way to God. What things in particular would cause offence?

✤ (*Go round the group.*) What have you learned about God, about Jesus, about yourself, about the Holy Spirit, and about your friends who claim to be agnostics, atheists, etc.?

John 4:1–54
The Saviour of the world!

CONTEXT

In chapter 2 John showed us that the messianic age really had arrived. In chapter 3 this was confirmed as Jesus explained to Nicodemus *how* a person could enter His kingdom. Now, in chapter 4, the question shifts from *how* to *who*. Who belongs? So far Jesus has been dealing only with Jews. So is He just a Jewish Messiah? Jesus has already told us (3:16) that 'whoever believes' will enter God's kingdom, but we know that the faith of many, including Nicodemus, is confused and that numbers of people will reject Him. This chapter, in which Jesus begins to reap 'a harvest' among the Samaritans, confirms once more the arrival of the messianic age and also identifies the beneficiaries of this age.

STRUCTURE

4:1–26   'I who speak to you am He!' Jesus is the Messiah, God's king.

      1–15   Jesus is the Christ: God gives eternal life through Him – a person, not a place.

      16–26 Jesus is the Christ: God seeks true worship focused in Him – a person, not a place.

4:27–42 Harvest time! Jesus gives an explanation of why He is going to the Samaritans: He really is the Saviour of the whole world and the Samaritans really are expressing a true response.

4:43–54 The second sign: the healing of the official's son. This confirms the arrival of the messianic age and reminds us that this age is for Jews too – although not all Jews exercise growing faith.

Old Testament background

One nation, one king, one sanctuary: Carson provides an excellent summary of the Samaritan issue (p. 216). The prophets had promised a day when the bitter rivals, Samaria and Judah, would be reunited under one king. Ezekiel 37:15–28 provides a clear picture of all that was promised: Judah and all Israelites associated with him, and Joseph and all Israelites associated with him, would be made into one nation under one king (v. 22), saved from backsliding into idolatry, cleansed, and restored to a relationship with God (v. 23), with God dwelling amongst them in His sanctuary (vv. 26–28). None of these promises had yet been fulfilled. But every part of the prophecy by Ezekiel finds an echo in this passage.

Living water: Jesus' words about living water resonate with another passage in Ezekiel, in which the prophet is shown the living water that flows out from the temple, after the return of God's glory to the temple (Ezek. 47:1–12; 43:1–12). Living water is also a picture of eternal life and the pouring out of God's Spirit in the day of God's salvation (Isa. 44:3; 55:1–3).

Saviour of the whole world: In Isaiah 42:6 the Servant of the Lord is seen as being 'a light to the Gentiles'. The idea of God rescuing people from many nations is not new: the ingathering of the nations will be part of the messianic age (Isa. 2:2–4).

Text notes

1–26 'I who speak to you am he!'

Jesus is the Messiah who brings life to all, Samaritan as well as Jew. He reunites Jew and Samaritan in 'true worship'. The *main* point of this part is in verse 26. Jesus' calling of a Samaritan woman is further evidence of what has been taught from the beginning of the Gospel, that He is the longed-for Messiah (see Old Testament notes).

1–6 Scene change to Samaria. The scene change and the geographical notes all ensure that the reader is in no doubt, in the following verses, about the implications of Jesus' actions and His offer of living water. We are not told why He 'has' to go through Samaria. Note the humanity of Jesus, that He was tired, thirsty and, presumably, hungry.

7–15 Jesus is the Christ: God gives eternal life through Him – a person, not a place! Jesus takes the initiative in calling this woman, whose character and identity both suggest she shouldn't stand a chance. She realises this. She is a Samaritan, to whom a Jew would not speak without risking defilement, and a woman, to whom a rabbi should not have spoken (v. 27). The Samaritans and Jews hated one another bitterly. There is a deliberate contrast between Nicodemus and the woman: he respectable, Jewish, religious, pure; she immoral, Samaritan (see Old Testament notes), female and an outcast. This passage is intended to make us sit up and take notice!

In verses 10–12 Jesus introduces the main issues of the conversation – who He is, and the nature of God's gift. Both these ideas had come into the conversation with Nicodemus, and there are real comparisons to be drawn between the ways they are discussed, with him and with her. But the *new thing* (and it is surprising) is that Jesus is now offering God's gift of eternal life to a Gentile woman. She questions both His identity and His ability – like Nicodemus she does not realise that Jesus is speaking about spiritual issues.

In verses 13–15 Jesus brings the conversation back to the point. The issue He is dealing with is God's gift of eternal life. The gift of eternal life lies with Him and He is offering it to *this* woman. He really is the Saviour of the whole world. Jesus implies that He is much greater than Jacob and that He can give something far greater than Jacob ever gave the Samaritans. In addition, this gift is for whoever drinks the water that He gives. Again, there is a comparison here between the Samaritan woman, who presumes that she is one of God's people because she can claim Jacob as her spiritual father, and Nicodemus, who fails to understand his need for anything other than his religion.

16–26. Jesus is the Christ: God seeks true worship focused in Him – a person, not a place! In verses 16–20 Jesus' exposure of the woman's background serves primarily as a means of identifying Himself to her. Like Nathanael (in 1:49), the woman realises that she is not speaking to any ordinary stranger. Here is someone who 'told me everything I ever did' (v. 29). Once she begins to realise who Jesus is, then the spiritual nature of the conversation begins to make sense. The fact that Jesus pinpoints her sin is not commented upon, so we should beware of making it a major point. For the reader, Jesus' supernatural knowledge of this individual provides a mark of His divinity. It also gives a further emphasis to the word 'whoever', as in the promise of eternal life for 'whoever believes' (3:16): He knows this adulterous Samaritan woman through and through, and yet still He offers *her* the salvation that earlier He had offered to Nicodemus.

In verses 21–25 Jesus brings the conversation to a focus. God is seeking 'true worshippers' who will worship in spirit and in truth. The phrase 'God is spirit' controls our understanding of what Jesus means: God is divine and other; He is everywhere and He knows everything. True worshippers, therefore, cannot tie Him down to a place, they cannot regulate Him or control Him. He cannot be confined by a simple set of legalistic codes, nor can He be confined just to one race. He must be worshipped in spirit because *He* is Spirit. He should be worshipped all the time, everywhere, and by all people. And yet, as 'spirit' He has revealed Himself in 'the truth', and so He must be worshipped as *He has revealed Himself*, first to the Jews in the Old Testament and now in Jesus. Now that Jesus is here, He will unite Jews and Samaritans as true worshippers who will worship in spirit and in truth. This means that religious places for worship are declared redundant – a deeply shocking concept for both Samaritan and Jew – and also that the same kind of response is demanded from both Jew and Samaritan.

Verse 26: Jesus really is the Messiah, for the Samaritans as well as for the Jews (Ezek. 37:15–28).

27–42 HARVEST TIME!

The structure of these verses helps explain why Jesus was going to the Samaritans (vv. 1–26).

27–30. The disciples are astonished, but the woman displays true signs of discipleship (just as Andrew and Philip had done, 1:35ff).

31–38. Jesus explains that He is doing God's work and that God's harvest has come. Like the woman and Nicodemus, the disciples are preoccupied with physical matters, but Jesus urges them to open their eyes and see God's true harvest, the approaching Samaritans. Eternal life is being offered to the Samaritans and they are receiving it! An entirely new age, with opportunities that are altogether new, has begun.

39–42. As if to prove that it really is harvest time, the Samaritans display true growing faith. They believe without a miracle, simply by hearing the woman's testimony and then Jesus' words (v. 42). The 'whoever', in 3:16 and 3:36, really does mean anyone in the world!

43–54 THE SECOND SIGN: THE HEALING OF THE OFFICIAL'S SON.

This sign provides a closing bracket to the section that began at 2:1 (see section notes). The section closes with further proof that Jesus really is the Messiah and further evidence of His glory – He can heal the dying even at a distance. At the same time, the Galileans' failure to believe is contrasted with the Samaritans' faith, and Jesus rebukes them (in verse 48 the 'you' is plural). But the royal official does exhibit a growing faith.

Observing, in this chapter, the two types of response to Jesus, we are better prepared for the stark polarisation of response that comes in chapters 5–10.

KEY THEMES

- ♉ Jesus reveals Himself as the Saviour of the world:
  - ↘ Through Him the Father calls true worshippers, whatever their race or background.
  - ↘ He fulfils the Old Testament promises and will gather in the harvest, both now and at the end of time.
  - ↘ He has divine omniscience and divine authority over all.

✥ Different people react to Jesus differently:

  ↘ The disciples are perplexed and appear not to recognise that Old Testament prophecies are being fulfilled.

  ↘ The Samaritans respond in faith.

  ↘ The Jews and the Samaritans, Nicodemus and the woman, are compared and contrasted.

✥ The nature of true faith:

  ↘ Jesus does not make it easy to respond to Himself. He is provocative and searching with everyone He meets.

  ↘ He defines 'true worship'. A true response to God means worshipping Jesus in all places and at all times (i.e. in spirit) and as He has prescribed (i.e. in truth).

Application

To them then: This passage contains confirmation that Jesus really is the Messiah. By revealing Himself as the one true Saviour of the world who calls both Jew and Samaritan to worship Him, Jesus shows Himself to be the One promised in the Old Testament. This has implications for the disciples in their relationship with others (they need to recognise that Jesus offers life and membership of the kingdom of God to *all*), and also in their own response to Jesus (they need to demonstrate growing faith). Are they, like the Samaritan woman, beginning to see the spiritual implications of Jesus' identity? Or are they, like the Galileans, in need of rebuke?

To us now: We should join with the original hearers, and John's readers, in realising the implications of what Jesus is doing. He is claiming to be the Saviour of the world, and that His harvest time has begun. He calls true worshippers from every spiritual, racial and moral background to the same response of growing faith in Himself, the Messiah, the Saviour of the world (see Old Testament notes). The most direct application concerns our response to Him. Do we have this growing faith? Or are we, like the Galileans and other Jews that we have come across in this section, unwilling to believe in anything except the *spectacle* of the miracles?

THE AIM OF THIS STUDY

To realise that Jesus is the Christ, the Saviour of the world who brings spiritual life to all, Gentiles as well as Jews. We should respond to Him appropriately by believing His words and coming to Him as our Saviour and Lord.

SUGGESTED QUESTIONS

1–26 JESUS REVEALS HIS IDENTITY

- ✤ Jesus' encounter with the Samaritan woman follows His meeting with Nicodemus.
  - ↘ What are the similarities between the two episodes? (What are the main issues?)
  - ↘ What are the most striking differences between the two?
  - ↘ What point is John making by placing one encounter after the other?
- ✤ How does John make sure that we do not miss the 'new thing' that is being taught here?
- ✤ What does God seek, according to these verses, and what does He give? How are His purposes fulfilled in Jesus?
- ✤ What do these verses have to teach us about eternal life?
- ✤ What do they teach us about true worship?
  - ↘ How does Jesus' statement that 'God is spirit' (v. 24) explain what He tells the Samaritan woman? What are the implications for the way we view aspects of church life, church buildings, worship services, etc?
  - ↘ What are the implications for our time at home, in the office, at college, etc?
- ✤ Read Ezekiel 37:20–23. In the light of this promise, what is the main point of verses 1–26?

27–42 THE SIGNIFICANCE OF JESUS' ENCOUNTER WITH THE SAMARITANS

- ✤ In verses 31–38, what are the teachings that challenge and change the disciples' understanding about who Jesus is, and also about God's purposes?

✧ How are these lessons confirmed by the woman and the villagers?

✧ In what ways do the woman and the villagers show that they have understood what Jesus was teaching in verses 1–26?

   ↘ How do they exercise the 'growing faith' that we have been learning about since chapter 1?

43–54 THE SECOND SIGN: THE HEALING OF THE OFFICIAL'S SON

✧ *(Explain that this miracle is paired with 2:1–11.)*

✧ From this section (2:1–4:54), how may we summarise the issues of who Jesus is, what He has come to do, and who will gain entry into His kingdom?

APPLICATION

✧ From the whole of today's passage, what would you say is the correct response to Jesus?

✧ Why do you think John included this chapter, with its focus on the Samaritans, at this stage in his book?

✧ What do we learn from the Samaritan woman's misunderstandings about Jesus and also from her correct response to Him?

Section Notes : John 5:1–10:42

The two signs in 5:1–15 and 9:1–41, together with their discourses, form the brackets for this section. Both consist of a healing performed in Jerusalem on a Sabbath. Both result in a prolonged exchange, back and forth, between the person healed and the Jews. In both cases the story ends with the Jews wanting to take violent action against Jesus: persecution and the desire to kill Him in 5:16-18 and, in 10:32,39, attempts at stoning and arrest.

The following incidents and explanations occur in these six chapters:

5:1–18   The healing of the lame man, and controversy over the Sabbath.

5:19–47   Jesus speaks of His equality with the Father as the Son from heaven.

6:1–70   Jesus and the Passover: the feeding of the five thousand, the walking on the water, and the discourse about the bread of life. Jesus is the true manna and the genuine sacrificial Lamb of the Passover. The disciples are tested, the presumption of the Jews is exposed, and Jesus teaches that unless God draws a person, no-one can enter the kingdom.

7:1–52   Jesus at the Feast of Tabernacles: the Jews are divided and confused by Jesus. They attempt to seize Him. He responds by offering living water to all who will drink.

8:12–59   Jesus at the Feast of Tabernacles: Jesus continues to expose the Jews' real attitude, pointing out that those who are hostile to Him are not His people, they belong to this world. At the same time He offers light to all who will follow.

9:1–41   The healing of the man born blind, and controversy over the Sabbath. Jesus explains His work: the giving of sight to the blind, and the blinding of the sighted. It takes a miracle to 'see' spiritually.

10:1–42   'I am the Good Shepherd.' Discourse about the blind man's healing. Jesus explains how He can and will save.

Recurring themes

- ✤ The identity of Jesus: He is the Son who has come from the Father, He is the Passover Lamb, the true manna, the water of life, the light of the world, the Good Shepherd and the 'I AM'.

- ✤ The rejection of the Son by His people. The Jews cannot accept His equality with the Father – He explains that they are not His people. They cannot see their need of true manna, and they cannot stomach His 'bread', which is His death on behalf of the world. They try to seize Him. He asserts that they hate Him because they are of the world. They are simply unable to 'see' because they refuse to admit their own sin and their need of His intervention. They are shown to be utterly blind and under judgment – selfish shepherds out for selfish gain.

- ✤ The miracle of sight worked by the Son for His people who respond by listening to His words and accepting His Father's works. Throughout the section Jesus continues to hold out His offer of life to all those who will accept it. At the same time He demonstrates that this offer can only be accepted by those whom the Father draws, and to whom He gives sight as they listen to His word.

Note that the two signs in chapter 6 and the sign in chapter 21 do not act as brackets. Chapter 6 is remarkably dense, summing up most of the main ideas contained in the Gospel. The two signs in this chapter highlight the significance of what is going on, stressing the true identity and mission of Jesus, and exposing the true nature of the Jews and also their destiny.

APPLICATION

Having established the themes and purpose of the section, it is important that our application is in line with John's intention.

Jesus' identity: Jesus is the long-awaited Son of God to whom all the Old Testament feasts and ceremonies point. He has come to deal with sin through His sacrificial death as the true Passover Lamb.

Warning: The response of God's historic people to God's Son is the major surprise of the section. We need to realise that the Jews are not, by birth, members of God's family. And we need to heed the warnings for those who, like them, will not accept God's Son. The reason the Jews reject Him is that they cannot stomach His teaching about their sin; nor can they stomach His 'hard teaching' about the necessity of dependence on His death for forgiveness. They want to follow an earthly Messiah, with an earthly agenda – a Messiah of their own making. We need to be asking ourselves whether we are following a different Christ to the Christ revealed in these chapters.

Invitation: At the same time as the warning, there is great hope and promise for anyone who is prepared to accept Christ's offer of light, life, and freedom from judgment. That is, the person who will come to Him and listen to His word. Such a person is assured that they have been drawn by the Father and given sight to see. He or she must then listen to the Good Shepherd.

STUDY 6

John 5:1–47
He came to His own (1)

CONTEXT

Chapter 5 opens a new section that runs right through to 10:42. In chapters 2–4 Jesus is presented as having come from heaven to earth; He announces the arrival of His messianic kingdom and teaches about membership of it. In chapters 5–10 the issues dealt with all relate to Jesus' claim to be the Messiah and equal with God. His claims are challenged by the Jews who already consider themselves to be God's covenant people. The question is, What will happen in this extraordinary conflict between God's Son and God's historic people who want to kill Him?

In chapter 5 the presenting issue is the Sabbath. By setting out and expounding His claim to equality with God, with the right to give life and to judge, Jesus shows the Jews what is at stake if they reject Him. We are left wondering why they reject Him, and what will happen to them.

STRUCTURE

5:1–18   Proof of equality with God: the healing by the pool.
5:19–30   Claim: Jesus is the Son, equal with God, who gives life and judges.
5:31–47   Jesus' equality with God: affirmed or rejected.

OLD TESTAMENT BACKGROUND

The lame shall leap! Isaiah 35 looks forward to a day when God will rescue His people, at which time 'the lame will leap like a deer' (35:3–7). In selecting the paralytic from a group of lame, blind and paralysed people, Jesus clearly shows that the time of God's rescue has come.

The Sabbath: The day of rest when God's people were meant to remember God's rescue of them in the past, from the slavery of Egypt (Deut. 5:12–15). However, for the Jews of Jesus' day, the Sabbath had become an end in itself. The keeping of the Sabbath rules and regulations was more important than the God whom they should have been honouring on the Sabbath day. They should have recognised, in Jesus' healing of the paralytic, the clear sign that the 'future rest' of the messianic age was at hand; instead, they quibbled about the keeping of rules.

The Son of Man: From Daniel 7 we have already seen that the term 'Son of Man' speaks of Jesus' role as king after the final judgment. John has already added to that that He is the gateway to heaven (1:51; 3:15). Now further meaning is loaded into the title as we see the Son of Man as life-giver and judge.

TEXT NOTES

1–18 PROOF OF EQUALITY WITH GOD: THE HEALING BY THE POOL

The signs in John are significant. This sign again announces the arrival of God's king and His rescue (see Old Testament background). However, it also sparks off a controversy with the Jewish authorities which runs through chapters 7–10. The controversy is about Jesus' action of healing on the Sabbath, which He claims is justifiable on the basis of His equality with God (v. 17). The purpose of this sign is entirely to illustrate Jesus' claim to be the giver of spiritual life and the judge of all mankind on the Last Day.

John makes no comment on the state of the man's faith – we should not allow ourselves to get sidetracked by that issue. Instead, we should recognise how the claims of Jesus are being substantiated. First, the man is healed just by Jesus speaking authoritatively to him (v. 8). Here is the powerful voice of the judge on the Last Day (explained in v. 25). Secondly, the man's illness is part of the general condition of men living in a fallen world. (The 'something worse' of verse 14 is almost certainly a warning of final judgment, rather than some worse illness.) Here is evidence of the Son of Man's power to reverse the effects of human fallenness on the Last Day. Thirdly, this all happens on the Sabbath (see Old Testament notes). Here is the Son of Man accomplishing, for the paralytic, all that the Sabbath pointed to in terms of rest and rescue.

In verses 16–18 we see that the sign, and the resulting discourse (with its claims and accusations), spark off the controversy that results in Jesus' death. Jesus' authoritative action on the Sabbath struck at the heart of the Jews' religion (see Old Testament notes). As Jesus justifies His action in healing the paralytic on the Sabbath, He makes a most radical claim: God has always worked on the Sabbath, and in healing the paralytic Jesus was simply engaged in His Father's work. The Jews see this as a claim to equality with God – which it is! But His claim needs explanation. On what basis does He have the right to do this sort of thing?

19–30 CLAIM AND EXPLANATION: JESUS IS THE SON, EQUAL WITH GOD, WHO GIVES LIFE AND JUDGES

In John's Gospel this is the most important passage concerning the deity of Jesus. He Himself explains the nature of His work on earth, and the implications of His claim to be equal with God. A clear grasp of both these points will be vital to our understanding of the rest of the Gospel. The passage begins with a 'therefore' in verse 19 (not shown by the NIV) and is structured around the three '*I tell you the truth*' sayings. The central saying, in verse 24, contains the key point of the whole chapter, the assertion that whoever responds to Him *now*, genuinely trusting His words and His Father who sent Him, has *already* crossed from death to life. The other two sayings mirror each other.

19–23 He is the life-giver and the judge – so honour Him. In this passage Jesus explains the basis of His relationship with His Father. He is dependent on the Father's revelation to Him. He restricts

Himself to doing only what His Father reveals. He has chosen, in obedience (v. 30), to limit His divine power and to do exactly what He sees His Father doing. This relationship of obedience and submission guarantees the Father's love, and so guarantees that the Father shows the Son 'all He does'. The Son's perfect dependence (in obedience) *guarantees* rather than *limits* His equality. Because He only does what He sees, so the Father loves Him completely and reveals everything to Him. This is how the Son perfectly accomplishes His Father's work and, at the same time, perfectly reveals the Father to us.

But in verse 20b Jesus claims that the Father will show Him two greater 'works' (NIV 'things'). These greater works are to be shown to the Son *in order* that people may be amazed (v. 20b) and that they may 'honour the Son' (v. 23). These greater works are

- ♉ the divine work of giving eternal life
- ♉ the divine work of judgment

24 He is the life-giver and the judge – so believe in His words and in His Father who sent Him. This verse emphasises both the necessity of belief and the present possibility of 'crossing over'. Having told us what sort of 'Son' He is, Jesus now promises eternal life to anyone who takes His words seriously. Anyone who hears and believes now the words of God's appointed judge may be assured of salvation both *now* and *then* (the Day of Judgment).

25–30 He is the life-giver and the judge – so do not be amazed! Verses 25–26 tell us that Jesus gives eternal life now to the spiritually dead, and verses 28–30 give us two reasons why we should not be amazed ('marvel') at what Jesus does in the present. First, He is to be the Great Judge of the Last Day. He has already made that clear (vv. 19-23), but here He amplifies it. Secondly, His perfect relationship with His Father guarantees the perfection of His judgment, both now and then.

31–47 JESUS' EQUALITY WITH GOD:AFFIRMED OR REJECTED
Jesus has made massive claims as to His own identity. Now He points to what will validate these claims. *John the Baptist* (vv . 33-35) was

one witness, but Jesus makes it clear that the Baptist's testimony has been surpassed by the witness of *His work* (v. 36) and *His Father's words* (vv. 37–39). His work is seen in the sign of verses 1–9, which ought to be proof enough! His Father's words, contained in the scriptures, also testify to the identity of Jesus.

All this points to the reality of who Jesus is, and yet the Jews, who claim to be God's people, refuse to believe. These verses begin to explain why 'His own did not receive Him' (1:11). Jesus multiplies the negatives as He exposes the Jews' failure to believe. Their reaction to Him proves that they have never really listened to God's voice in scripture (vv. 37–40), and therefore they have never really believed Moses whom they claim to follow (vv. 45–47). Had they listened they would have understood the prophecies about Jesus and so they would have recognised Him. Also, they do not really love God wholeheartedly (vv. 41–42), and therefore they make no real effort to please Him. By their reaction to Jesus, the Jews show that they are not the people they claim to be. In short, their religion is a hypocritical farce.

Stand by for chapters 6–10! What will happen in the inevitable head-on collision between God's Son and God's historic people?

Key themes

This chapter contains the fullest account of how Jesus is equal with His Father. It unlocks and explains the next four chapters and, as we shall see, it casts a long shadow: it is on account of the claims made in this chapter that the enemies of Jesus seek His death.

 ℔ Equality with the Father:

  ↘ Jesus claimed it, and the Jews recognised the claim for what it was. John the Baptist, Jesus' own works and the Father's words in scripture are cited in support of this claim.

  ↘ Jesus is the life-giver and the judge. He gives eternal life to all who make a genuine response, hearing His words and believing the Father who sent Him.

⬎ Equality means that Jesus is entitled to honour with the Father; no-one can honour the Father who does not honour Jesus.

⬎ Jesus is dependent on and submissive to the Father. Because of His obedience His equality is guaranteed.

✤ Jesus' work on earth is to judge and to give life through His word. Our response to His word, therefore, has enormous significance. This point will recur throughout the Gospel.

✤ The response to Jesus' claim:

⬎ His claim is attested by John the Baptist, by His own works, and by His Father's words in scripture.

⬎ The Jews will not listen to God, nor seek His approval, for they do not accept the One He has sent. They will be judged for their behaviour towards Jesus, which shows that they are not God's people.

APPLICATION

We need to experience afresh the impact of Jesus' claims to equality with God, and to 'marvel' at who He is. To do this will require close study of verses 19–30.

We need to grasp that God's work on earth now is to rescue people for eternal life. This will come about when people listen to Jesus' life-giving words about Himself and His mission, and trust in them. God is at work, therefore, through Jesus' words. We need to be galvanised into taking Jesus' words more seriously as we trust and obey them ourselves, and we also need to have confidence in them as God's power for His work in the world.

The works of Jesus and the words of God in scripture testify to the truth of what Jesus is saying. We need to ask ourselves whether we pass the test of believing where the Jews failed.

THE AIM OF THIS STUDY

To see that Jesus is equal to God, and that we can only honour God and have eternal life by believing in the powerful words of Jesus, the eternal life-giver and judge. The Jews did not do this and so they are not God's people.

SUGGESTED QUESTIONS

✤ Read through the whole passage and, as you read, see if you can spot how the passage might divide naturally.

1–18 PROOF OF EQUALITY WITH GOD: THE HEALING BY THE POOL

✤ The healing of the man at the pool seems like a great miracle. Why do the Jews find Jesus' action so very offensive?

19–30 THE CLAIM: JESUS IS GOD'S SON WHO DOES GOD'S WORK OF GIVING LIFE NOW AND ALSO OF JUDGING

✤ In verses 19–23 Jesus implies that the healing is only a foretaste of two far greater things. What are they?

↘ What is the Father's purpose in showing Jesus these 'greater things'?

↘ What is it about Jesus' relationship with the Father that enables the Father to show Him these greater things?

↘ What light does this shed on the miracle of verses 1-9 and the reactions to it?

✤ What does verse 24 teach us about the nature of a right response to Jesus, and the implications of a right response? How does this tie in with verses 1–18? How do verses 25-30 substantiate the claim that Jesus has made in verse 24?

✤ So, what great truths have we learned about Jesus and His role, in the present and in the future, and a correct response to Him?

↘ How do verses 1–18 provide proof of these truths?

✤ How do verses 19–30 help us to understand verse 14?

✤ chapter 5 contains both 'good' and 'bad' news for our friends. How should these words change the way we talk to them?

31–47 JESUS' EQUALITY WITH GOD: ATTESTED OR REJECTED

✤ Jesus now calls at least three witnesses. Who are they, and how does each one help support His claims? Why are they so appropriate to Jesus' audience?

✤ What are the different points that Jesus makes in His assessment of the Jews? At this point in the Gospel, what should we be learning from these negatives?

⤷ How do these verses bring Jesus' message to a Christian person who is plagued by doubts about what Jesus claims in verse 24?

⤷ What are the implications of verse 39 for your group?

✤ How do we need to pray for one another in the light of this chapter?

John 6:1–40
He came to His own (2)

CONTEXT

In chapter 5 Jesus showed Himself to be equal to the Father, the one with authority to give life and to judge. In this passage we see Jesus identifying Himself as the true Redeemer who is able to give life (5:24). He is the one about whom Moses wrote. As the chapter proceeds Jesus presses home the implications of His identity and His rescue. As He explains the nature of His rescue operation, those who appear to be following Him start to fall away. Eventually we shall see that even some of His disciples are unable to accept what Jesus says about His work of rescue.

This chapter answers two of the big questions raised in chapter 5:

✤ Why are the Jews stumbling?

✤ What has God's Son come to do *now* – to give life or to judge?

STRUCTURE

6:1–21   The signs: evidence that Jesus has come to perform God's rescue.

6:22–40   Why did the crowds follow Jesus? Motives exposed, signs explained, and an invitation extended.

OLD TESTAMENT BACKGROUND

The Exodus: God rescued His people from slavery to the Egyptians, leading them out of Egypt and into the land He had promised to their forefathers. The rescue was accompanied by signs and wonders, of which one of the most crucial was the Passover (described in Exodus 12) when God passed through Egypt in judgment, striking down every first-born among the Egyptians. There then followed a period of testing, trial, and also further miracles, as the Israelite nation wandered around the wilderness before being brought into the Promised Land. The whole Exodus period was key to Israel's understanding of herself as a nation belonging to God, and of her God as a God who rescues.

Around the time of the exile, when Israel was driven away from the Promised Land, God promised a new rescue which would take the form of a new Exodus under a new leader (Isa. 11:15–16). Since then the Jews had been longing for God to bring about this promised rescue.

At the time of the Exodus, God had provided certain key events which enabled Israel to look back and remember the character of their God as Rescuer:

The Passover feast. This was an annual festival instituted by God to ensure that His people remembered the night of escape. (More on this in the next study.)

Manna. The miraculous provision of bread – the bread was called 'manna' – sustained the Israelites day by day. It also served other purposes of God, reminding His people of their rescue and testing them, to see whether they really would continue to depend on their Rescuer alone, by keeping His commands (Exod. 16:4).

The Prophet. In Deuteronomy 18:15–18, God promised Israel a new prophet 'like Moses' who would lead them as Moses had done.

Walking on water. The rescue of the Exodus involved two miraculous partings of water: Moses parted the Red Sea, so that the Israelites could cross over safely, and Joshua parted the River Jordan, in order to bring them into the Promised Land. There is an allusion to this in Isaiah 11:15.

Psalm 78: This long psalm, containing many references to the Exodus and the desert wanderings, contrasts the Israelites' stubborn, unbelieving behaviour with the continued goodness and mercy of God. The reference to this psalm in verse 31 is highly ironic.

Text notes

1–21 THE SIGNS: EVIDENCE THAT JESUS HAS COME TO PERFORM GOD'S RESCUE

Chapter 5:24-30 taught us that Jesus is the life-giver, but left us wondering how He is going to give that life and what exactly He is going to do now – give life, or judge? This passage is designed to teach that Jesus is God's promised Rescuer. The events echo the events of the Exodus and provide evidence that Jesus is the one about whom Moses wrote (cf. 5:46). First, John tells us that it is Passover time (v. 4), so the context, we realise, is one of heightened expectation, that God's promises of rescue for His people will soon be realised. Secondly, in this context Jesus feeds the crowd miraculously. The people are quite clear that this shows Him to be 'the prophet who is to come into the world' (vv. 5-15); they have made the link between Jesus and Moses, the one through whom God rescued and provided. Thirdly, Jesus later walks on the water of Lake Galilee, providing immediate confirmation to His disciples that He is the deliverer of Isaiah 11, who will enable men to cross the waters in sandals.

The crowd are obviously expecting a Rescuer and they appear to have identified Jesus correctly. But John's comment in verse 2 about the reason why the crowd are following, and Jesus' withdrawal in verse 15, leave us slightly uneasy. We have already been told that people who respond to Jesus purely on the basis of the miracles they have witnessed are highly suspect (2:23–25). John tells us twice (vv 2,14) that the crowd are responding on that basis. Verse 15 gives us a partial clue as to what is wrong: their expectation of the nature of His Rescue seems to be unsatisfactory. Jesus does not want to be made king *by force*, so He withdraws.

Verse 6 shows that the disciples, as well as the crowd, need to make a response to Jesus. Just as the manna in the wilderness was a test for God's people (see Old Testament notes), so the feeding of the five thousand will be some sort of test for His disciples, to see whether they have begun to trust Jesus' teaching.

22–40 WHY DID THE CROWDS FOLLOW JESUS? MOTIVES EXPOSED, SIGNS EXPLAINED, AND AN INVITATION EXTENDED

In the dialogue of this passage a number of themes are dealt with simultaneously. The best way to tackle them is to focus on them one at a time.

Motives exposed. Verse 26 presents us with a problem. In verses 2 and 14 John told us that the crowds were following Jesus because they had seen the miraculous signs. In verse 26 Jesus tells the people that they are following Him not because they saw the signs, but because they had had their fill. The problem is resolved when we realise that Jesus is criticising them for not having fully seen the significance of the sign. They have seen *something* but not everything. One commentator puts it this way: 'instead of seeing in the bread, the sign; they see in the sign, only the bread ...' They are looking for a rescue and a rescuer, but Jesus' analysis of them is that they are looking for a different type of rescue to the one He has come to bring. Their agenda is entirely materialistic, so they want a political king (v. 15) who will meet their materialistic needs (v. 26), through their religious works (v. 28).

Their motives are further exposed in verses 28–30, when they ask what they need to do. Jesus tells them to believe in the One God has sent, but their reply immediately reveals that they are willing to do this only if He conforms to their ideas of what a Messiah should be. His analysis of their condition is shown to be accurate in verse 31: He has just done a miracle such as Moses did, but they do not see the significance of it and will not believe His claims, so they ask for another miraculous sign! They are so obsessed with their own ideas of what the Rescuer will be like, and what He will do, that when Jesus comes they do not recognise Him. He summarises their failure in verse 36.

Signs explained. At the same time as He exposes the wrong motives of the crowd, Jesus describes the nature of the rescue He is going to provide. He does this in terms of the Father's 'work' (vv. 27ff), the Father's gift (vv. 32ff), and the Father's will (vv. 38ff). The Father's 'work' – in other words, what the Father requires – is to believe in the Son of Man, who provides food that endures to eternal life (v. 27). The Father's gift is 'the true bread from heaven',

Jesus Himself. And the Father's will is that those whom He gives to Jesus should never perish but be saved. In replying to the crowd, Jesus identifies the nature of the bread they *should* be looking for: not ordinary bread at all, but the man whom the Father has sent from heaven and who will give spiritual life to all. By verses 35–36 Jesus has taken the crowd beyond their focus on manna, showing that manna was only ever intended to point beyond itself, both backwards in time, to their rescue by God, and forwards, to Jesus who will accomplish God's new rescue on God's terms.

An invitation extended. Having seen the crowd's failure to understand, we may be wondering whether anyone at all is going to be rescued. But in verse 35 Jesus extends an invitation to all who will come, urging them to come to Himself and be satisfied. Note the generosity of the offer, in contrast to the peevishness of the crowd's response in verse 41. Verses 37–40 assure us that the Father is interested in rescuing and that His rescue will be accomplished through the perfectly obedient Son (cf. 5:19ff).

KEY THEMES

⚲ Jesus is God's Rescuer who fulfils His Father's will and rescue plan.

↘ He fulfils Old Testament types and prophecies – indeed, He far surpasses them.

↘ He really is God's Rescuer; He has His Father's approval.

↘ His Father's plan is to give eternal life, which comes only through Jesus.

↘ He continues to offer life to all who will come on His terms.

↘ His Father's will is to draw His people to His Son who will keep them for eternity.

✤ Jesus' miracles and words are a test for the people, just as the manna was in the Old Testament; the contrast between the two agendas, the will of God and the will of humanity, is exposed.

↘ The people's motives and will are exposed. A Rescuer who conforms to their image of the Messiah is what they want, not God's genuine Rescuer with His agenda of eternal issues.

↘ The people are only really concerned with earthly things. They want instant and physical satisfaction *now*, hence their insatiable desire for miracles.

↘ In the end they are not interested in what Jesus is doing; they do not want His sort of rescue because they want to remain 'in control' of God.

APPLICATION

To them then: The Jews were clearly expecting a rescue. As God's people they were therefore on the right tracks. However, it rapidly becomes apparent that they are looking for the wrong sort of rescue. Their concern is entirely for something physical to meet their immediate needs. They have missed the point of the lessons to be learned from the Exodus, failing to recognise the events that the Exodus foreshadowed (i.e. God's provision of eternal life through Jesus). He makes it clear that the rescue they need, the rescue that He has come to provide, is eternal life. He will not be influenced by their agenda. Instead, He continues to make His offer to anyone who is prepared to come to Him.

To us now: This passage presents us with the challenge of accepting Jesus on His terms. It presents a real challenge to the world, which is not interested in God's spiritual rescue but is preoccupied with present material needs (social gospel, political gospel, God to sort out immediate problems). There is also the challenge to *the church*, preoccupied as it is with present material concerns – power in this world, status, health, wealth, prosperity. Often the church is only interested in miraculous signs and in forcing Jesus' Spirit to meet an earthly agenda. And frequently it shapes its evangelistic message to the world's felt needs rather than its real needs as identified by Jesus. *My life* is challenged too: do my prayers and requests to God reflect my present needs, rather than being shaped according to His agenda and His future kingdom, with Him in control?

THE AIM OF THIS STUDY

To see that Jesus has come as God's Rescuer to bring eternal life, and that we need to look to Him to provide that sort of rescue, not a rescue of our own design.

SUGGESTED QUESTIONS

- ♨ What have we learned about Jesus' identity and function from chapter 5?
- ♨ What were the major surprises about the Jews in chapter 5?
- ♨ (*Before discussing chapter 6, quickly make a list of the main issues that you tend to pray about, as a group and as individuals. Then put it to one side!*)
- ♨ (*Give a brief explanation of the four components of the Exodus, from Old Testament notes.*)

1–21 EVIDENCE THAT JESUS HAS COME TO PERFORM GOD'S RESCUE

- ♨ How are the four Exodus themes picked up in these verses?
  - ↘ How does this affect our view of the crowd, as shown in these verses?
  - ↘ John tells us twice why the crowd were following Jesus. What is the reason?
  - ↘ What pointer does this reason give us as to what will happen in the rest of the chapter?
  - ↘ How will verse 6 affect the way we read this chapter?
- ♨ How do the events of verses 16–21 reinforce the lessons of verses 1– 14?
  - ↘ What does this teach the disciples?

22–40 EXPOSURE OF THE MOTIVES AND EXPECTATIONS OF THE SECULAR CROWD

- ♨ What do verses 22–24 tell us about the crowd? How does Jesus interpret this frenetic activity? What is the contradiction between verse 26 and verses 1–15? Can anyone give an explanation?

✤ What do we learn about the crowd from the demands they make of Jesus in verses 30–31?

✤ What do we learn about the crowd from verses 27–31?

✤ At the same time as criticising the crowd, Jesus tells them what sort of Rescuer He is. What does He tell us about the work of God, the gift of God and the will of God?

✤ How does the rescue He describes differ from what the crowd expected and desired?

✤ The reaction of the crowd to Jesus leaves us wondering whether anyone is ever going to be rescued! How do verses 25–40 help us address that question?

✤ How does this passage help us in identifying those whom God has given Jesus?

APPLICATION

In this passage we see a conflict between the crowd's materialistic agenda concerned with the present and God's spiritual agenda concerned with the future. How do we see this conflict in the world, in the church, and in our own lives? Look back at those prayer requests! What warning does the passage have for us? What *should* we look to Jesus for?

John 6:41–71
He came to His own (3)

CONTEXT

Chapter 5 raised several major questions. First, why are the Jews stumbling? Secondly, what has God's Son come to do *now* – to give life or to judge? Thirdly, what then will happen to the Jews? In the last study we saw the first two questions being answered, as Jesus exposed the Jews' motives in looking for a rescuer, and explained what it means for Him to be 'the bread of life'. In this study we see those answers developed. He explains *how* it is that He is the 'bread of *life*' – His origin and His death are central to His explanation.

Jesus continues to expose the Jews' unwillingness to accept His offer of life on His terms. They will not 'eat this bread' (i.e. they will not believe) because the ideas of His divine origin and of His death are deeply offensive. And they will not accept that they are sinful. Verse 63 is the key verse which summarises Jesus' response to the argument: the Jews' best works are useless and a divine rescue is needed if they are to have life.

He begins to provide an answer to the big question of what will happen in the conflict between God's people and God's Son, by teaching us that the Father will give Him all whom the Father draws, all who listen and learn. This third question is not fully answered in the chapter but is further developed in chapters 7 and 8.

Structure

The structure is based around the response to two 'hard teachings'.

6:41–51   Jesus' supernatural origin: 'How can He say "I came down from heaven"?'

6:52–59   The scandal of the cross: 'How can this man give us His flesh to eat?'

6:60–71   The response: 'This is a hard teaching. Who can accept it?' Division among those who will not accept that 'the Spirit gives life but the flesh counts for nothing'.

Old Testament background

The Passover feast: This was an annual festival instituted by God to ensure that His people remembered their miraculous rescue from Egypt under Moses' leadership. On the night of the Israelites' escape from Egypt, each family had had to kill a lamb and daub its blood on the lintels of their door, marking out the family as one that belonged to God. The lamb's death protected the family's eldest son from the wrath of God's angel, who came that night in judgment on the Egyptians (Exod. 12:1–13) Every year, at the time of the feast, the killing and eating of the Passover lamb would remind God's people of this event. The mention of 'eating flesh and blood' in connection with the Passover would immediately conjure up images of this substitutionary lamb, sacrificed on behalf of the eldest son. The blood of the lamb had marked out God's people so that they were safe.

Grumbling: One of the most notable characteristics of the Jews during the Exodus period was their constant refusal to trust God for their rescue. Instead of trusting they grumbled, against Moses and against God (Exod. 16:2,7,12).

'They will all be taught by God': The people of God have always been set apart by the one great fact that they possess, listen to, and obey the Word of the Lord. This quote from Isaiah 54:13 pictures the people of God, redeemed by the Suffering Servant, standing in God's presence and being taught by His word of truth. It is a picture of the true family of God, with God forever. The point is that those who truly belong to God will listen to God's words about Jesus.

TEXT NOTES

41–51 'HOW CAN HE SAY "I CAME DOWN FROM HEAVEN"?'
THE 'HARD TEACHING' OF JESUS' SUPERNATURAL ORIGIN

The central features of this passage are the Jews' unwillingness to believe that Jesus is 'from heaven' and Jesus' insistence that He is from God.

The Father's drawing work. Verses 43–46 provide an explanation as to why the Jews do not believe: coming to the Son for life is entirely dependent upon the Father's 'drawing work'. The quote from Isaiah 54:13 demonstrates that the true people of God have always been those who willingly listen to, and learn from, His word. The Father does His 'drawing work' through His revelation. So, it is by paying attention to the Father's word that people are drawn to His Son. (See also v. 65.)

The Jews' presumption. The Jews refuse to listen and learn, and so they do not come and receive the life that the Son offers. The negatives in this passage (the two 'no-one's) provide the explanation of this and also expose the problem: the religious Jews are presumptuous because they assume that they already have all they need. Jesus emphasises that no-one can come *unless ...* and that no-one has seen *except ...* (vv. 44, 46). The Jews need to learn the lesson of verses 29–31, that their works, and the bread Moses gave them, have failed to bring life, for 'the flesh counts for nothing' and only the Spirit can give true life (v. 63). In verses 47–51 Jesus exposes their presumption even more by pointing out that the manna eaten by the Jews' forefathers was insufficient to provide life; something else must be required.

Jesus' supernatural origin and mission. Jesus points to Himself as that 'something else', the only one who has seen the Father, and the true 'bread of life'. He begins to explain *how* the bread He provides is superior. The bread is His 'flesh' which will be given *on behalf* of the world, as a substitutionary sacrifice to bring life (see Old Testament notes).

52–59 'HOW CAN THIS MAN GIVE US HIS FLESH TO EAT?'
THE 'HARD TEACHING' OF THE OFFENCE OF THE CROSS

At Passover time, mention of eating the flesh of the Son of Man and drinking His blood in connection with 'this bread' would tie

Jesus' death to the sacrifice of the Passover Lamb (see Old Testament notes). While the Jews cannot work out what Jesus is saying in verse 51, He replies by stressing the essential nature of His death for the obtaining of eternal life. His death is vital to the work of rescue.

Negatively, Jesus insists that unless a person depends on His death they have no life (v. 53). Again He stresses that the manna provided in the desert was insufficient to give life (v. 58). The Jews must realise that their presumption – that they are acceptable to God because they were born Jews – is fatal.

Positively, Jesus teaches that His death achieves the eternal life that is lacking. First, anyone at all (i.e. 'the world', verse 51) who does 'feed' on Jesus' death will be rescued and given eternal life, for this bread is truly life-giving (vv. 54, 55). Secondly, anyone at all who 'feeds' on Jesus' death will have an intimate personal relationship with Jesus, who takes up residence and lives within a person (v. 56).

By the end of this passage (vv. 57–59) the development of the 'bread types' is complete. The chapter began with the feeding of the five thousand and physical bread. Jesus has shown that physical, material food is entirely insufficient to meet the Jews' real need, which is for eternal life. This need can only be met by God coming to earth and giving His life on behalf of the world. The Jews need to stop being so presumptuous, and to start depending on Him and on His solution to their real problem.

The big question throughout the passage is, What does Jesus mean by 'eating', or 'feeding on', His flesh? That question is answered by verses 35, 40, 47 and 63. Throughout the chapter 'feeding' has been a metaphor for 'believing' His message. His message has been shown to include the prediction of His death on behalf of the world. (On the question of whether this passage can be taken as referring to Holy Communion, Carson, p. 297, is excellent.)

60–71 'THIS IS A HARD TEACHING. WHO CAN ACCEPT IT?'

Up to now it has been the Jews who grumble. Now the disciples are unable to take Jesus' teaching. The 'hard thing' to accept is His supernatural origin and His death as the Passover Lamb. They can't handle the idea of God coming to earth in human form, or of following a dying Messiah. These ideas 'scandalise' them, or cause them to trip up. Jesus criticises them for being unable to see His divine nature and divine mission. He has come from heaven to die and He will return to heaven (v. 62). If the first idea horrifies them, they'll never grasp the second!

In verse 63 Jesus explains the whole chapter by showing that the Spirit is the One who will bring spiritual life. The Spirit brings this life through the words of Jesus. It is a great error either to drive a wedge between the Spirit and the words of Jesus, or to expect God's Spirit to work apart from Jesus' words. The eternal life that Jesus offers can come no other way than by His Spirit through His word, for all our human efforts are useless – 'the flesh counts for nothing.' (The word 'flesh' is used here in a different sense from that in previous verses; here it means earthly understanding and earthly life.) The disciples have still not grasped the lessons of 3:1–8.

By verse 66 it becomes clear that some who have been following Jesus as 'disciples' are, like the Jews, only interested in following Jesus on their own terms; they have failed to see Him as He really is, God's true Rescuer. It is now even clearer than before why Jesus does not entrust Himself to people who believe only on the basis of miracles (cf. 2:23–25).

When Jesus asks the Twelve if they too want to leave, Peter answers, identifying Jesus correctly.

KEY THEMES

✤ Jesus is God's Rescuer.

> ⬎ He alone has seen God, He alone has come from God, He alone can give eternal life.

> ⬎ He will accomplish God's rescue of 'the world' by giving His life on our behalf.

> ⬎ His offer of life is extended to 'everyone who listens to the Father', and 'whoever' eats His flesh.

> ⬎ His offer of life is explained as an intimate union with Him now and certain rescue by Him at the Resurrection.

> ⬎ Rescue, or eternal life, is only available to those who 'eat His flesh'.

> ↘ 'Eating Jesus' flesh' is a metaphor for believing in His death on our behalf.

↯ The Jews and the disciples grumble.

> ↘ The idea of Jesus' death is deeply offensive both to the Jews and to some of the disciples; they cannot accept Jesus' assertion that 'the flesh counts for nothing'. They are proud and presumptuous and will not accept God's solution to their problem. They cannot see beyond their own earthly agenda, nor can they see their need. They fall away once they realise that this Messiah is going to die.

> ↘ The Twelve, represented by Peter, recognise Jesus' identity and also their need.

↯ Predestination.

> ↘ Only God can enable a person to come to Jesus on His terms.

> ↘ A person can only come to God if he or she comes to Jesus and learns from Him.

APPLICATION

To them then: The shock of this passage, to Jesus' audience and to John's readers, is on account of the nature of Jesus' mission and also the exclusivity of it. He is the Bread of Life because He is going to die on behalf of the world. No-one else can provide God's rescue because no-one else has come down from heaven and no-one else has seen God. Jesus exposes the failure of all past systems to achieve a real rescue that lasts, and points to Himself and His death as the only and essential solution for anyone who wants to be rescued. Once again, like in the last study, this teaching proves highly offensive, not just to the Jews but also to His disciples. They are not ready to follow a Messiah who will die; this prospect proves to be a stumbling block to them. Nonetheless, Jesus continues to extend His offer of life to all who will believe. The benefits are enormous: intimate union with Him now *and* then (cf. 5:24).

To us now: Are we like the Jews, people who grumble? Are we presumptuous, or are we scandalised by a suffering Messiah? It is all too easy to impose alternative agendas onto Jesus, and make Him into a 'here-and-now, political, social, me-and-my-immediate-needs Messiah'. If we are tempted to do this, it is because we have failed to see the seriousness of our sin, and our urgent need of His divine, substitutionary rescue. If we are dependent on His death for eternal life, then the benefits, both now and then, are immeasurable.

THE AIM OF THIS STUDY

To see that following Jesus means believing in His death as the central point of His rescue mission, without which we have no hope of life.

SUGGESTED QUESTIONS

- ✢ What did we learn about the crowd and about Jesus in the last study?
- ✢ In verse 60 Jesus' disciples complain about His teaching. Look back over verses 41–59, and try to identify some of the things that they find hard.

41–51 HARD TEACHING NUMBER 1: THE SCANDAL OF THE INCARNATION

- ✢ What are the different negative and positive things that Jesus says in these verses?
  - ↘ How do these negatives and positives help us to understand (a) the Jews to whom Jesus is speaking? (b) the answer to the question of verse 42b?
- ✢ Read verse 63a. How does it help us to understand what is going on in the synagogue?
- ✢ The Jews of the synagogue were the most religious people in the nation. What, then, is the surprise of this passage and what does it have to teach us?

52–59 HARD TEACHING NUMBER 2: THE SCANDAL OF THE CROSS

- ✢ How does the proximity of the Passover, and the location of the discussion, help to make sense of what Jesus has to say about His flesh and blood? (*Explain the Passover Lamb.*)
- ✢ There are more negatives and positives in these verses. What are they?

↘ How do the negatives address the attitude of the religious Jews?

↘ How do the positives address the person who is prepared to listen to God and learn from Him?

↘ From the chapter, what does it mean to eat His flesh and drink His blood?

60–71 DIVISION AMONG THOSE WHO WILL NOT ACCEPT THAT THE FLESH COUNTS FOR NOTHING

✤ What is it about Jesus' teaching that proves so offensive to so many?

↘ How do verses 62–65 explain what is going on?

↘ Why is this such a warning to us?

↘ How do we try to evade the 'hard teachings' of Jesus in our discipleship?

✤ What does Peter's response teach us about the nature of genuine discipleship?

John 7:1–52
His own did not receive Him

CONTEXT

In chapter 7 Jesus returns to Jerusalem where He finds hatred, on account of His healing on the Sabbath (vv. 20–25). This fact helps us see how all of these chapters are part of a major section which began at chapter 5, with the description of that healing. In chapter 6 Jesus claimed to be the long-promised Rescuer to whom the Old Testament festivals pointed and for whom God's people should have been waiting. However, God's people 'grumbled' at the kind of Rescuer He claimed to be. They were scandalised at His exposure of their sin and at God's solution (6:63). The questions left in the air are, is He really God's rescuer? And, are they really in need of this sort of rescue? This is the background to the hostility, confusion and division that runs right through chapter 7 and into chapter 8, as the confrontation continues between God's historic people and God's Son.

In answer to the second question, chapter 7 sees a development in the exposure of God's people's motives and hearts. Verse 7 sums it up: the Jews hate Jesus and are therefore of the world. The next two chapters will see a rapid downward spiral among the Jews as Jesus exposes the true nature of even the most religious human heart.

In connection with the first question, the discussion about Jesus' 'right time' is very important. Jesus' words and actions demonstrate that He is in complete control of all that is going on, that He is working to an agenda specifically laid down by His Father, and that He has come down from above to accomplish a task among God's people. At 'the right time' He will return to His Father and fulfil the Rescuer's promise, namely the pouring out of the life-giving Spirit of God upon the people of God (see verse 39).

Structure

7:1–10	Setting the scene: Jesus has 'a time', and knows when that time is. As He heads towards it He is always in control of His agenda. The world remains hostile, hating Him for exposing its sin.
7:11–31	He is from above: they are of the world.
7:32–52	He is returning to His Father: they cannot come to His Father.

Old Testament background

Feast of Tabernacles: This feast dominates chapters 7–10. It was a harvest festival, a time of great joy and celebration. During the eight day feast all Israel gathered in Jerusalem and camped in 'booths' or 'tabernacles' made from branches. This was to remind the people that they had lived in tents in the wilderness during the time of God's rescue. During the feast the two themes of water and light played important parts. The people looked back to the past, remembering God's provision of water from the rock in the desert, and also His presence in the pillar of cloud or light that went ahead of them to lead them.

At the same time they looked forward to the future, to the time when God's Spirit would be poured out, as promised, in the last days. The prophet Zechariah, in the period after the exile, had urged God's people to look forward to a future great Feast of Tabernacles when all God's promises to His people would be fulfilled, through an act of cleansing, restoration and judgment, and His sovereignty over the whole world would be established (Zech. 13:1; 14:6–21).

The feast culminated in a large gathering on the last day, an opportunity that Jesus uses to maximum effect.

Text notes

1–10 SETTING THE SCENE

This introductory passage serves the important function of showing us the background to the action in chapters 7 to 10. The failure of Jesus' brothers to believe in Him reminds us of the 'hard teaching' and the 'scandals' of chapter 6. Even those closest to Jesus want Him to be championed by the people and to have a wide public ministry. We realise that the questions left in the air at the end of chapter 6 – Is Jesus really 'the Christ'? Are God's historic people really so completely wrong? – are still very much in the frame at the start of chapter 7

Verses 7–8 are key verses that begin to explain the answers to the two questions. Verse 7 explains the reason for the Jews' rejection of Jesus and summarises the shocking failure of 'God's people'. Their hatred of Jesus shows them to be part of 'the world' that is in rebellion against God, by virtue of its natural human tendency to reject God (see 1:10). This verse introduces the exposure of God's historic people, a theme that continues through to chapter 10. (Jesus' analysis of His brothers, that they too belong to the world, at least at this stage, underlines the seriousness and universality of human sin. There is no favouritism in God's family.)

Verse 8 raises again the theme of timing which will run through chapters 7 and 8. Jesus begins to explain what He means by His 'right time', and later we shall see that He has been sent by His Father, and will return to His Father, after accomplishing all that God's true people should have been looking forward to. Jesus' refusal to comply with His brothers' request, to go up to the Feast with them, is because He is working to His Father's agenda, in obedience to His Father's will (5:19). *He will* select the 'hour', not them. He needs to be at the Feast on the last day, so that His offer of 'streams of living water' (v. 38) may have maximum impact, but He cannot afford to spend too much time in the public eye because of the Jews' plan to arrest and kill Him. This matter of 'timing' highlights Jesus' total control of the situation, even amidst the complete confusion and the conflicting claims that await Him in Jerusalem.

11–31 HE IS FROM ABOVE: THEY ARE OF THE WORLD

This passage, with its first mention of 'widespread whispering' (literally *grumbling* – in the Greek it is the same word as in 6:41), contains three main areas of material.

The exposure of the Jews. This continues in the round of questions and answers that follows, as Jesus testifies to the real attitudes and plans of the 'people of God'. Briefly, He explains in three steps the reasons behind their refusal to recognise Him: they choose not to do God's will and so have no hope of recognising Him (vv. 16–19); in fact, they so misunderstand God's law as to be able to make only human judgments from a human perspective (vv. 21–24). Their claim to know God is therefore shown to be as false as their hypocritical religion (vv. 28–29). Jesus' logic is ruthless and His assessment of the Jews is confirmed by their action – they are plotting murder, despite claiming to be God's people (vv. 25, 30 and 32), and so they are making a sham of the Sabbath.

The identity of Jesus. In contrast to worldly behaviour, Jesus' integrity is absolute: He keeps God's law because He seeks God's honour and not His own (vv. 16–19). He fulfils God's law by healing the whole person, in anticipation of the Sabbath rest (vv. 21–24). He knows God because He is from God and was sent by God (vv. 28–29). The major emphasis in this passage is on the identity of Jesus, the fact that He is *from* God (v. 29).

The response of the crowds. Jesus' teaching in verses 12–31 is met with hostility, as some try to kill Him (v. 19) or seize Him (v. 30), confusion, as some try to work out what is going on (vv. 25–27), widespread whispering (vv. 12–13), and a kind of faith (v. 31).

32–52 HE IS RETURNING TO HIS FATHER: THEY CANNOT COME TO HIS FATHER

32–36 Exposure of the Jews. Jesus is on His way back to the Father. Time is running short for the Jews to respond to Him. A time is coming when they will no longer be able to find Him and His offer of life, and nor will they be able to come to His Father. His greatness comes not only from the fact that He has come from the Father, but also from the fact that He is going back to the Father.

The Jews still fail to understand what Jesus is saying. Note the irony of verse 35.

In verse 32 comes the first mention of the Jews taking active steps to arrest Jesus – the pace is hotting up!

37–39 Jesus' mission. Even as the Jews fail to understand what Jesus is saying, He makes His offer to the world, to the 'anyone' and the 'whoever' who believes. This offer, coming at the end of the Feast of Tabernacles, is a claim to be the fulfilment of all that the Feast signified, all that it pointed back to and all that it anticipated. Jesus is the one true Rescuer who will provide the outpouring of the Spirit of God. The Spirit's rich abundance of life will be like a self-replenishing stream in the believer; this will be the 'eternal life' that has been spoken of from the start of the Gospel. But note the key reference to Jesus' 'time' which John provides in his interpretative comment (v. 39). Once again we are being shown that Jesus is the true Christ who has been sent by His Father to accomplish a specific mission at a specific time and through a specific action. Amidst all the division and confusion Jesus stands firm, continuing to develop His teaching that He has come to provide eternal life for God's people. As He teaches it becomes increasingly evident that without Him there is no hope of life, but that with Him life is possible.

40–52 The people's response. The people respond to this teaching in a whole variety of ways: they are divided, confused, and amazed. Their leaders deny that Jesus is the Christ.

The shock of this chapter lies in the gradual and sustained exposure of the Jews. They are shown to be God's enemies who do not, in fact, listen to Moses. They may *appear* to be religious people, serving God, but their reaction to Jesus and their attempt to arrest Him give them away. They are evil people.

Of course, there is nothing new about this. It has always been God's verdict on His people that they cannot keep the Law and that they need rescue. The remarkable thing is that Jesus continues to offer to rescue anyone who will believe in Him. And it appears that there are some who are beginning to respond in genuine faith.

KEY THEMES

    ✤ The exposure of the hypocrisy and failure of God's people. They cannot recognise Jesus, for the following reasons:

        ↘ They do not keep Moses' law.

        ↘ They have failed to understand the Law and so can only make ungodly human judgments.

        ↘ They do not know God, and they will not go to Him.

    ✤ The offer of Jesus to provide rescue as He steadily pursues His God-given mission.

        ↘ He is the One from God who is going back to God.

        ↘ He alone can provide the cleansing and spiritual life that His questioners need; this He does through the giving of the Spirit.

        ↘ He is only here for a short time. He demands a response.

        ↘ His offer is to 'anyone' who will believe, and to 'whoever' will believe, in Himself.

    ✤ The polarisation of those who would call themselves God's people as they respond in confusion, denial, hostility, and also faith.

APPLICATION

To them then: The confusion, division and growing polarisation recorded in the chapter demonstrate how Jesus' claims applied to the people He was speaking to. He exposed the failure of the most religious people imaginable. In spite of all their claims and pretence, they did not know God. John's inclusion of Jesus' explanatory comment in verse 7 makes it all clear: 'it [the world] hates me because I testify that what it does is evil'. John's descriptive comments also help us to see the points that he wants his original readers to realise. God's people appear to be unable to respond to this uncomfortable Messiah in repentance and faith. They are *not* God's people. At the same time, Jesus purposefully pursues His God-given mission. He *is* God's Son, sent from God and returning to God. Those who turn to Him will have eternal life.

To us now: The application to us now is parallel. The shock of the passage, for us as for the Jews, is that Jesus is an uncomfortable

Messiah who exposes the hypocrisy of all human beings towards God. Even the most religious people need His rescue. This has relevance for us, both in our own attitude to Jesus and in what we should expect when we teach the 'real Jesus' to our friends. We should expect to find confusion, division, and polarisation. We should expect hatred of Jesus from people to whom we bring the gospel, however *religious* they may appear to be. And yet we should realise that His response to that rejection is to continue to extend His offer of rescue. Therefore we should be unmoved as we continue to hold out His offer of life.

The aim of this study

To see that even the most religious Jews are 'of the world' and are therefore evil, whereas Jesus is from God and is pursuing His God-given mission to bring life to God's people. His mission will therefore meet with a variety of responses.

Suggested questions

✤ What causes both the Jews and Jesus' disciples to grumble in 6:40–71?

↘ How do these two scandals contrast with the Jews' preferred agenda for a Rescuer?

↘ If these agendas conflict so severely, what questions are we left asking at the end of chapter 6?

1–10 SETTING THE SCENE

✤ How do Jesus' brothers pick up on the issues and questions left at the end of chapter 6?

✤ How does verse 7 begin to answer these questions?

✤ Verse 8 appears confusing. What *can* we learn from the verse? How might this help with the questions from chapter 6?

11–31 WHERE IS HE FROM? WHERE ARE THEY FROM?

✤ What is it that characterises the atmosphere at the feast in Jerusalem? (*NB Explain that* whispering *in verse 12 is best translated* grumbling *as in 6:41.*)

↳ What major issue is presented by the three questions in verses 15, 20 and 25?

   ↘ In response to these three questions Jesus provides three reasons why His questioners cannot recognise Him. What are they?

   ↘ What are we to conclude about God's historic people gathered for this major religious feast?

   ↘ How is Jesus' assessment of them confirmed by their actions? How does this tie in with verse 7?

↳ How does Jesus measure up to the issues of truth, judgment and knowledge of God?

   ↘ So how does this help to answer the questions about who Jesus is and where He is from?

32–52 WHERE IS HE GOING? WHERE ARE THEY GOING?

↳ What do we learn about the Pharisees, from Jesus and from their own actions, in this passage?

↳ How does Jesus' teaching in verses 33–39 help us to understand His destination, His identity and His mission? (*You will need to explain the purpose of the Feast.*)

   ↘ What is God going to do, when, and for whom?

↳ There are more confused responses to Jesus in this passage. Make a list of all the responses recorded in the whole chapter.

↳ What has Jesus done to answer each of these responses?

   ↘ How will today's passage help us in our evangelism?

John 8:12–59
Children born not of natural descent

CONTEXT

Chapter 8:12 follows directly from 7:52: Jesus is still at the Feast of Tabernacles speaking to the crowds and once again He extends His offer of salvation beyond the hostile Jews to the 'world' and to 'whoever' will follow Him. In chapter 7 God's historic people appeared to be divided on account of God's Son and many rejected Him. Jesus had already explained this rejection in chapter 6, by exposing the fact that the Jews were concerned with earthly priorities and an earthly Messiah. In the first half of chapter 8 He reiterates the fact that those who are hostile are from this world and therefore cannot follow Him. But the second half of the chapter contains a far greater shock: even the faith of those 'many' who appear to accept Him turns out to be phoney faith. These are the people who pick up stones to stone Him. The shock is this: God's historic people seem *incapable* of expressing genuine, growing faith, the faith that would lead them to acknowledge their sinfulness and accept Jesus' Messiahship (cf. 2:23ff). They neither listen to Moses (ch. 7) nor belong to Abraham (ch. 8). They show by their response to Jesus that they are not God's people – indeed, they are children of the devil. We are left wondering what is going to happen, now that God's historic people have rejected His Son? If *they* can't express proper faith in God's Son, who can?

STRUCTURE

8:12–30   Jesus is from above: the Jews are 'of this world'.

8:31–59   Jesus exposes their phoney faith. They are 'children of the devil' because they do not acknowledge their need and Jesus' ability to meet it. Jesus is the Son of the Father.

OLD TESTAMENT BACKGROUND

Light: This has a vast array of symbolic meanings in the Old Testament. Chapters 8–9 combine the meanings of light to be found in the story of the Exodus, when the pillar of light led God's people to freedom, and also in the book of Isaiah, where the prophet relays God's promise of a 'servant' who will be 'a light for the Gentiles, to open eyes that are blind, to free captives from prison and to release from the dungeon those who sit in darkness' (Isa. 42:6–7). As 'the light of the world' Jesus offers freedom to the people of God (8:31) and sight for the blind (ch. 9). The Jews reject both offers and so are *blinded* by the light.

Abraham: The Jews believed that their racial descent from Abraham guaranteed for them all the blessings of God's covenant with Abraham. They were fiercely proud of their membership of his family and saw belonging to Abraham as synonymous with belonging to God. Jesus has already exposed the Jews for not listening to Moses or doing what Moses says. He now goes a step further and denies even their membership of Abraham's family, because they do not exercise the faith that Abraham had in Him (8:56).

TEXT NOTES

7:53–8:11

Carson explains why this passage is left out. In short, almost all of the earliest and most reliable manuscripts do not include it. Those that do include it have it in different places. It is most likely that this incident did occur but that John did not have it as part of his original Gospel. (See Carson, p. 333.)

12–30 JESUS IS FROM ABOVE: THE JEWS ARE 'OF THIS WORLD'

With the exclusion of verses 1–11 the chapter begins at verse 12, which may be translated literally as, '*Again, therefore*, He spoke to them.' This shows that these verses are a response to the Pharisees' condemnation of the soldiers, the crowd and Nicodemus in 7:45– 52. The Pharisees despise the mob. Jesus, who has not left the feast, responds by announcing that He is the light of *the world* and that *whoever* follows Him will never walk in darkness. (For the meaning of 'light' see Old Testament notes.) Given the reference to the cross (v. 28), and Jesus' exposure of the Pharisees as being in desperate need of rescue (8:21, 24), the life that Jesus promises must be *eternal* life, i.e. rescue and salvation.

The dialogue that follows divides into two sections, in which Jesus restates first His divine origin (vv. 13–20) and then His divine mission and destiny (vv. 21–30). As He does so, He continues to expose the darkness of the Pharisees and the Jews. It is deeply offensive stuff (v. 20b). He condemns God's historic people as being ignorant, unable to make anything but human judgments, having no relationship with God, destined to die in their sins and, finally, being 'of this world'! God's historic people are in desperate need of rescue. If they do not *follow* Him they will never find the rescue they need. Jesus, on the other hand, claims that He stands with the Father and has the Father as His witness, that He has come from above and has been sent from above by the Father. He *is* the promised Rescuer who has come to accomplish His mission in His Father's time (vv. 20, 28).

We, the onlookers, wonder what on earth is going to happen to God's historic people. Is there any hope for God's people who refuse to follow His Son? Jesus closes by teaching that the ignorance of God's people can only be dealt with at the cross (vv. 27–29) after they have crucified Him. *Then* they will realise that He is on His Father's mission. This is the clearest suggestion yet that Jesus' 'time' will be His death, by which means He is going to rescue His people. (Later in the Gospel, when John relates Jesus' crucifixion, he will carefully record certain details of the event, pointing out how they fulfil scriptural prophecies. Understanding all this will enable people to realise that Jesus was fulfilling His Father's purpose by redeeming the world.)

'Many' people in the crowd appear to believe in Jesus, and so He turns His attention to them.

31–59 JESUS EXPOSES THEIR PHONEY FAITH: 'YOU ARE CHILDREN OF THE DEVIL, I AM THE SON OF THE FATHER.'

We saw earlier, in 2:24,25, that Jesus knew what was in a person and therefore would not entrust Himself to anyone. In chapter 2 it was not altogether clear what was required, if a response to Jesus was to be genuine, other than that some sort of 'growing faith' was needed. In chapter 6 Jesus tested the disciples and many proved not to have this kind of faith. Here in chapter 8 Jesus continues to show us what real faith is all about: it is a matter of 'holding' to His teaching. This implies much more than the cliché of 'stick close to Jesus'. The word for 'hold' is literally 'remain in' (cf.15:1–7). And so 'holding to His teaching' is the mark of true faith and of real disciples, even when His teaching proves to be as searching and uncomfortable as it is here.

In the verses that follow, Jesus exposes the 'faith' of the Jews on two counts. First, the Jews are unable to accept the unpalatable truths about their own sinfulness and, it follows, about their own need of rescue. Secondly, they are unable to accept the truths about the identity of Jesus and His claims. They could not persevere. We often hear verses 31–32 used in evangelistic talks, in order to point to this benefit of following Jesus, but when Jesus spoke these words He was face to face with people who were *already* professing faith. Their response was to try to stone Him. Some follow-up meeting! The point is this: it is the same gospel that both creates faith in the first place, and keeps the Christian later on.

31–48 Who is the Jews' Father? Will the faith of these Jews who 'put their faith in Him' prove to be genuine? Will these people 'hold to His teaching'? The ensuing discourse shows that their faith is not genuine because, as Jesus points out:

✤ Genuine children of God are set free from sin's penalty, but these Jews are still enslaved by it.

✤ Genuine children of God do the things Abraham did (i.e. have room for His word, the truth that He has heard from God), but these Jews have no room for His word and are plotting to kill Him.

✤ Genuine children of God love Jesus, but these Jews are plotting to kill Him and so betray their true family membership. They are 'children of the devil'.

Jesus' argument is so strong that the Jews can only respond with abuse (v. 48).

49–59 Who is Jesus' Father? With their true identity exposed by Jesus, the Jews resort to insult (v. 48). Jesus rebuts their insults and then offers eternal life to anyone who will actually *keep* His words – unlike these people who have professed a phoney faith. The Jews are deeply offended by Jesus' claim to be able to save from death, to provide the solution to the greatest of all human problems. Jesus closes the debate with a claim to divinity, the clearest claim yet, but the Jews are simply unable to handle it. To a monotheistic people this claim by a human to equality with God must be blasphemous. There is only one solution. Earlier, in chapter 7, they had taken active steps to arrest Jesus, but now they try to stone Him.

Key themes

✤ Jesus makes a devastating appraisal of God's historic people:

↘ They belong to this world and so are only able to make worldly judgments about Jesus.

↘ They are unable to reach eternal life. They are in real need of rescue but cannot see it.

↘ Their inability to express genuine faith proves that Jesus is correct in His analysis.

↘ They are not, in reality, members of God's people. They are slaves to sin and therefore children of the devil.

✤ The claims of Jesus Christ, the Son of God:

↘ He speaks the Father's words, not His own.

> ↳ He has been sent by the Father, who testifies to Him and glorifies Him.
>
> ↳ He is one with the Father (8:58), and honours Him.
>
> ↳ He is the One who is able to save the people of the world from sin, to set them free, to give them light, and to keep them from death.

✤ This passage shows Jesus sifting the faith of His hearers to see 'what was in a man' (cf. 2:25):

> ↳ Genuine faith is a matter of accepting one's total inability to provide for one's own rescue, and total dependence on the Son to set one free.
>
> ↳ Genuine faith perseveres to the end. It means holding on to Jesus' teaching, however uncomfortable that may prove to be.

APPLICATION

To them then: The shock of this passage, both to the Jews in Jerusalem and to John's original readers, is that God's historic people are utterly incapable of responding adequately to the arrival of God's long-awaited Son and Rescuer. Jesus' explanation of this failure is highly offensive to them. They are unable to respond correctly because they are 'children of the devil'. But Jesus does not leave it there. Even those who appear to respond in faith find that they cannot stomach the grim realities of their utter helplessness and their absolute need of rescue. Pride and self-sufficiency prove to be insurmountable obstacles for those who think that they can call themselves 'Abraham's children', simply on the basis of their birth certificate.

To us now: This passage presents us with 'the Christ' who is exceedingly uncomfortable and who seems to raise more questions than He answers. He prompts us to ask ourselves whether our own faith is genuine. The faith that *keeps* the Christian is faith in exactly the same gospel as the gospel that saves the Christian. New Christians don't need an addition to the gospel. Rather, Christians new and old need to be challenged to allow the same gospel to shape and reshape their thinking and lives. Do we still realise that we are, in fact, enslaved unless Jesus sets us free? Are we still prepared to admit that by nature we are children of the devil? Are we prepared to recognise that we are, by nature, blind, unable to see? If we cannot still say this then we are not holding to His gospel teaching and we need to ask serious questions about the genuineness of our faith. In amongst all the challenge is real hope: if we do admit these things, then we may have light, freedom and life.

THE AIM OF THIS STUDY

To see that even God's historic people were utterly unable to respond to Jesus adequately, owing to their blindness and the hardness of their hearts. The correct, genuine response to Jesus involves a lifelong commitment (or holding) to His gospel, with its hard teaching about human sin and His role as divine Rescuer.

SUGGESTED QUESTIONS

‣ What have we learned in chapters 5–8 about God's historic people and about Jesus?

12–30 JESUS IS FROM ABOVE: THE JEWS ARE 'OF THIS WORLD'

‣ Verse 12 begins, 'Again, therefore ...' What is Jesus' new claim in these verses, and why and to whom is He making it?

↘ How does Jesus summarise the reason for the Pharisees' response to His offer in verses 13-20 and in verses 21-29?

↘ How does He authenticate His claim in verses 13–20 and vv. 21– 29?

‣ How does this passage help develop our understanding of Jesus' 'time'? What will His 'time' achieve?

‣ What grounds for hope are there in this passage?

31–59 JESUS EXPOSES PHONEY FAITH THAT WILL NOT 'HOLD TO' THE GOSPEL

‣ To whom is Jesus' offer of verse 31 made?

↘ Try and restate His offer in your own words.

‣ Jesus' listeners react very strongly to what He is saying. What are the specific things that they find most unpalatable?

✤ Verse 31 tells us that Jesus is speaking to those who had believed. Would you describe His 'Christian Basics Course' as a success or a failure? Explain your reasons.

✤ Chapters 7 and 8 have been about the response of God's historic people to God's Son. What new and shocking truth do these verses teach us about God's historic people? Which verses of the Prologue do these chapters most obviously expound?

APPLICATION

✤ 'I made a commitment to Christ several years ago, so I know that I'm saved.' How would you respond, from the passage, to this statement?

  ↘ What are the marks of a true believer? What good news is there for the true believer?

✤ What must we include in our gospel message if our evangelism is going to be faithful to John's presentation of Jesus and His message?

✤ How does this passage fit in with John's purpose statement in 20:31? What does this tell us about ourselves and about our own claims to be God's people?

John 9:1–41
Born of God

CONTEXT

Three broad headings help to summarise what we have learned in chapters 5–8:

What we discover about Jesus: He is from God, He is equal to God, and He is the One who provides God's rescue – though He is radically different from what the Jews expected. He has been described as 'the Son of Man', who has authority to execute judgment (ch. 5) and who gives His flesh and blood for people to eat and drink (ch. 6); He is also described as the Christ, the Son of God, and the eternal 'I am'.

How the Jews respond to this Rescuer: Their response was hostile. Jesus exposed the true state of their hearts and that they were really 'children of the devil'. They were rebels in need of rescue. But instead of repentance, the Rescuer met rejection. It began to emerge that God's historic people were unable to accept His Son because they did not really belong to God. The shock of these chapters is enormous – especially to John's audience. John wants to persuade his readers that they must acknowledge Jesus as the Christ. John's point is that *they* must believe, even if the Jews won't: he makes it clear that the Jews' unbelief is a reflection of their own sin, and not of Jesus being false.

How then will anyone 'see'? Throughout chapters 5–8 we find a number of answers to this question. People will 'see', or recognise Jesus as the Christ, if they listen to Moses and so to God (5:46), if they listen to the Father and learn from Him (6:45), if they choose to do God's will (7:17), and if they hold on to Jesus' words (8:31,32). But we have seen that even the most promising among God's historic people (i.e. those who initially 'believed') have failed to do these things. How then will *anyone* be able to see?

Chapters 9 and 10 answer this question. They summarise and close the section that began with a Sabbath healing in chapter 5 (see section notes). Spiritual sight requires the miraculous intervention of Jesus, the Messiah. The self-sufficient, who consider themselves healthy and who therefore reject the Messiah, will remain blind forever. As the chapter progresses we witness the blind man becoming progressively more spiritually sighted, and the Jews becoming progressively more blind. Jesus really is 'the light of the world' and in this chapter He expounds the meaning of that title. In chapter 10 Jesus completes His mission to Jerusalem, pronouncing a final condemnation of the Jews and holding out, to all who will turn to Him, the prospect of complete assurance of salvation.

[handwritten margin note: blindness / darkness ∫ sight ∫ light]

STRUCTURE

This chapter divides most easily into a series of 'interviews':

9:1–7   The significant sign: the healing of the blind man and its significance.

9:8–38   Different responses to the sign:

         8–12   Interview with the blind man's neighbours.

         13–17   Blind man's first interview with the Pharisees.

         18–23   Parents interviewed by the Pharisees.

         24–34   Blind man's second interview with the Pharisees.

9:35–41   Jesus' explanatory interview with the blind man and the Pharisees.

OLD TESTAMENT BACKGROUND

'*I am the light of the world*': Blindness in the Old Testament is more than just a physical thing. It is used as a metaphor to illustrate total spiritual failure. This is a major theme in Isaiah:

- ✧ Blindness is a sign of refusing to see and believe God (Isa. 29:9; 42:18–25).
- ✧ In fact God, in judgment, spiritually blinded those who rebelled (Isa. 6:9,10)
- ✧ This blindness will be remedied for God's people when the Messiah comes to rescue them (Isa. 29:18; 32:3; 35:5; 42:7).

In chapter 9 Jesus is developing the 'light of the world' theme, which first appeared in 8:12. In chapter 8 He had offered freedom to His people but they had rejected Him because they were blind. Now, in chapter 9, He gives sight to the blind but blinds those who rebel.

TEXT NOTES

1–7 THE SIGNIFICANT SIGN: THE HEALING OF THE BLIND MAN AND ITS SIGNIFICANCE

As with all the signs in John, the healing of the man born blind has a purpose. Jesus identifies that purpose in verses 3–5. Other translations of 'displayed' are 'become visible', 'known' and 'revealed'. So the purpose of the man's blindness is to make God's work visibly apparent; the man was born blind so that Jesus could display what His work is. It is to bring people to believe. Verse 5 encapsulates and explains part of John's Prologue, 1:4–9 – Jesus really is 'the light of the world' who gives sight to the spiritually blind, and blinds those who consider themselves sighted. Verse 4 looks tricky, but 13:30 explains it: 'night' comes when Jesus is betrayed and taken to the cross. Following His ascension His 'work' will continue (14:12).

8–38 DIFFERENT RESPONSES TO THE SIGN

8–12 *Interview with the blind man's neighbours.* The previous chapter had ended with a violent confrontation between Jesus and the Jews, leaving us with the shocking realisation that God's Son was being rejected by God's historic people. At this point we need to be assured

[Handwritten margin notes, left side, top to bottom:] CANNOT SEE & BLIND CAN SEE. • WHAT THE BLIND CAN DO WHAT CAN THOSE WHO • WHAT IS LIGHT THAT IS INTERESTING

that Jesus really is who He says He is. The giving of sight to the blind is something that only God can do, but did Jesus really perform this miracle? It is important that the *fact* of the miracle is backed up by clear evidence that it really did happen – hence the value of the blind man's neighbours (and later his parents) as witnesses. At the same time we are given our first glimpse of the blind man's understanding about Jesus. At this stage he sees 'the man they call Jesus'.

13–17 Blind man's first interview with the Pharisees. In chapters 7–8 we saw the division and blindness of the Pharisees. Both are on display again here. Healing and kneading were both forbidden on the Sabbath (see Carson). The Pharisees appear to be unable to see beyond the immediate event to the wonderful reality of wholeness that the healing symbolised (see Old Testament notes on the Sabbath for chapter 5, p. 70). They remain preoccupied, throughout the chapter, with how the blind man was healed (v. 26). *He* begins to see more clearly – 'He is *a prophet*' (v. 17).

18–23 Parents interviewed by the Jews. This part provides further authentication that Jesus' miracle was genuine. At the same time we see the stubbornness of the Jews who will not believe, despite the evidence; they have already made up their minds. For the first time we see their hostility being transferred to someone who has decided to follow Christ. Eventually this hostility will lead to action against the blind man.

24–34 Blind man's second interview with the Pharisees. This part is full of tragic irony. The Pharisees refuse to see who Jesus really is, and so they urge the man to 'give glory to God' by condemning Jesus as a sinner. Their illogical position (see v. 33) drives the man one step further towards his conversion, as he gives glory to God by saying, 'If this man were not *from* God, He could do nothing.' The harshness and bitterness of the Pharisees, these 'false shepherds' (cf. ch. 10), is confirmed by their reaction both to the man and to his parents. They throw him out of the synagogue. As in chapters 5–8, the Pharisees continue to claim to be Moses' disciples, but even the man born blind can see that their claim is hollow.

excommunicated?

35–41 JESUS' EXPLANATORY INTERVIEW WITH THE BLIND MAN AND THE PHARISEES

The reappearance of Jesus makes us wonder why He hasn't been around to help the blind man. He seems to have healed him and then left him to it! We are not given the answer to this question, but the man's perseverance, sticking with Jesus in spite of hostility, shows that he has the persevering faith we read of in chapter 8, e.g. verse 12b. Once a genuine work of God has begun in a person, then no-one can snatch that person out of God's hands – Jesus will 'lose none of all that He [the Father] has given me' (6:39). Jesus seeks out the blind man because he is ready to believe, in spite of opposition, and his faith grows. Once again, Jesus gives Himself the title 'Son of Man'. In chapter 5 we saw that it is the Son of Man who speaks God's final words of life and judgment *now* (5:27), and later we understood that unless a person eats and drinks the Son of Man's flesh and blood that person has no life (6:53). The blind man now 'sees' and worships this life-giving, self-giving Son of Man.

In explaining His action (v. 39) Jesus enables us to understand what has been going on all through chapters 5–8. He is 'the light of the world', but His light does two different things. It blinds the hard-hearted who, like the Pharisees in this chapter, are convinced that they see everything, but who are in reality blind. But it illumines those who are willing to believe in the significance of the signs. Thus 'the light of the world' brings rescue and fulfils the prophecy in Isaiah 42. The work of the Son of Man is to bring this judging, life-giving light.

[handwritten marginal note: → not those who are merely "seek after signs"]

KEY THEMES

- ✥ Jesus is 'the light of the world':
  - ↘ His coming fulfils the prophecy in Isaiah 42:6–7.
  - ↘ *He* does what God alone can do: He opens blind eyes, enabling people to see. Restoring physical sight is the sign that He, and He alone, can give spiritual sight and rescue.
  - ↘ He blinds the hard-hearted who reject Him.
  - ↘ He is the means by which anyone can come to believe and to persevere in belief.

✤ The response of the Jews:
- ↘ They refuse to accept Jesus as the Christ, despite the evidence.
- ↘ They are unable to see beyond God's Old Testament revelation to the person to whom it testifies, because they are convinced that they already have the last word.
- ↘ This response means that they will be judged.
- ↘ Their failure to respond rightly should not hinder our belief; it will not stop God's work.

✤ The blind man's response – and his example of 'growing faith':
- ↘ Jesus works in him and 'keeps' him; the initiative is God's.
- ↘ He obeys from the beginning.
- ↘ He perseveres in acknowledging Jesus, despite opposition.
- ↘ He grows in understanding as he acknowledges Jesus and, remarkably, as he is persecuted.

APPLICATION

To them then: Jesus' explanatory comments in verses 39–41 indicate how He intended the sign and following dialogue to be interpreted. His words help us to make sense of the shock of chapters 5–8. The sign has provided clear and convincing proof that Jesus is the Messiah, and that the messianic rescue really has come. But the surprise is that Jesus' work as 'the light of the world' is *both* to give sight to the blind *and* to blind those who think they can see. The application of this to John's readers is clear: it means that they should not be disturbed, shaken, or put off by the fact that God's historic people have rejected His Son. Nor should they be unnerved by the hostility of God's people. They should not be dismayed at the apparent impossibility of anyone being able to recognise God's Rescuer, because it is Jesus Himself who gives sight to the blind, and He will 'keep' those in whom He is working. The only qualification required, for sight to be given, is a recognition of blindness. But, for those who think they can see there is no hope.

To us now: Once we see the application to John's readers then, the application to us now should be very clear. This passage explains what has been going on in the previous four chapters: after studying it we should come away *convinced* that Jesus really is the Messiah, *humbled* as we understand why and how we have believed, and *clear* that His work as 'the light of the world' involves spiritual blinding as well as the giving of spiritual sight. This should *encourage* and *reassure* us in our evangelism, because the opening of blind eyes is *His work* and He will do it completely, whatever the world's reaction to those who believe.

THE AIM OF THIS STUDY

To be assured that, despite the negative reaction of the Jews in chapters 5–8, Jesus really is the long-awaited Messiah. His work involves giving sight to those who recognise that they are in need of rescue, and blinding the spiritually self-sufficient.

SUGGESTED QUESTIONS

- ✠ Why was the rejection of God's Son in 8:59 so devastating?
  - ↘ How does this miracle, of giving sight to a man born blind, answer some of the questions about Jesus' identity that were raised in chapters 5–8?
- ✠ Chapter 9 can be divided into a series of interviews. What are they?
  - ↘ What is the point of the interview with the neighbours?
  - ↘ What is revealed about the Pharisees as they investigate the healing, and as they interview the parents and the man born blind? How does their understanding develop in the course of the chapter?
  - ↘ What is revealed about the blind man during the action of the chapter? How does his understanding develop? What can we learn from his 'right response'?
  - ↘ Very often we worry about the danger of new or young Christians falling away, because of persecution or hardship in the early stages of their Christian lives. How does this chapter address our worries?

❧ There are two places in the chapter where Jesus tells us how we should interpret the sign. What interpretation should we give to what is going on?

  ↘ If you had to describe the 'work of God' (v. 3) what would you say it is?

  ↘ What are the negative and the positive aspects of Jesus being 'the light of the world' and how do we see them developing through the chapter?

  ↘ Jesus appears to be absent for most of the incident (vv. 8–34). What does this tell us about 'the work of God'?

  ↘ How does this passage challenge the way we normally think about Jesus?

❧ Why do you think John includes this passage in his Gospel?

❧ What lessons does this chapter contain?

  ↘ For Christians like us, who claim we can see, what lessons are there? And how do we avoid verse 41?

  ↘ How might our attitudes and approach to evangelism, and to those we evangelise, be changed by this chapter?

  ↘ For someone weighing up whether or not to believe in Jesus, what pointers are there in this chapter?

(5.21.21)

How can I know what is real & what is true when there are so many "authorities" telling me so many different opinions? Just keep looking at & listening to Jesus — what does He say about himself, his work, his people, you & ? And place yourself under his authority. If a man born blind in the first century living in Jerusalem, a small colony of Rome, can have sight, anyone who wants to see can be given sight!

116

John 10:1–42
The Good Shepherd

CONTEXT

In chapter 9 Jesus has been expounding what it means for Him to be the 'light of the world'. Primarily it means that He gives spiritual 'sight', or understanding, to those who are being rescued. Simultaneous with this work of rescue is the exercising of God's judgment on those who oppose His purposes, and this takes the form of blinding. Despite the negative reaction of the Jews, in chapter 9, the story of the blind man has assured us that people can and will be saved.

In chapter 10 John rounds off the section with Jesus' declaration that He is the Good Shepherd, who can and will save His sheep. There is a close connection of thought between chapters 9 and 10: in chapter 9 the temple authorities behave as bad shepherds would, mistreating the 'sheep' of God's people. By contrast, Jesus introduces Himself as the Good Shepherd. He picks up the prophecy in Ezekiel 34, in which God had promised that when He came to rescue His people, He would provide a true shepherd from the house of David who would call out and rescue God's true people (Ezek. 34:23). This chapter explains *how* Jesus is the true Shepherd. It also demonstrates how, in the conflict between Jesus and the Jews, Jesus is in the right and the Jews are in the wrong.

Structure

10:1–21   The Good Shepherd:
1–6 The parable.
7–18 The explanation:
7–10 He is the true Gate.
11–13 The Good Shepherd and the hired hand.
14–18 The Good Shepherd and His flock.
19–21 The response from the Jews.

10:22–39   The Jews prove that they are not God's sheep. In spite of the miracles that Jesus has worked before them, the Jews prove by their actions that they are not God's sheep.

10:40–42   Jesus goes back across the Jordan.

Old Testament background

The Good Shepherd: There are a number of references to sheep and shepherds throughout the Old Testament, but the closest parallels with this chapter in John are found in Ezekiel 34. In the book of Ezekiel chapter 34 represents a turning point. Up to this point Ezekiel has been preaching judgment on God's people and the destruction of Jerusalem. But, just when God's people appear to be doomed, God promises a Good Shepherd who will rescue His true sheep. The chapter promises two things. First, judgment on God's failed shepherds, who should have been feeding the sheep but who have in fact exploited them, with the result that the sheep had become scattered. Secondly, God promises to rescue the sheep who have been lost and scattered among the nations. When He has done this He will provide a shepherd, from the family of David, to tend His flock.

Text notes

1–21 THE GOOD SHEPHERD

1–6 *The parable*. This contains three metaphors: the gate, which is the correct entrance to the sheep pen; the true shepherd, who calls his own sheep by name and leads them out; and the shepherd's own sheep, which recognise his voice and follow him. Verse 6 shows that this discourse is still part of the response to the sign of chapter 9, so Jesus' audience includes the Pharisees of chapter 9:40 and others, and probably the blind man too.

7–18 The explanation. Jesus' listeners fail to understand the meaning of verses 1–6, so He explains the three metaphors.

He is the true gate (vv. 7–10). Jesus has already told His disciples that when they come to Him they will see 'heaven opened' (1:51). This metaphor of the gate probably picks up on that idea, with its resonance of Genesis 28. The 'thieves and robbers' refers to the Pharisees and their structures and rules and regulations which cannot provide salvation. In fact the Pharisees only desecrated the sheep (as has been vividly illustrated by their treatment of the blind man and his parents). Jesus is the genuine gateway into salvation and everyone who enters through Him finds rescue and security. 'Life to the full' (v. 10) is interpreted by 'come in and go out, and find pasture' (v. 9), which is a picture of security and provision for those who have been rescued – shorthand for Ezekiel 34:11–16.

The Good Shepherd and the hired hand (vv. 11–13). The first 'good shepherd' statement contrasts the genuine shepherd with the hired hand. The key distinction is about commitment to the sheep. The thing that will ultimately authenticate Jesus' ministry is that He will never abandon the sheep; more than that, He lays His life down for them. The hired hand is like the false shepherds of Israel (Ezek. 34:1–6) who 'only take care of themselves'.

The Good Shepherd and His flock (vv. 14–18). The second 'good shepherd' statement expands on the Shepherd's vital relationship with His flock. The Good Shepherd knows His flock, and they know Him, as intimately as He and His Father know each other. A second time, Jesus speaks of laying down His life for the flock. The extent of His flock goes beyond the 'sheep pen' of Israel but, importantly, whatever 'pen' the sheep come from, the genuine response to the Shepherd is still that of listening to His voice. Verse 18 focuses on the death of Jesus: His self-sacrifice is quite voluntary – 'I lay it down of my own accord' – because He really does love the sheep; He retains absolute control over His death and resurrection, since

He is no puppet or robot, and He submits to death out of perfect obedience – 'This command I received from my Father' – because He always submits fully to His Father. This is the Shepherd whom the Father loves, and whom the sheep know and listen to.

19–21 *The response from the Jews*. The Jews' response to this clear warning from Jesus shows that nothing has changed on their part. The 'again' of verse 19 is the first of three – verse 31 'again the Jews picked up stones' and verse 39 'again they tried to seize Him'. As Jesus comes to the end of His public ministry, John emphasises how the Jews are a divided and hostile people, intent on doing away with God's Son. They will not listen to any warning.

22–39 THE JEWS PROVE THAT THEY ARE NOT HIS SHEEP

The Jews of Jerusalem repeat the question that they asked the Baptist (1:19ff). In the discourse that follows the issue that has kept the Jews from turning to Jesus becomes sharply focused: they are not His sheep.

In answer to their question about His identity Jesus makes it quite clear that His miracles, which have been done in public, speak for Him. These miracles have one clear message, which Jesus twice puts into words: He is one with God the Father (vv. 30 and 38).

The Jews do not object to the miracles (works) – they are happy with a miracle-working Messiah! But they will not accept what these miracles imply about Jesus, even though they have clearly understood it (vv. 31, 39). When Jesus makes the point of the miracles explicit, they want to kill Him. The Jews want 'a Christ' of their own devising, not 'the Christ' who challenges their practices and presuppositions! This proves that they are not His sheep, for His sheep listen to His voice and are rescued and kept by the Shepherd.

Jesus maintains that their objections are entirely unreasonable, both in view of scripture (vv. 34–36) and in view of the clear public message of His works. In Psalm 82:6 God addresses His people as 'gods' and 'sons of the Most High'. If God can call His people His son (cf. Exod. 4:21–22) then it is entirely reasonable for Jesus to speak of Himself as 'God's Son'. But His authority to do this is all the greater in view of His works and words which make Him uniquely the Son of God.

a warning for anyone!

40-42 JESUS GOES BACK ACROSS THE JORDAN

This geographical note is a significant marker, showing us that this section is now being drawn to a close. The reference to John the Baptist reminds us of his purpose (see 1:7), the purpose that is now being fulfilled as people come to believe in Jesus.

KEY THEMES

✤ Jesus is God's Rescuer.

↘ He is the only way into God's kingdom. All other ways of trying to get to God are futile.

Hope

↘ He is the true Shepherd who cares enough for the sheep to die for them, in contrast to the false shepherds who run away.

↘ He is the true Shepherd who will be recognised by the sheep. He will call them out from wherever they are and guarantee them eternal life; they will never perish.

↘ His works support His claims that His Father loves Him and is with Him, and that the Father has set Him apart and sent Him into the world.

✤ Those who oppose Jesus do not belong to God.

↘ Anyone who attempts to lead God's people any other way than to Jesus is a thief and a robber, but such a person will not succeed with the true sheep.

Warning

↘ Anyone who does not respond to Jesus is not one of His sheep.

↘ The Jews, by their actions, prove that they do not belong to God: they will not recognise Jesus, they will not accept His miracles, and they will not listen to the Scriptures.

APPLICATION

To them then: Jesus is the Good Shepherd who provides rescue for His people even when they are in the grip of false teachers. He alone is the Good Shepherd – all others are hoaxers – and He is the only way to God. His credentials are plain for all to see – He alone is committed to His sheep to the point of death. The chapter provides great hope of rescue just at the point when the leaders of the Jewish nation appear to be under judgment. There is also great assurance for His people and especially for the man born blind, who would appear still to be in the audience. Even though he has been rejected by his family and cast out of the synagogue by the Jews, he has real life, to the full, in Jesus.

The Jews' [...] people to doubt [...] will have eternal [...] them. The Go[...] them and pro[...]

To u[...] urce of great co[...] inated by the r[...] le. We can know [...] e and shepherd [...] e and follow H[...] now, which ma[...], but which in [...]

THE A[...]

To be assu[...] rtain salvation t[...] [listen] to His voice and follow Him. All who oppose Him are certainly thieves and robbers.

SUGGESTED QUESTIONS

✤ Read Ezekiel 34. What themes and ideas in Ezekiel 34 are picked up in chapter 10? How does this chapter help us to understand what Jesus is claiming?

1–6 THE GOOD SHEPHERD

✤ Verse 6 tells us that Jesus' hearers do not understand His parable. Who are they?

↘ How do these verses continue Jesus' condemnation of the Pharisees that began at the end of chapter 9 (vv. 39-41)?

↘ How do these verses reassure people who, like the man born blind, had begun to believe in Jesus?

✤ From your reading of chapters 9 and 10, do you think there should be a chapter division at 10:1? Justify your answer!
(*The parable changes slightly as Jesus comes to explain it in verses 7–18. Don't try to read it as if it had a developing storyline from verse 1 to verse 21. Jesus picks up each of the concepts in verses 1–6 and deals with them in a new way.*)

7–10 THE GOOD SHEPHERD AND THE GATE

✤ How does Jesus' explanation of the 'gate' influence your view of other religions?

↘ How does the experience of the man born blind influence our interpretation of what 'life to the full' means?

↘ What should we expect if we enter through the true gate?

11–13 THE GOOD SHEPHERD AND THE HIRED HAND

✤ What are the marks that distinguish the Good Shepherd from the hired hand, thief and robber?

↘ How does this passage add to our picture of Jesus as 'the only gate'?

↘ How should Jesus' teaching on 'the gate', and also on the Good Shepherd in verse 11, affect our assessment of the leaders of other religions ... and likewise our assessment of the leaders of our own churches and Christian organisations?

14–17 THE GOOD SHEPHERD AND HIS FLOCK

✤ What does Jesus teach about His sheep in this passage?

✤ It seems that all of this was spoken in the presence of the blind man and the Jews. What has each party learned from the parable and its explanation?

↘ Of what help will this be to the blind man, as he continues in his witness to Jesus?

↘ How does this help us to deal with criticism and opposition from religious authorities?

22–39 THE JEWS PROVE THAT THEY ARE NOT GOD'S SHEEP

✤ How do these verses prove that the Jews are not the true sheep of God?

✤ What reassurance is there here for those, like the blind man, who are His genuine sheep?

✤ Christians say that they have a personal relationship with Jesus. How does this passage explain what that relationship involves, on His side and on our side?

Jesus	the True Church
the Good Shepherd	the true sheep
selfless love	trust
gives full life, provision, security	receives full life, provision, security

the Rulers of the Jews
bad shepherds, hired hand, thieves & robbers

self-interest & pride

oppression, condemnation,

Section Notes: John 11:1–20:31

The two signs forming the brackets for this section are the two resurrections, of Lazarus and of Jesus, in chapters 11 and 20. Thus the main subject matter deals with the demonstration and revelation of God's glory through the completion of His plan to bring life through the death of His Son. The section can be summed up as follows: the achievement of Jesus' death is life!

The following incidents and explanations occur in these ten chapters:

11:1–57   Lazarus is raised from the dead and Jesus identifies this miracle as a demonstration of the glory of God. Jesus announces to Mary that He is the resurrection and the life. Caiaphas prophesies that it is better for one man to die on behalf of the people than that the whole nation should perish.

12:1–50   Jesus the king prepares for His death at the time of the Passover. Jesus explains that His death will bring life, and also judgment.

13:1–30   The foot washing: Jesus' death is essential to life.

13:31–16.33   'The Upper Room Discourse': what life will be like while we wait. Jesus explains, for the first time, that when He goes away His disciples will not be able to follow Him immediately but will have to wait for His return. This provokes a series of questions about His departure. He explains that His departure is the way to the Father, and that when He is gone His disciples will continue to 'see' God and to 'do the work' of God by bringing life to His people through their teaching of His word.

Once He has gone (to the cross) He will send His Spirit who will enable His apostles to record His word accurately. His people will remain in Him through remaining in this word. As they remain in Him so they will bear fruit. In spite of the persecution they will experience, His going will be for their benefit, for the Spirit will come to testify to the world and to enable the apostles to testify. His going will bring them peace and joy in an open union with the Father through the Spirit.

17:1–26 Jesus prays that His Father would glorify His name, through completing His plan to call together a people, a people who would belong to Him for eternal life.

18:1–27 His death, on behalf of His people, will mean that He, instead of them, bears His Father's wrath against sin.

18:28–19:16 He is the king from above who has come to establish His heavenly kingdom through His death as the innocent 'Passover Lamb'. His death establishes the guilt of the world, represented by the Jews. They will not listen to the truth and prefer an earthly kingdom to the kingdom of Jesus' Father.

19:17–42 Jesus' death as the Passover Lamb accomplishes His Father's sovereign plan to overthrow the effects of the Fall and bring life to His people.

20:1–31 Jesus' resurrection demonstrates that the cross has indeed been the means of fulfilling the Father's plan. He commissions His apostles to take the message of His achievement on the cross to all the world.

21:1–25 Jesus reinstates Peter and commissions the apostles to feed His sheep.

RECURRING THEMES

✤ Jesus teaches what His death will achieve, namely the glory of the Father through the bringing of life to His people.

✤ Jesus teaches that His death as a substitute will achieve life, because in it He will be bearing His Father's wrath at sin, wrath that would otherwise bring destruction to sinners. At the same time this death will judge the world and overthrow Satan.

✤ Jesus teaches that once He has gone His people will be drawn together through the work of His Spirit. The Spirit will enable His apostles to record His words accurately. And so the Spirit will do the work of God (i.e. bringing life to His people) through His word as it is proclaimed by His people.

✤ Jesus teaches that once He has gone His people will experience the benefits of His death: they will be indwelt by Him, and they will also experience the joy and peace of a relationship with the Father.

APPLICATION

The main application is to believe that Jesus has achieved what had long been looked for, the overthrow of the effects of the Fall.

Death has been conquered. The Father's wrath has been dealt with, and life is now available. Next we must understand what the normal experience of life should be in this world. Life now is experienced through remaining in Him as we listen to His words, accurately recorded by His apostles. We are promised the joy and peace that come from knowing that God's wrath has been dealt with, and from the reality of knowing God and being able to pray to Him. We are also promised intense hatred and persecution from the world.

John 11:1–54
'I am the resurrection and the life'

CONTEXT

As with the previous two sections, this last major section begins and ends with signs that introduce and sum up its main subject material. The signs that bracket this section are the raising of Lazarus and the raising of Jesus. In this way John indicates what is the subject matter of the section: the giving of life. The material of chapters 11–20 can be grouped under two headings: the whole question of what Jesus' death achieves – life, and the Gospel's developing narrative – the plot to put Jesus to death.

John introduces the section's key themes in chapter 11 by showing us that those who already believe still have a great deal to learn about Jesus. Martha, like Peter in chapter 6, may recognise Jesus as 'the Christ, the Son of God', but she hasn't yet understood what it means for Him to be 'the resurrection and the life'. For people like Martha and Peter, the first half of John's purpose statement in 20:31 has by now been achieved, but the second half needs fleshing out. John is going to do that in this section by showing that 'the glory of God' is revealed in His dealing with the greatest problem facing the human race – death.

The direct link between the raising of Lazarus and Caiaphas' prophecy, at the meeting of the Sanhedrin, indicates to the reader that Jesus' substitutionary death is going to be the means by which the effects of the Fall are reversed and *life* is given. And so the reader is driven forward to find out how Jesus' death will achieve this life, and where the plot of the Sanhedrin will end.

STRUCTURE

11:1–16 The purpose of the sign, the raising of Lazarus, is God's glory. Jesus performs the sign in order to bring glory to God and His Son. He delays for a reason.

11:17–37 The significance of the sign. Mary, Martha and others express disappointment at Jesus' failure to be present to heal. Jesus tells Martha, 'I am the resurrection and the life.'

11:38–44 The sign: Lazarus is raised to life.

11:45–54 The outcome of the sign. Many believe in Jesus, but the Jews plot His death. God's plan is the substitutionary death of His Son.

OLD TESTAMENT BACKGROUND

Death and life: Ever since Adam and Eve were banished from the Garden and from the Tree of Life, at the time of the Fall, the issue of death and life has been a major theme in the Old Testament. Isaiah speaks of the 'shroud (of death) that enfolds all peoples' (Isa. 25:6ff) and looks forward to a day when death will be swallowed up forever.

Substitution: In Leviticus 16 the principle of substitution is established. In order for sin and guilt to be taken away from God's people, something has to die in their place to satisfy God's just wrath. In Leviticus 16 the sins of the Israelites are transferred to one of the sacrificial goats which is then killed. Leviticus 17:11 explains that 'it is the blood [i.e. death] that makes atonement for one's life'. Much later the prophet looks forward to God's Servant coming into the world and dying on behalf of many (chs. 49 and 53).

TEXT NOTES

1–16 THE PURPOSE OF THE SIGN, THE RAISING OF LAZARUS, IS GOD'S GLORY

God's glory. The sign is designed to reveal God's glory and to glorify Jesus (v. 4). These words of Jesus in verse 4 give us the first indication as to how we are to interpret the raising of Lazarus; we need to be asking *how* it reveals God's glory.

The disciples' faith. Jesus also tells us that the sign will enable the disciples to believe (v. 15). But the odd thing is that He is speaking to a group of people who *already* believe. This indicates that there is much more for the disciples still to learn and suggests that the raising of Lazarus points forward to the new things that Jesus is about to teach them. All the way through the previous sections John has been teaching that genuine faith continues to grow (e.g. 2:22, 4:42 and the blind man in chapter 9). There are further lessons still to learn. As we apply the lessons of chapter 11 we shall need to be asking how this miracle stretches our faith.

The delay. Verse 6 suggests that Jesus delays deliberately. The literal translation goes: 'When *therefore* He heard ... He stayed where He was two more days.' The delay guarantees that when Jesus gets to the tomb everybody recognises that there is no hope for Lazarus – he is well and truly dead (vv. 37–39). But the comment in verse 5 that 'Jesus loved Martha and Mary', and the mention of Jesus' uninhibited grief (vv. 33–36) combine to ensure that the delay is not seen as a callous act, but as a genuine act of love, enabling Martha and Mary, the disciples and many others, to believe.

His death. There are hints in this first part that Jesus' going to Judea will result in His death (vv. 7–10; v. 16).

17–37 THE SIGNIFICANCE OF THE SIGN

Disappointment at Jesus' failure to heal. First Martha, then Mary, and finally the Jews express disappointment that Jesus did not heal Lazarus. Martha and Mary react to Jesus' arrival with exactly the same words (vv. 21 and 32). Both of them express faith in Jesus' ability to heal, but also anguish that He didn't arrive in time to save their brother, anguish that is echoed by their friends (v. 37). Martha's recognition that God will give Jesus whatever He asks shows that she sees Jesus as more than just a healer, but we cannot go so far as to say that she was definitely expecting Jesus to raise Lazarus because of her objection in verse 39.

Jesus' teaching on who He is. Jesus is explicit with Martha. She, and the others, still have a great deal to learn. Martha is rightly looking forward to a final 'resurrection' (the final resurrection of all people at the Last Day, the Day of Judgment). But she hasn't yet been shown the connection between an abstract belief in the resurrection and a personal belief in Jesus. Jesus, God's Rescuer, does not simply procure or promise the resurrection – He is the resurrection and He is the life. Those who come to Him in belief now have found life forever and they have found it now! They will never die in the fullest sense, even though they will die physically, because He is God's Rescuer who overthrows death. He is God's answer to the greatest problem facing humanity.

This statement, 'I am the resurrection and the life', leaves us with a host of questions. What exactly is this life that He gives? How does He give it? How can He be 'the resurrection'? While the disciples may believe in Him already, they still have a huge amount to learn about what their belief really means. Later on in the Gospel, in chapters 12–21, we shall learn what it means to say that 'the Christ, the Son of God' is 'the life'.

Jesus' indignation and grief at death. Verses 33–36 show Jesus expressing indignation at the sadness, pain and suffering caused by death. The word translated 'deeply moved' expresses indignation, outrage and anger. Jesus is rightly indignant at the presence of death in a fallen world. This is not how things ought to be – Jesus recognises that and, unlike us, He is able to do something about it.

38–44 THE SIGN: LAZARUS IS RAISED TO LIFE

This miracle reveals God's glory, showing that Jesus is the One who can overcome the great enemy of the human race (see Old Testament notes). He raises Lazarus simply by His word (cf. 5:25). Martha's response to the opening of the tomb (v. 39) shows that, though she does believe Jesus to be the Christ, the Son of God (v. 27), she has yet to see that He can give life now.

45–54 THE OUTCOME OF THE SIGN

Some believe in Jesus at once, just as the disciples did in 2:11. God's glory has been revealed and the result is the awakening of faith. But the very miracle that 'reveals God's glory' also precipitates the crisis of the death of His Son; the raising of Lazarus provokes a violent reaction among Jesus' enemies, and drives the plot forward towards His death (note the causal link, 'therefore', in verse 45). In showing us this, John is indicating that the giving of 'life' and the 'glory of the Son' cannot be separated from the Son's substitutionary death.

The 'prophecy' of Caiaphas is, on the face of it, simply a politically motivated remark about the most expedient way to deal with Jesus. It is better for Him to be killed than for the whole nation to go through political upheaval as a result of Him continuing His ministry. But, as John points out, the suggestion is in fact a prophecy of Jesus' substitutionary death (see Old Testament notes). The plot to take His life will result in Jesus, 'the Lamb of God', giving His life on behalf of many nations. This idea has come before (6:51), but by making such a plain reference to substitution, here, John ensures that the explanation of what Jesus' death achieves, which comes in chapter 12, will be understood in the context of His death being a substitutionary death. Caiaphas' comment is also loaded with irony: it is 'better' that Jesus dies, but not for the reason Caiaphas thinks! Verse 48 is the absolute give-away as to the reasons for the Jews' response to Jesus in chapters 5–9: they want a Christ, but not this uncomfortable Christ.

Jesus withdraws until the time is right (v. 54).

KEY THEMES

♫ What Jesus' death achieves. Issues of life and death.
  ↘ Death is a horrifying thing, the greatest enemy of mankind.
  ↘ Mary and Martha believe in Jesus as 'the Christ'. They even seem to believe that He will bring about the resurrection

at the Last Day, but they don't yet see that He is able to give eternal life now – though this is the kind of rescuer He is.

↘ God's 'glory' and the 'glorification' of God's Son will be seen in the overthrowing of the horrors of death.

↘ Jesus' substitutionary death is going to be at the heart of His achievements for the 'scattered children of God' (11:52) and is part of the revelation of His glory.

↯ The developing narrative. The Jews plot to kill Jesus. The highest authorities, when confronted with His miracles, see only a reason to put Jesus to death.

APPLICATION

To them then: Jesus tells the disciples how this sign applies to them (vv. 1–15). Through it they will see God's glory revealed and so their faith will be strengthened. The general coming and going of the funeral scene indicates a much closer contact with death than we have in the twenty-first century, so the scandal of death being present in God's world may have been more vivid in those days than now.

Martha, it seems, does believe that Jesus will bring life at the general resurrection on the Last Day. But Jesus shows, in the raising of Lazarus, that He has come to bring eternal life now to those who believe in Him. He shows the disciples that while they may recognise Him as 'the Christ', they have yet to see the full significance of who He is, that He is, in the present, the resurrection and the life. Through faith in Him, the scandal of death is reversed already – and will therefore be reversed fully in due course.

To us now: We should rejoice in the revealed glory of Jesus – He really is the one who can deal with death and reverse the effects of sin in a fallen world. He brings life *now*; He does so through His substitutionary death, as prophesied by Caiaphas. We should expect our faith in Jesus to be strengthened, as a result of studying this account, and we should also expect our faith to grow, as did the disciples' faith, as we grow in our understanding of who Jesus is and what He came to do.

THE AIM OF THIS STUDY

To see that Jesus, as the Christ, brings life and resurrection because He is the resurrection and the life.

SUGGESTED QUESTIONS

✎ What words would you use to describe the emotions that a funeral generates? Why does death make us feel like this? What does the Bible say about the reasons that death exists?

1–16 THE PURPOSE OF THE SIGN, THE RAISING OF LAZARUS, IS GOD'S GLORY

✎ In these verses Jesus gives two reasons for the sign that is about to follow. What are they?

↘ How will the answer to this question help us when it comes to applying this passage?

↘ We've already looked at some of the feelings generated by death. What would you say to someone who suggested that Jesus' delay in going to Martha and Mary was callous?

↘ What does this tell us about Jesus and His attitude to sin in a fallen world?

✎ What clues are there in the passage to suggest that Jesus' decision to go to Judea will result in *His* certain death? Why do you think John includes these hints?

17–37 THE SIGNIFICANCE OF THE SIGN

✎ In what ways do Martha, Mary and their friends show signs of real faith?

✎ In spite of these signs of faith in the disciples, there is clearly something lacking in their faith. What is it, and how does Jesus expose this lack?

↘ How will His answer to Martha affect the way you view Jesus and what He offers? How will it affect the way you view death?

↘ How does Jesus' knowledge of who He is and what He offers affect His attitude to death in this world? What does this tell us about our emotions at the death of a believer?

38–44 THE SIGN: LAZARUS IS RAISED TO LIFE

- How does the sign achieve its stated purpose?

45–54 THE OUTCOME OF THE SIGN

- How do the verses develop our understanding of the way in which Jesus is going to 'give life'? What is the irony attached to the response of Caiaphas and the Jews?

- Jesus told us the purpose of the sign in verses 1–15. How has the sign and the dialogue surrounding it served to reveal God's glory to you?

  - How does it add substance to your belief in and understanding of Jesus?

  - In what way will it change your commitment to Him?

- How would you use these verses to evangelise your friends?

John 11:55–12:50
Death in this world – life in eternity

CONTEXT

Chapters 11–20 form a section which begins and ends with a 'resurrection' sign, the raising of Lazarus and the resurrection of Jesus. Within these two events the narrative weaves together two 'strands' of material.

ᕧ The unfolding narrative. In chapter 11 the Sanhedrin again plot to kill Jesus. Their plot will end in His death, but as yet there is no indication of this.

ᕧ The explanation of what Jesus' death achieves – life. In chapter 11 Jesus began to explain what His death will achieve by teaching that life was far more than the general resurrection of all people to face judgment on the Last Day. His words in 11:25–26 taught us what He means by 'life': eternal life that is to be found only in Him. It can be experienced now, for He is the resurrection and the life. Caiaphas' prophecy made a link between His substitutionary death and 'life' (11:50).

Throughout chapter 12 the achievements of Jesus' death are emphasised. As we follow Jesus' explanation of His death and glorification, and take note of the events and actions that are pushing the narrative forward to the Passover, to Jerusalem and to the cross

– these are especially evident in the first half – we begin to see that the 'life' of chapter 11 can only come through the 'death' foretold in chapter 12.

STRUCTURE

11:55–12:11 Preparation for Jesus' death.

12:12–19 The arrival of the rescuing king on the way to His death.

12:20–36 His death explained: the hour of Jesus' death is the hour of His Father's glory, for death leads to life.

12:37–50 Jewish unbelief explained.

OLD TESTAMENT BACKGROUND

'Blessed is He who comes in the name of the Lord': Psalm 118, from which this line comes, is one of a group of psalms that look back to the rescue of the Exodus. These psalms were always sung to celebrate the Passover, and Psalm 118 was used to welcome pilgrims arriving in Jerusalem for the Passover feast. In the context of today's passage the crowds were using the psalm to welcome the one they perceived to be the Messiah, come to rescue His people.

'Your king is coming, seated on a donkey': Zechariah 9:9–13 prophesies the arrival of God's rescuing king, who will ride a donkey, not a warhorse. Three features about the arrival of this gentle king are worth noting: His arrival will bring the end of war (v. 10), He will proclaim peace to the nations, extending His reign to the ends of the earth (v. 10), and His arrival will release prisoners, on the basis of the blood of God's covenant (v. 11).

Isaiah 53:1: This verse expresses the astonished reaction of the nations to the means God uses to rescue His people – the suffering and death of His beloved servant.

Isaiah 6:10: This is a key verse in the book of Isaiah. It is picked up in all four Gospels and also in Acts; we have already seen it in John 9. God hardens the Jews' hearts in judgment so that they cannot see or understand the message.

TEXT NOTES

11:55–12:11 PREPARATION FOR JESUS' DEATH

This is now the third Passover recorded in John's account. By mentioning the feast at this point, John establishes a link between Jesus' approaching death and this festival, which is so significant in the life of God's people. The expectations of the people in verse 56 only heighten the sense of Jesus' control over His planned arrival in Jerusalem for the feast. At the same time, Jesus' explanation of the anointing (v. 7) shows Him to be fully aware that His journey to Jerusalem will end in His death. Note the contrast with Jesus' progress to the feast of Tabernacles in chapter 7. At that point His 'hour' had not yet come and He resisted any attempt to impose an agenda upon Him. Now His 'hour' has come and He heads up to Jerusalem with full knowledge of all that awaits Him.

The narrative of verses 1–11 helps us identify the key issues of life and death. Lazarus, once dead but now living, sits at table with Jesus, now living but soon to die. As with Caiaphas in chapter 11, Mary's action signals more than she realises. Together with Jesus' explanatory comment in verse 7, her action introduces the major theme of this chapter: Jesus is going to His death.

12–19 THE ARRIVAL OF THE RESCUING KING ON THE WAY TO HIS DEATH

This passage is sandwiched between the preparation for Jesus' death and the arrival of the Greeks, an incident that signals the approach of His death. The great crowd hail Jesus as their rescuing Messiah. *Hosanna* means 'Give salvation now', and the people greet Him as 'King of Israel' and one who 'comes in the name of the Lord'. He is the long-awaited king. In contrast to the other occasion when the crowd wanted to 'make Him king' (6:15), Jesus both allows and accepts their adulation. But while they see Him as Messiah, they fail to see that in coming on a donkey Jesus was fulfilling Zechariah's prophecy; and so, once again, they fail to see what kind of Messiah He is and what He is going to achieve (see Old Testament notes). He knows the agenda of the next few days and so allows them to hail Him as their king, but John acknowledges that even the disciples failed to see the significance of the donkey until after Jesus' death (v. 16).

20–36 HIS DEATH EXPLAINED: THE HOUR OF JESUS' DEATH IS THE HOUR OF HIS FATHER'S GLORY, FOR DEATH LEADS TO LIFE

20–23 The 'hour' has come. The arrival of the Greeks causes Jesus to announce that the hour has now come. This is the 'hour' that we have been waiting for, all through the Gospel, since it was first mentioned at Cana (see 2:4). The request to see Jesus, coming from the Greeks, symbolises the ingathering of the nations by God's Messiah. It stands in stark contrast to the rejection of the Messiah by the Jews. But Jesus' delay in speaking makes the reader aware that there is more to 'see' before they can 'come to Him'. In the events that follow (Jesus' death and resurrection) the reader will see the full glory of God.

24–26 The explanation. The explanatory metaphor about the grain of wheat introduces the key principle underlying all Jesus' actions in the next few days. It outlines the central truth that the only way to have life in eternity is to hate life and lose life now. Jesus Himself lives out this principle, achieving rescue and life for His disciples. But in verses 25–26 He makes it plain that this is the way of discipleship that all must follow – discipleship therefore entails great cost and great reward. This does not mean that His followers should become spoilsports who are unable to enjoy God's good gifts. Rather, they should learn from the cross that life lived out in rebellion against God in this world stands under judgment, and is what took Jesus to His death (see verses 31–33).

For the people in the crowd, this short paragraph contains major correctives to their understanding, about the kind of Messiah that Jesus is, and also about the nature of true discipleship.

27–30 The Father's witness. These verses show clearly that Jesus' death was part of God's overall plan for achieving His glory. They also make it clear that Jesus did not somehow escape from all the physical and emotional agony involved in crucifixion. His death was not a mistake, and He did not draw on supernatural powers to avoid the pain and agony of suffering His Father's wrath. His death, which conquers death itself and brings life to the world, really is the supreme moment when God's glory is revealed. The voice from heaven is for the benefit of the disciples: they hear it and are convinced, but the crowd, though they hear it, do not understand it (cf. verses 37ff).

31–33 The achievements of the cross. Jesus' death will bring judgment on the world, drive out Satan, and draw all kinds of people into His kingdom. By 'all men' He does not mean 'all people without exception', but rather 'all without distinction'. This reminds us of the significant arrival on the scene of the Greeks and Jesus' immediate response about His death; Gentiles as well as Jews would be rescued through His death (vv. 20–23).

Note that Jesus does not yet tell us *how* these things will be achieved; we must be careful not to pre-empt the narrative. Nevertheless, we are encouraged to recognise that the events of the next few days will be full of significance; looking back we will understand what was going on in this fulfilment of the Passover.

34–36 The final appeal. Interestingly, the people in the crowd understand Jesus' reference to being 'lifted up' to be an explicit reference to His death. They do not understand how the Messiah could possibly die, so Jesus appeals to them to learn from Him and trust in Him before it is too late. Judgment is a real threat and they, together with John's readers, need to respond to Jesus' offer and accept the opportunity of becoming children of God before the time has passed. Jesus withdraws; His public ministry will soon come to an end.

37–50 UNBELIEF EXPLAINED

John's comments show us that the Jews' unbelief has been foretold, and so is not unexpected (v. 38), and that it is from God, and so is not outside God's sovereignty (v. 40). Nevertheless, there are exceptions; many Jews, even leaders, do believe, though secretly (vv. 42–43).

Jesus' final public words (vv. 44ff) summarise His message to the Jews. They contain yet another appeal to those who are unbelieving to change their minds, on account of who He is and what He offers. The major emphasis is that the unbelief of the Jews will lead to their judgment (v. 48). Note the *would not* (v. 37) and *could not* (v. 39).

KEY THEMES

↳ The developing narrative: the major development is Jesus' decision to move, voluntarily, towards His death. He sees that His hour has now come.

↳ The significance of Jesus' death:

> It is the death of God's chosen king who has come in fulfilment of the Old Testament prophecies.

> It will achieve much fruit in the next world.

> It is *the thing* for which He came, yet it is something He dreads.

> It is the supreme moment of revealing God's glory.

> Through His death He will bring judgment on the world and drive out Satan.

> Through His death He will draw all kinds of people to Himself, bringing God's peace, rule and freedom to all nations.

> It is the model for genuine discipleship.

↳ Responses to Jesus (John is still focusing on this):

> Some (the Greeks) respond rightly, others (the Pharisees) wrongly.

> Jesus highlights the urgency and necessity of a right response to Him, in order to obtain eternal life and avoid judgment.

APPLICATION

The events of the first twenty-three verses show Jesus to be in complete control of the timetable of His death. He enters Jerusalem as king, though not the kind of king the crowds are expecting. His death will be a voluntary sacrifice, timed and enacted deliberately (though not without huge personal anxiety) by Him, in order that eternal life might be made available to all. Our response should be modelled on Mary's response to Jesus – uninhibited devotion. Unlike Mary, however, and the disciples of verse 16, we should be fully aware of *why* we respond the way we do.

Verses 20–36 increase our understanding about Jesus' death, as He teaches what it means and what it will achieve. Meditating on these things (see the points in Key Themes) we should be prompted to praise God for His death, and to make His death our lifelong study. Jesus' death should become the continuing focus of our faith and discipleship as we learn to hate all our rebellious attitudes and actions that led to His death.

Verses 37–50 show us the reason why people failed to respond to Jesus and also the urgent reason for responding to Him. Verses 42–43 are extremely challenging to us as we seek to live as Christians in the world.

THE AIM OF THIS STUDY

To see the significance of Jesus' death in bringing eternal life, and as a model for Christian ministry.

SUGGESTED QUESTIONS

11:55–12:11 PREPARATION FOR JESUS' DEATH

- ✤ How does John draw our attention, in this passage, to Jesus' impending death? Note how he presents the various characters, their actions and their motives, and note the timing of the incidents.
  - ↘ Back in chapter 7:1–8 Jesus prepared to 'go up to Jerusalem' for a similar feast. What is different about this occasion?
  - ↘ What does all this tell us about Jesus and His ministry?

12–19 THE ARRIVAL OF THE RESCUING KING

- ✤ In what ways is the crowd's reaction to Jesus in keeping with the way they have treated Him so far in the Gospel?
- ✤ In what way is Jesus' treatment of the crowd out of keeping with the way He has treated them so far in the Gospel?
  - ↘ In the light of 11:55–12:11 and 12:17–19, is it really out of keeping? (*Note: verse 17 begins with 'therefore' – not translated by the NIV.*)
  - ↘ Look up Zechariah 9:9–13. How do these verses, coupled with the events of the cross, help the disciples understand all that is going on?
  - ↘ So what do these verses tell us about the nature of God's rescuing king?

20–36 HIS DEATH EXPLAINED

✤ How does Jesus' explanation of what His hour will involve (vv. 24ff) correct the crowd's expectation of Him and His ministry? And how does it correct their expectation of what following Him will involve? (*See chapter 6.*)

    ⬎ In what way does Jesus model this kind of discipleship in verses 27–28?

    ⬎ How do verses 29–32 help us understand why Jesus' death is the hour of His glory and also His Father's glory? How does this help explain Jesus' refusal, throughout the Gospel, to meet the crowd's agenda for Him?

    ⬎ What difference does it make to you today that Jesus would not conform to the crowd's agenda but, rather, chose to do His Father's will?

✤ In verse 36 Jesus appeals to the crowd to receive Him and become children of God. From this passage what will it mean for a person to 'put their trust in the light'?

    ⬎ What is it that you would 'cling on to', and why would it be worth dropping it?

    ⬎ Why do people tend to drift away from the centrality and application of the cross to a different message and an alternative lifestyle? Why is it so foolish to do so?

37–50 UNBELIEF EXPLAINED

✤ How do these verses explain the message of the chapter, to the Gentiles as well as to the Jews?

John 13:1–30
The cross is central!

CONTEXT

This section (chs. 11–20) contains two major subjects. First, there is the unfolding narrative – the plot against Jesus which leads eventually to His death (followed by His resurrection). Secondly, John gives us the theological explanation of what Jesus' death and resurrection achieved. Chapter 12 contained both these elements: the plot intensified, and Jesus explained the achievements of His death in terms of 'life', His Father's glory, the judgment of the world, the driving out of Satan, and the drawing of many people to Himself.

The footwashing is an acted parable performed in the presence of the disciples that both explains the cross and is explained by the cross – the cross cleanses from sin and is itself the ultimate in service. Another vital aspect of the footwashing is that it shows the personal application of Jesus' death to His disciples – the cross must be central in the discipleship of every individual believer. In this way the footwashing is an illustration of the truth of Jesus' metaphor about the grain of wheat in 12:24; it applies the principles, taught there universally, to the individual disciples. Without the footwashing, the explanation of the achievements of Jesus' 'hour' in chapter 12 remains on a grand, universal scale; with it, we see the need for the cross to be appropriated by every believer, individually. In addition we see the importance of understanding Jesus' example for the life of the believer.

Interwoven with this graphic illustration is the plot against Jesus, with the climax of Judas going out into the night. Throughout the chapter, however, John makes it clear that it is Jesus who is in control, not Satan, and that Jesus lays down His life – it is not taken from Him. This point is forcefully made by John's contrasting of the disciples' failure to understand events with Jesus' complete awareness of what is going on.

STRUCTURE

13:1–17   The footwashing – the cross in the life of the believer.

        1–11   Being 'washed' by Jesus is essential to belonging to Him, and is also sufficient.

        12–17   Jesus' washing of the disciples' feet is an example for His true 'messengers' to follow.

13:18–30   Jesus' control of the situation – He identifies the betrayer.

OLD TESTAMENT BACKGROUND

'You will be clean from all your sins.' The idea of being 'clean' is often found in the Old Testament as a picture of being forgiven (see Lev. 16:30; Ps. 51:7).

TEXT NOTES

1–17 THE FOOTWASHING – THE CROSS IN THE LIFE OF THE BELIEVER

The footwashing as an explanation of the cross. The narrative of the developing plot against Jesus could flow quite naturally from verse 2 through to verse 18, missing out the footwashing incident altogether. So, we need to ask why John includes an incident which all the other Gospel writers leave out. The answer becomes clear when we realise that the footwashing is an explanation of the cross. But is this really so? Three things show us that it is right to understand the footwashing as an acted parable of the cross.

First, John introduces the chapter by telling us that the cross is imminent. The mention of the Passover, and of the time having come for Jesus to leave this world and return to the Father (His 'hour'), points the reader unequivocally to the fact that Jesus is now focusing on the events of His death.

Secondly, John contrasts Jesus' understanding of events (vv. 1, 3, 11) with the disciples' lack of understanding (vv. 7, 12, 28). He also shows us how Jesus is educating the disciples so that they will see the place of the cross in the life of the believer. At this stage the disciples do not understand what Jesus is doing, but He assures them that 'later' (v. 7), i.e. after His death, they will understand.

Thirdly, by telling us that Jesus 'now showed them the full extent of His love' John is surely indicating that we should look ahead to the cross. The footwashing does show Jesus' love, but with the events of the cross only a day away verse 1 cannot be read without understanding it to refer to the cross. And so the footwashing must be understood within the context of the cross.

NB It is helpful to realise that the footwashing has a similarity with the 'shepherd' metaphor of chapter 10: in both cases Jesus develops the metaphor as He makes a number of slightly different points.

1–11 *The cross is essential to the believer's cleansing.* Peter's horror (v. 6) is understandable when one realises that footwashing was a task given only to the most menial slave. Some Jews held that even Jewish slaves should never be allowed to do it. The streets were full of animals, and since shoes, if worn, were open sandals, feet got pretty dirty!

Verse 3 is a very significant verse. It shows Jesus' *humility* – He is so great, yet He stoops so low; His *love* – He even washes Judas' feet; His *knowledge* – He knew that God had given Him the position of supreme power, and He knew that Satan had prompted Judas, yet He proceeded with God's plan of action because He knew that this was the way for Satan to be driven out (12:31); and His *power* – as Jesus gives up His life, so He accomplishes God's supreme purpose (12:24).

At first Peter questions Jesus' action – perhaps understandably – but then he reacts with embarrassment as he objects to his master's words. Later (literally 'after these things') Peter will understand what Jesus is doing. Following the cross, when Jesus has shown the full extent of His love, and when the Spirit has come, Peter will realise that he can have nothing to do with Jesus unless he allows Jesus to wash his sins away. He cannot serve his master until he has first been served by his master. (The key word in this paragraph is 'unless', in verse 8.)

Once Peter begins to understand that being washed by Jesus is essential, he reacts with characteristic enthusiasm. Jesus uses this to make a second point about the sufficiency of the cross for the believer. People going out to dinner didn't need to bath again when they arrived, it was just their feet that needed cleansing. Similarly, once believers have come to Jesus for washing, they don't need to keep on going back to the beginning and starting all over again each time they sin. Once clean, Jesus' own people remain clean. But, at the same time, they need to remain dependent on Jesus' cross for the washing off of dirt that is picked up after the first bath. (Here the key word is 'only', in verse 10.) Confidence in the sufficiency of the cross, however, must not lead to complacency.

12–17 The example of Jesus in washing the disciples' feet is to become a central model for all believers who wish to be called blessed. A distinguishing feature of those who follow Jesus should be that they humbly follow His example and lower themselves in order to serve others (cf. 13:34). By drawing a parallel between His disciples and a servant or messenger Jesus shows how absurd it would be for a believer to refuse to serve someone. If Jesus has lowered Himself to the point of death on a cross, His disciples must follow His example, however hard they may find it to love their brother or sister. 'Blessed' (v. 17) means 'highly favoured' (by God). The point is that faith will only be seen to be genuine if it is matched with obedient action – this is the proof that a person has understood the gospel. Here is another instance of the way Jesus explains the cross and then immediately points to the application, in the life of the believer, of His example in submitting to the cross. (For other instances of this see 12:23–26 and 13:34.)

18–30 JESUS' CONTROL OF THE SITUATION – HE IDENTIFIES THE BETRAYER

These verses continue the unfolding narrative of the plot to kill Jesus. Judas, of course, has been present during the footwashing, his presence adding a *frisson* to the story and increasing its dramatic irony: Jesus knew exactly what was going on and, indeed, was in control of what was going on. This point is emphasised by John, as he records the disciples' lack of awareness and their failure to understand. The contrast highlights Jesus' sovereignty and also His love: even though He is fully aware of what is going to take place, He continues with this course of action.

Jesus' foreknowledge also enhances His credibility and, later on, the credibility of the disciples (vv. 19–20). The cross was not a huge accident. It took place according to the Father's plan and with Jesus' full knowledge, and also it was foretold in the scriptures. This is a point that Jesus has made before (8:28ff), but now in verse 20 He envisages the message of His pre-ordained death being spread abroad by His disciples; this is how He will 'draw all men to Himself'.

Verse 30 is deeply significant, alerting us to the close of the 'twelve hours of daylight' (11:9; 12:35). The final chapter in the plot against Jesus has opened and the darkest hour of history is upon us.

KEY THEMES

ℵ The achievement of the cross for the individual believer, as shown in the footwashing:

  ↘ The achievement of the cross is applicable to individuals who believe, and not to those who refuse to accept the necessity of Jesus' death on their behalf.

  ↘ The cross accomplishes the once-for-all washing away of the believer's sins, which brings that person within the scope of Jesus' work. Without this washing no person can belong to Jesus.

> ↘ Once washed, the believer does not need to keep going back to the beginning again. There is no room for complacency, however; that person must continue to rely on the cross for forgiveness.
>
> ↘ The cross, like the footwashing, provides the model for genuine Christian discipleship. It is not enough just to understand this; genuine faith involves taking action on what is understood.
>
> ✤ The developing plot that brings about Jesus' death.
>
> > ↘ With Judas' departure the hour of 'light', when Jesus is in the world, draws to a close.
> >
> > ↘ Throughout the chapter John has made it clear that Jesus is fulfilling what He had said in 10:18. He is in control and His life is not being taken from Him; this alone would be proof of His identity.

APPLICATION

To them then: The initial reaction to the footwashing – that Jesus should take on the task of a slave – is one of horror. But, following the events of the cross the disciples understood what Jesus was teaching them. John's presentation of the incident shows that he had understood how the cross must be central to membership of God's people and also central in the ongoing life of the believer. The whole passage emphasises the intimacy of Jesus' love for His own and His commitment to His own, even when He knew what was about to happen.

To us now: The overriding application of this passage concerns the place of the cross in the life of the believer. No person can serve Christ unless they have first been served by Him. The cross is central to our membership of Jesus' family, to our assurance, to our day-by-day forgiveness, and to our life and witness as His servants and messengers. As we study the passage, seeing what Jesus has achieved through the cross and what it cost Him, His determination knowingly to go to His death ought to move us to a deeper and more real love for Him. Similarly, the teaching of 12:25–26 cannot simply remain as an abstract truth that we assent to: Jesus going to His death should affect every part of our lives as we lay them down in His service.

THE AIM OF THIS STUDY

To see that the cross must be central if individuals are to become believers and belong to Jesus. We must be 'washed', we must trust His 'washing', and our discipleship must be modelled on Jesus' humble service of us.

SUGGESTED QUESTIONS

- ✎ What are the two major themes of the section we are in at the moment?
  - ↘ According to 12:20–36 what did Jesus' death and resurrection achieve?
- ✎ How would you subdivide the passage? And why? Give titles to your subdivisions.
- ✎ Only John records the washing of the disciples' feet. What does this incident add to the explanation of the cross that Jesus gives in chapter 12?

1–11 JESUS' DEATH IS ESSENTIAL TO BELONGING TO HIM AND SUFFICIENT FOR REMAINING IN HIM

- ✎ There are several indications as to why the footwashing should be understood as an enacted parable about the cross. What are they?
- ✎ John tells us several things about Jesus in verse 3. Why is Jesus' action in verse 4 such a surprise, given what John tells us in verse 3?
  - ↘ How do verses 1 and 2 help to explain His action? What do they tell us about Jesus?
- ✎ Peter misunderstands Jesus in two different ways, in verse 8 and again in verse 9.
  - ↘ Why are his misunderstandings so understandable?
  - ↘ Peter has not yet grasped two key lessons of discipleship. Why do we find these lessons so hard to learn?

↘ What difference would it make to our relationship with Jesus and our service of Him if we really understood them?

↯ How would these lessons apply to Peter, following his denial of Jesus?

↘ How would these lessons apply to a friend of yours who felt he/she had let Jesus down really badly?

12–17 JESUS' DEATH IS A MODEL FOR HIS PEOPLE'S DISCIPLESHIP

↯ What does verse 16 tell us about the nature of genuine discipleship?

↘ In the course of an average week, what opportunities do you have to serve other believers out of love?

↘ How will Jesus' attitude, position and action affect the way you serve?

↘ How will this teaching affect our priorities and the way we use our time?

↘ What, in this passage, keeps us from re-entering the world of legalism?

18–30 JESUS' DEATH WAS NOT AN ACCIDENT OF HISTORY

↯ How would this passage help you reply to someone who considered Jesus to be just a 'victim of circumstances'?

John 13:31–14:4
'Lord, where are you going?'

CONTEXT

It was noted, at the beginning of this section, that two main strands of material are interwoven throughout the section: the unfolding narrative, and the explanation of the theological significance of Jesus' death and resurrection. With the departure of Judas, Jesus is now left alone with His faithful disciples and a conversation known as 'The Upper Room Discourse' begins. The narrative is placed on hold for the next few chapters, as Jesus uses this opportunity to explain what His death and departure will mean for His disciples. In summary, He teaches His disciples:

- ♫ that His imminent departure via the cross is a good thing and not, as it might appear at first, a disaster. It will achieve salvation.
- ♫ that His disciples will not go with Him immediately. They will continue to live 'in the world' as His people when He is gone, and this will involve both the privilege of intimate friendship with God and the pain of the world's hostility.
- ♫ that after His departure His disciples will need to persevere in following Him. This perseverance will require continuing faith and obedience.

✤ that after His departure His people have a mission to accomplish while in the world, namely, to bear the lasting fruit of more disciples.

✤ that His departure will lead to the sending of the Holy Spirit to dwell in His people. His Holy Spirit will equip and enable His people to accomplish God's purposes for them in the world and to experience God's presence with them.

✤ that God's new people will be constituted around the words of Jesus (which are the words of the Father), and the Holy Spirit will guarantee these words by enabling the apostles to remember, understand and record Jesus' teaching.

Chapters 13–17 are particularly important to our understanding of what it means to be a disciple of Jesus between the time of His ascension and the time of His return. Throughout the Upper Room Discourse Jesus continually reassures His disciples and teaches them about this period when He will be separated from them. The Discourse is essential to the overall purpose of John's Gospel; it explains what it means to believe and to 'have life' *now*, in this life, and then, after death. The discourse is divided into two parts by the phrase 'Come now; let us leave' of 14:31. The passage 13:31–14:31 is best studied by following the structure provided by the words of four disciples: Peter in 13:36, Thomas in 14:5, Philip in 14:8 and Judas in 14:22.

STRUCTURE

13:31–35 The shock of His departure. Jesus announces the hour of His glorification and the imminence of His departure.

13:36–14:4 Peter: 'Lord, where are you going?' Jesus' reply: 'You will follow later.' Jesus assures the disciples of the *eternal* achievement of His death, the rescue of His disciples for a place in heaven.

TEXT NOTES

31–35 THE SHOCK OF HIS DEPARTURE

31–32 *The hour of His glorification.* The NIV misses an important 'therefore' in verse 31. The text should read, 'When therefore he was gone, Jesus said ...'. The 'therefore' links verse 31 back to Judas' leaving and John's statement that 'it was night'. This ties the 'Now' of verse 31 to Judas' act of betrayal and thus to Jesus' death. Jesus announces that the act of betrayal has set in motion the events of the cross which will bring about His glorification. Two points should be made:

First, what Jesus is teaching. When Jesus explains that the moment of God's glorification is 'now', and 'at once', He is referring to His imminent death. The sentence structure of verses 31 and 32 points to the key thing that is about to happen, which is the glorification of God in the Son; the phrase 'God is glorified in Him' lies at the heart of the two verses. The glorification of the Father and the glorification of the Son – the two are tied inextricably together – take place at the cross where the Father and the Son stoop to save humankind.

We must allow the impact of this to strike home to us: God's moment of supreme triumph is achieved through the betrayal, humiliation and weakness of His Son as He is nailed up to a tree by humankind, the people He has created. The cross may look weak but it is actually the point at which God undoes all of humankind's sin and reverses the consequences of the Fall.

This is the point of 'glory' and the 'hour' that the whole Gospel has been anticipating. It can only really be understood by taking an eternal perspective. If we want to see God honoured by any means other than the exploration and explanation of the cross, we shall have missed the Jesus of John's Gospel and we shall be making the mistake that the crowds made in 2:23–25 (see chapter 6:26–33 and also Application).

Secondly, the 'therefore' indicates a deliberate move by Jesus to set about teaching those who remain (His true disciples): they need to know what will happen next, before the events of His crucifixion overtake them. There is also an urgent need for them to understand what it means to be part of His rescued people, so Jesus explains at length to His disciples, and also comforts them.

Verse 33 The imminence of His departure and the necessity of their remaining. From Peter's response to this verse it is clear that Jesus' announcement of separation causes the disciples great surprise. They had heard Jesus tell the Jews that they wouldn't be able to go with Him – 7:34 and 8:21 – and in the light of the Jews' hardness of heart that statement had made sense. But now the disciples themselves are forbidden to join Him. Notice, though, the highly significant omissions. Jesus had told the Jews, 'You will look for me', and had then added, 'but you will not find me' (7:34) and 'and you will die in your sin' (8:21), but He does not repeat these last two phrases to His disciples.

34–35 The mandate for His disciples. The command Jesus gives His disciples is not, in fact, new – see Leviticus 19:18. The thing that is new is the way in which they are to love. Jesus qualifies His command with the words 'as I have loved you'. So, this is the new command for His new people: their lives should be marked by a love for one another that is modelled on His self-sacrificial act of love for them (cf. 13:14). Christian love is not about emotion or likes and dislikes; it is about the challenge of self-sacrifice (12:25), service (13:14ff) and obedience to Jesus' commands (14:15) (see Application). This kind of genuine Christian discipleship is one of the most potent forms of evangelism.

13:36–14:4 'LORD, WHERE ARE YOU GOING?'

36–38 The dialogue between Peter and Jesus contains two elements:

First, Jesus' reply to Peter's question, which contains great reassurance. When the Jews had had a similar conversation with Jesus (8:21) He had told them, 'you will look for me, and you will die in your sin. Where I go, you cannot come.' Now Jesus assures Peter that he will follow Him, but later.

Secondly, Peter's bold pronouncement in verse 37 which, translated literally, means 'the life of me *on behalf* of you I will lay down'. The irony is that Jesus has told the disciples that they must eat His flesh given *on behalf* of the life of the world (6:51), and, that the Good Shepherd will lay down His life *on behalf* of them (10:11). But Peter has failed to understand his own need, and now that the hour for Jesus' death is at hand Peter wants to die *on behalf* of Jesus, to engage in heroics rather than gratefully receive Jesus' death on his behalf. It seems Peter has still not understood the lesson he was taught at the footwashing. By repeating Peter's offer word for word Jesus encourages Peter to reconsider. His prophecy of Peter's denial throws doubt on Peter's ability even to persevere as a faithful disciple, let alone to die on Jesus' behalf.

14:1–4 Jesus then speaks to all the disciples, to reassure them. It is important that we realise just how troubled the disciples are. They have left everything to be with Jesus, and now He is telling them that they are going to be separated from Him. The remedy for their anxiety is that they should trust both God the Father and Jesus Himself.

Much has been written about the word translated 'rooms' (NIV). The point Jesus is making is that there is plenty of room in heaven for each of His disciples to join Him there. However, Jesus' 'going' (which must involve the whole process of His death, resurrection and ascension) is precisely so that He may prepare a place for His people. Until now Jesus has focused on why and how they need to be rescued; now He explains what they are rescued for. This is the perfect comfort for a troubled people. He reassures them by pointing beyond the present trouble to the eternal reality of what His death is going to achieve.

KEY THEMES

- ✤ The eternal implications of Jesus' death.
  - ↘ It will bring His glorification and God's. It seems a failure but is in fact God's greatest victory.
  - ↘ It will mean the preparation of a place in heaven for His disciples. Unlike the Jews, who will die in their sin, they will join Him later when He returns to take them to be with Himself.
- ✤ The present implications of Jesus' death.
  - ↘ The disciples will be separated from Him.
  - ↘ It will demonstrate His love for them, giving them a pattern for the way they should love each other.

    ↘ It will mean that, in His absence, the disciples will need to keep trusting Jesus as well as the Father.

  ♭ Peter's confusion.

    ↘ He doesn't understand that Jesus must die on his behalf.

    ↘ He hasn't understood the depths of his own weakness. He wants to die on Jesus' behalf and believes he has the strength to do it.

APPLICATION

First, God's supreme moment of glorification is at the cross. Peter's reaction to Jesus' announcement shows that he hadn't really grasped this – it *is* a hard lesson to take on board. We need to learn, and re-learn, that God is glorified by the teaching of the cross, not by 'signs and wonders', magnificent buildings, large numbers at meetings, big budgets, clever rhetoric and argument, or even our singing. It is Jesus' death that achieves God's glory, through the reversal of all our failure. All through history the church has stumbled when it has drifted away from this truth, either by thinking we are good enough to achieve God's glorification (like Peter), or by failing to view history from an *eternal perspective* and looking for God's glorification in a visible way through our work now.

Secondly, the time of physical separation from Jesus may cause dismay and 'troubled hearts' as we experience the pain of life in a fallen world. The way to tackle these emotions is through gaining an *eternal perspective*. Jesus' departure secures our salvation, a place in heaven.

Thirdly, Christian love is distinctive and a powerfully effective form of witness in the world, while we wait for Jesus to return. The Christian community should be highly attractive. Whether we find individuals easy or hard to get on with, the way to love them is to learn from Jesus' death for us on the cross.

All these lessons need learning and re-learning throughout our Christian lives. We should not be surprised at our own, or others', slowness – discipleship is all about growing in understanding. Peter had to learn the hard way and it took him a long time.

THE AIM OF THIS STUDY

To see why having an eternal perspective is essential, both for understanding what Jesus' departure achieves and also for living now, as we await His return.

SUGGESTED QUESTIONS

13:31–35 JESUS' GOING AND HIS FATHER'S GLORY

- ✤ Complete the sentence: 'If only the church was more ... then my friend would believe in God's power and majesty.'
  - ↘ Verse 31 begins 'When *therefore* he was gone'. What do verses 31–35 tell us about *when* and *how* God will be glorified?
  - ↘ How do the sentence structure, content and context of verses 31 and 32 make the point?
  - ↘ In what ways does this lesson run counter to the way we often expect God to be glorified? How would this change the way we might complete the sentence we were considering just now?
- ✤ What is new, and what is not new, about the command in verse 34?
  - ↘ If you were to look in the dictionary, what definitions would you find for the term 'love'? How does Jesus' definition differ?
  - ↘ How will this affect the way we love others, those we like and those we find it harder to like? What real differences would it make to the group if we were to love one another in this way?
  - ↘ 'It's more important that I spend all my time with my non-Christian friends than that I encourage my Christian brothers by meeting with them.' Discuss this in the light of verses 34ff.
  - ↘ How will the application of this verse lead to further glorification of God on earth?

13:36–14:4 JESUS' GOING AND HIS DISCIPLES' FUTURE

✢ In 14:1 the word 'troubled' is the same word as in 11:33 and 12:27. What does this tell us about the intensity of the disciples' mood at this point in the Gospel?

  ↘ What has Jesus just said to cause such disturbance for His disciples?

  ↘ Compare verse 33c and verse 36 with what Jesus says to the Jews in 7:34 and 8:21. What is the *big* difference?

  ↘ How does this help to clarify Peter's concern in verse 37?

  ↘ Peter makes a bold statement in verse 37. How does Jesus' answer point to the irony of Peter's offer?

  ↘ What has Peter failed to understand about himself? And about Jesus' death?

  ↘ Look back to 13:8. What does this tell us about Peter's learning curve in understanding both himself and God's purposes in the cross?

  ↘ Why are these lessons so hard for us to learn?

✢ There are several promises in 14:1–4. How does each one address Peter's failure, and also meet the disciples' troubled hearts?

  ↘ How will these promises help us as we too live in the world as disciples of Jesus?

John 14:5–14
'How can we know? ... Show us!'

C O N T E X T

The Upper Room Discourse began at chapter 13:31 with Jesus' announcement of His imminent departure and physical separation from His disciples. Peter's reaction to this announcement indicates that the disciples were not expecting Jesus to leave them. The first part of the discourse, 13:31–14:31, deals with a series of questions about being a disciple that arise from this changed situation.

The main themes of the discourse are the identity of Jesus (Jesus summarises what He has already taught His disciples about Himself, and adds more), the reason for His death (what it will accomplish), and what it means to 'have life' in the period between Jesus' departure and His return. The subject matter at the beginning of the discourse is best divided up by the disciples' four questions, to give major divisions of material. In this study we shall look at Philip's request as well as Thomas' question, but since there is so much material in Jesus' answer to Philip we shall limit ourselves to just part of His answer.

S T R U C T U R E

14:5–7   Thomas: 'How can we know the way?' Jesus' reply: 'I am the means!'

14:8–21   Philip: 'Show us the Father!'

9–11   Jesus' reply, part 1: 'If you've seen me you've seen the Father' – listen and believe!

12–21   Jesus' reply, part 2: The answer broadens – further consequences of Jesus' relationship with the Father and of His imminent return to the Father.

Text notes

5–7 'HOW CAN WE KNOW THE WAY?'

Having answered Peter's question about His departure, Jesus assures the disciples that He is going away in order to prepare a place for them in His Father's 'house'. Thomas' question shows that, perhaps understandably, the disciples haven't grasped where Jesus is going. Nonetheless, wherever it is that He's going they want to go with Him! So Jesus moves on to tackle the subject of the way to the Father. His use of the familiar 'I am' shows us that the way is to be found in Himself. He explains why that is so by summarising what He has already taught about salvation, revelation and life.

Salvation. At the start of the Gospel, Jesus promised the disciples that they would see 'heaven open' (1:51). This was to come through the 'lifting up' of the Son of Man (3:14) and as He gives His flesh 'for the life of the world' (6:51). And so when He says, 'I, when I am lifted up from the earth, will draw all men to myself' (12:32) He anticipates His statement to Peter, 'you will follow later' (13:36). By dying on the cross He *is* the way to God.

Revelation. It was in the Prologue that John first alerted us to the fact that Jesus is the truth (1:17). He is the truth because His words are the Father's words (7:16; 12:49) and His deeds are the Father's deeds (5:19ff; 8:29; 14:10). So, all that He says about God is true and all that He does and says perfectly reveals His Father. Since His Father's work *is* salvation and judgment (9:3, 39), when Jesus says He is 'the Truth', He means that He is the truth about God's rescue. Hence verse 4, 'you know the way to the place ...'

Life. Life is in Jesus (1:4), He has 'life in Himself' (5:26), and He is 'the resurrection and the life' (11:25). So, 'whoever believes in the

Son has eternal life' (3:36), for He lays down His life for the sheep (10:15, 28). Again, since 'life' is eternal life, when Jesus says 'I am the life' He means that eternal life in relationship with God has its source in Him.

Jesus' statement in verse 6b that 'no-one comes to the Father except through me' shows that nothing else will do to gain salvation. A person needs to come to Jesus Himself if he or she is to reach the Father – there is no other way.

8–21 'SHOW US THE FATHER!'

Verse 7 provides the prompt for Philip's request. There are two possible ways of taking it. One is that Philip, like so many disciples and also unbelievers, seems to want to be given a unique one-off vision of the Father as proof of His existence; he wishes to be transported to heaven and be granted an exclusive viewing. In which case, Jesus' reply exposes Philip's shallow understanding of who He is and what He has done. If only Philip would realise what Jesus is doing, he would see that Jesus has provided him with a far greater privilege than a mere one-off glimpse of God, and that there is no need for further visions in the period of his separation from Jesus.

The other possibility is that Philip is exasperated by the ongoing complexity and apparent difficulty of knowing the Father, in which case his request is for a simpler and more straightforward means of revelation, something like, 'Come on! Can't you just show us right now?' Ironically, if Jesus were to have done that, Philip would have been left immeasurably poorer, for the only vision of God ever given to sinful humanity has been the merest glimpse of His back (Exod. 33:23) for 'No-one has seen God ...' (1:18).

9–11 Jesus' reply, part 1. Jesus begins by telling Philip that if he has seen Him he has seen the Father already. He commands Philip to look at Himself and to believe in Him as he listens to His words. Jesus' three questions, 'Don't you know me?'; 'How can you say, "Show us the Father"?' and, 'Don't you believe that I am in the Father ...' reveal the extent of Philip's ignorance, and He gently rebukes him. Jesus summarises His claims about Himself and His Father from earlier in the Gospel, and urges Philip to pay attention to His words and believe. The phrase 'seeing is believing' is wholly inappropriate when it comes to God. For, if a person *believes* in the *words* of Jesus they will see the Father. So instead of 'seeing is believing' we should say 'Hearing and believing is seeing.'

Jesus goes on to explain why this is so in verses 10b–11. We would expect the second part of verse 10 to read, 'the Father, living in me, *speaks His words*', but instead it reads, 'is doing His work'. *So, what Jesus says is the work of the Father.* If a person will only come to Jesus and listen to Him, then he will see the Father. Jesus continues with a command to believe His words, or at least to believe on the evidence of the works (meaning the totality of Jesus' signs, explanations and actions, not just the miracles).

12–21 Jesus' reply, part 2. Jesus now spells out further conse-quences of His own relationship with the Father and of His imminent return to the Father. What He says is to 'anyone who has faith in' Him – it is not limited to the apostles. It is a promise that believers will be able to do 'greater works' than Jesus. (The NIV unhelpfully translates 'works' as 'miracles' or 'things', but the Greek word *erga*, meaning 'works', is used throughout.)

This promise in verse 12 has been widely misinterpreted since the early 1980s to suggest that Christians today should expect to do greater miracles or more numerous miracles than Jesus Himself. A quick look at the context of 'greater works' in John's Gospel will show this to be wrong. In John 5:20ff Jesus speaks of how He will be shown 'greater works', and then goes on to define these 'greater works': they are, the giving of life (v. 21), and judgment (v. 22), in order that all may honour the Son (v. 23). Likewise, in 6:28 the works of God (same word, *erga*) are defined as belief in the One He has sent, and in 9:3 and 39 His work is seen to be salvation and judgment. All this teaching is summed up in 14:9ff where Jesus' work is making the Father known through His words.

So, these 'greater works' in 14:12 (again the same word, *erga*) point not to greater physical signs, but to the preaching of the words of the Father which accomplishes the work of the Father (as in v. 10b), namely proclamation of the gospel, conversion and judgment (cf. 9:3, 39). This will achieve 'life' for far greater numbers of people than Jesus was ever able to reach during His earthly ministry. Anyone who has faith, therefore, will do 'greater works'.

How on earth will this be achieved? Jesus gives part of the answer in the promise of verse 13. It is important to understand this promise correctly: it does not mean that anything 'named' and 'claimed' in the 'name' of Jesus will be given automatically to the believer. Such a ridiculously self-centred interpretation is prevented by two qualifying remarks: 'in my name' and 'so that the Son may bring glory to the Father'.

'In my name' indicates that the request must be in accordance with the character and teaching of Jesus. In the second phrase it is clear that the Son intends to answer prayer through which His Father will be glorified; Jesus' guarantee of answered prayers is restricted to prayers that will achieve this aim. Jesus does not promise to answer all prayers for happy, wealthy, trouble-free living; He does promise to answer prayers for the giving of glory to God.

Preliminary summary. If only Philip would believe it, the departure of Jesus is going to result in a far greater achievement than the one-off glimpse of God in heaven that he asked Jesus to give them. For Jesus has revealed God, and also opened the way to the Father for eternity, for the disciples now and for millions of others in the future, beginning at the day of Pentecost (Acts 2). That way is made available through the words of Jesus which are the work of the Father.

KEY THEMES

- ✤ The way to the Father is available to the disciples.
  - ↘ It is now made known through Jesus.
  - ↘ It is to be found through a genuine knowledge of Jesus.
  - ↘ There is no other way to the Father for only Jesus is 'the truth and the life'.
- ✤ Jesus' relationship with the Father has important consequences for the disciples.

> ↘ Jesus fully reveals the Father because He is in the Father and the Father is in Him.
> ↘ The Father's work can be seen in Jesus' words, which bring eternal life.
> ↘ Following His departure believers will go on to do more numerous works of the Father than Jesus did, namely, revealing the Father in order to bring people to eternal life.
> ↘ These 'works' will be done in answer to prayer, which will be answered because Jesus is going to the Father and continues to want to glorify Him.

APPLICATION

General note. In the Upper Room Discourse Jesus makes a large number of promises to His disciples. Some of these promises are specifically directed towards them as apostles, but other promises apply to anyone who believes. Therefore, we need to be very careful to note what the application was to them, and also whether the application is intended for all believers through all time, or just for the apostles. Taking care in these two ways will mean that we avoid misapplication and false expectations. Usually it is pretty clear when the point being made is to be applied generally, to *all* disciples; we have an example in this passage, when Jesus uses the phrase 'anyone who has faith in me'.

Application. The answer to Thomas' question would have struck home hard to the disciples. Jesus is making it clear that individuals cannot come to God unless they have a personal encounter with Him. No matter how religious they may be, or how strict their observance, or how good their deeds, or how orthodox their Jewish faith, He is the only way to the Father. For He alone has opened the gate to heaven through His death, He alone has come from the Father and is the truth from God, and He alone offers true life that will not perish. The applications of Jesus' words to our relativistic world are obvious.

The answer to Philip's request is *vital* for our faith today. Now that Jesus has gone to the Father, we need to realise that *the way* to 'see the Father' is through *the words* of Jesus. For, because of who Jesus is, He reveals the Father, and because He has gone to the Father we, as believers, will be able to continue doing the work of the Father through our teaching of His word and through prayer. Again, the application is obvious: through *hearing* His word and *believing* it we will be *seeing* the Father at work! We are supremely privileged!

THE AIM OF THIS STUDY

To grasp that Jesus is the only way to God, and that because of His relationship with His Father and His going to His Father, His disciples will continue to see God and to accomplish God's works today – through His word.

SUGGESTED QUESTIONS

(*For this study it would be helpful to have with you a copy of the* Book of Common Prayer, *known as the* Prayer Book, *or the* Westminster Confession.)

 ✤ We live in a pluralistic society. What are the features of our society that point to this pluralism? (*Record the answers on a sheet of paper.*)

5–7 NO-ONE COMES TO GOD EXCEPT THROUGH JESUS

 ✤ Jesus says three things about Himself in response to Thomas' question. Use your knowledge of what He has taught so far in the Gospel to explain how He can say these things.
  ↘ How do these things answer Thomas' question?
  ↘ How are the three parts of Jesus' answer affected by the negative statement in verse 6 and the positive statement in verse 7?

 ✤ Are you ever tempted to feel embarrassed about Jesus' uniqueness? If so, how and why?
  ↘ Living in a pluralistic world, how should our convictions be strengthened by what we have learned from John's Gospel?
  ↘ What difference will the words of Jesus make to conversations with your non-Christian friends?
  ↘ What difference will they make to your own commitment to Jesus and His teaching?

✤ Try to compose an 'Article of Religion' that summarises the positives and negatives of these verses. (*Now read Article 18 of the Thirty-nine Articles; use the index at the beginning of the Prayer Book to locate the 'Articles of Religion'. Chapter 10, Section 4 of the Westminster Confession contains the same idea.*)

8–11 HEARING AND BELIEVING IS SEEING!

✤ What do we learn about Philip from the three counter-questions from Jesus in verses 9 and 10?

✤ In verse 10 the second part of Jesus' reply to Philip begins, 'Rather, it is the Father, living in me, who ...'. How would we expect this sentence to end? The ending Jesus gives is unexpected: what does it tell us about how we come to 'see' the Father?

  ↘ It is often said by our non-Christian friends that 'seeing is believing'. How is this view corrected by what Jesus says to Philip?

✤ If, like Philip, you were someone who wanted a direct and dramatic experience of the Father, to prove His existence, how would these verses help you?

  ↘ How would you respond to someone who says, 'All this focus on Jesus' words is far too cerebral and dry!'?

  ↘ How would you respond to someone who says, 'It's all right for Philip, he could see Jesus face to face'?

12–14 JESUS' ANSWER NOW BROADENS OUT

✤ What two promises does Jesus make in these verses?

✤ Look up 5:20–23. How does Jesus' explanation of 'greater things' (in these verses) help us to understand His promise in verse 12?

  ↘ The promise in verse 12 seems to be a pretty tall order! How does Jesus guarantee that 'anyone who believes' will be able to pull it off?

✤ How does Jesus ensure that we don't turn His promise into an excuse for selfish praying?

✤ How do verses 12–14 relate to Philip's request? Do they provide an answer? If so, how does this answer help Philip and people like him?

John 14:15–31
'Show us... why us and not the world?'

CONTEXT

In this part of the Upper Room Discourse, Jesus' purpose is to instruct His disciples about His departure and what it is going to achieve. Peter has been told that it will achieve a place 'in my Father's house' for Jesus' disciples, and Thomas has been told that Jesus Himself is the way to the Father. Now Jesus is in the middle of addressing Philip's desire to 'see the Father'. In verses 8–11 He had explained to Philip that he had already seen the Father through being with Jesus and through listening to His words. Philip needs to understand that hearing and believing lead to seeing. In other words, Philip has already seen the Father!

In part two of His answer (vv. 12ff), Jesus broadens out the topic and assures the disciples of the privileges that will be guaranteed to them following His departure:

- ✤ They will do the works of the Father as the result of praying in Jesus' name (v. 12).
- ✤ They will receive the Spirit who will live with them and in them, so that they continue to 'see' Jesus (vv. 15–19a).
- ✤ They will therefore live (v. 19b) and so...

✤ They will understand Jesus' relationship with the Father and will themselves know the love of the Father and the Son as Jesus reveals Himself (vv. 20–21).

This answer provokes another troubled question, this time from Judas. Up to this point the disciples have had little reason to expect anything other than that Jesus' death would be followed immediately by the start of His messianic reign over all nations. All this talk of an interlude, and of Jesus revealing Himself to the disciples alone (v. 19), confuses them. Jesus' answers in the Upper Room presuppose that the messianic age will not come right away – there will be a delay. This has implications for three groups of people, and Jesus spells out these implications.

Structure

14:8–21   Philip: 'Show us the Father!'

           12–21   Jesus' reply, part 2 (cont'd): The disciples will not just see the Father; they are even more privileged than they understand.

14:22–31   Judas: 'Why us and not the world?'

           22–27   Jesus' reply, part 1: 'Don't be anxious – Father, Son and Spirit will be with you.'

           28–31   Jesus' reply, part 2: 'Don't be sad – my departure is better for me, for you, and for the world.'

Old Testament background

The Holy Spirit: Old Testament references to 'the Spirit of God' number just short of 100. The Spirit is God active as creator, controller and revealer. There are occasions in the Old Testament when the Spirit was said to enable and equip specific individuals, e.g. Bezalel, who was given artistic skill (Exod. 31:1–11), and Moses, Saul, David and many others who were equipped for leadership. The key, however, to understanding the NT significance of the Holy Spirit is to be found in the writings of the prophets. The prophets anticipated a day when the Spirit of God would be poured out on all His people, bringing them new life and giving them new clean hearts, so that they would be ready and able to obey God (Ezek. 36:26ff). While there are references throughout the Old Testament to the Spirit being God active in power, it is only the prophets who suggest that the Spirit could ever indwell and remain permanently with *all* God's people. Their prophecy was never realised in the Old Testament.

Isaiah 40:5: There was an expectation that the whole world would see the messianic age coming immediately, when the glory of the Lord was revealed.

TEXT NOTES

8–21 'SHOW US THE FATHER!'

12–21 Jesus' reply, part 2 (cont'd). In reply to Philip, Jesus continues to outline the privileges of discipleship. As He broadens out His answer and begins to describe the privileges, He makes sure that the disciples understand who His real followers are (vv. 15ff). The word translated 'obey' is a key word in today's passage (vv. 15, 21, 23 and 24). The same word was used in 8:51 where Jesus taught that the person who kept His word (literally kept watch, guarded), or persevered in His word, was the one who would see life. Here, in chapter 14, Jesus describes the person who loves Him as the person who keeps His commands. It is important to realise that obedience is an attribute of His true followers, and not a precondition for being one of His followers.

These are the privileges of those who love Jesus:

- ℘ They will receive the Spirit.
- ℘ They will live (v. 19b).
- ℘ They will be in relationship with the Son and the Father (v. 20).

It is important to identify what Jesus teaches His disciples about the Spirit:

The Spirit is the Paraclete. The word 'paraclete' is used of a legal friend who fights the cause of the defendant. He is 'another', of the same sort as Jesus, who remains with His disciples and will dwell in the believer forever when Jesus is gone. The English word 'counsellor' doesn't quite capture the sense of the one who comes alongside and pleads the cause of God in us. 'Paraclete' is *definitely* not 'counsellor' with the sense of 'therapist'!

The Spirit is the Spirit of truth. Jesus, who described Himself as 'the truth' (14:6), now describes the Spirit as the Spirit of truth. Truth has been a key and vital emphasis in John's Gospel: Jesus reveals the truth (1:18) and calls true worshippers who will worship 'in truth' (4:23), and the Spirit will lead the apostles in all truth, when Jesus is gone, by reminding them of Jesus' teaching (v. 26).

The Spirit's relationship with Jesus. Several points indicate that the Spirit is none other than the Spirit of Jesus. Though the Spirit is an independent operator within the Trinity, He does not have His own separate agenda. He is the Spirit of the risen, living, life-giving Jesus who comes to be with Jesus' disciples forever. When Jesus says, 'I am coming', He means that His Spirit is coming – He uses the two phrases almost interchangeably. The Spirit is given by the Father at the request of the Son. He is personal, a 'He', like Jesus. He will never depart from Jesus' words (v. 26), but will use Jesus' words to accomplish the Father's agenda. Indeed, the more we read the New Testament, the more we see that the three persons of the Trinity, though distinct, are very much one God. Like Jesus, the Spirit cannot be 'seen' or understood or received by the world, by people in hostile rebellion against God. (NB When Jesus says 'I will come to you', He cannot be referring simply to His resurrection appearances, for He promises that He will not abandon His disciples (v. 18) and also that He will come to 'whoever' (v. 21) and 'anyone' (v. 23) who loves Him and obeys Him.)

By verse 21 it is clear that Jesus' answer to Philip has broadened out to encompass a whole range of benefits that will be available to the believer following His departure. If only Philip will believe he will realise just how privileged he is.

22–31 'WHY US AND NOT THE WORLD?'

Judas' anxiety about the failure of the world to see Jesus can best be explained by Isaiah 40:5 (see Old Testament notes). In replying to Philip, Jesus has made it clear that, whereas His disciples will have a relationship of love with Himself and also with the Father, the world will not (v. 10). The messianic age, when the whole world will see and acknowledge the Messiah, will not come yet; there is to be a delay before this momentous era is fully ushered in. Judas cannot understand this. Jesus answers the question by first teaching the apostles what His departure will achieve for *them*. Having established this, He then answers the question with regard to the world.

22–27 *'Don't be anxious.'* What Jesus' departure will achieve for His disciples. *First*, an intimate union with the Father and the Son (vv. 23–24). The impact of this amazing prospect is reinforced when we realise that the word for 'home', that Jesus uses here, is the same word that He used when speaking to Peter in verse 2 – there it was translated as 'rooms'. (Literally, the word means 'dwelling place', with the connotation of permanence.) At that point Peter was promised a dwelling place in heaven; now Judas is promised that he will become the dwelling place of God on earth. Note that the promise in verse 23 is sandwiched between two reminders, one put positively and the other negatively, about the link between loving Jesus and obeying Him: this promise is specifically for disciples who have responded rightly to Jesus' revelation of the Father. Note too that Jesus underlines His promise by telling us that it comes from the Father.

Secondly, the sending of the Spirit will guarantee the accurate recalling of Jesus' words by the apostles (vv. 25–26). Note that the promise about teaching and reminding must apply initially to the apostles, for it is limited to 'everything I have said to you'. This has major implications for us today when the accuracy and the authority of scripture are questioned. The 'all things' and 'everything' of verse 26 show that the Spirit-inspired message of the apostles is both final and sufficient. The Spirit has no further words to add to the 'all things' He has taught Jesus' apostles. To suggest that He has more to say is to question Jesus' teaching in verse 26.

Thirdly, their peace, a unique peace with God their Father, which is established through their belief in the achievements of Jesus' death.

28–31 *'Don't be sad.'* What Jesus' departure will achieve for the world as well as for His disciples. In verse 29 Jesus tells His disciples that His instruction about His death now, *before* He dies, will enable them, later on, to believe in Him. He has already made this point twice (8:28; 13:19), but here He expands it in order to answer Judas' question about the world recognising Jesus as Messiah: His obedient and loving response to His God-given mission will be not only the way to convince His disciples, but *also* the way to convince the world of who He is. Thus the cross becomes the fulcrum on which the world is either saved or judged. Here then is the answer to Judas' question. The Spirit enables the apostles to record the message and meaning of the cross. The world will be enabled to respond correctly to Jesus through this message about the cross.

KEY THEMES

- ✤ Jesus' departure is not a tragedy for the disciples, whose love of Jesus is shown to be genuine by their perseverance in obeying His teaching. Following His departure:
    - ↘ They will receive the Spirit.
    - ↘ They will be the dwelling place of the Father and the Son.
    - ↘ They will be reminded of all the things that Jesus taught them.
    - ↘ They will be loved by the Father.
    - ↘ They will receive Jesus' peace.
- ✤ Those in the world will not receive these blessings, for they are still ruled by Satan.
    - ↘ They are unable to receive, see or know the Spirit because they do not love or obey the Son.
    - ↘ They will not see Jesus after His death.
    - ↘ They will see Jesus' love for His Father and His obedience to Him. They will either be judged or saved according to their reaction to this.
- ✤ The world will, however, be brought into a relationship of loving obedience to God through the Spirit-inspired message of the apostles – the gospel.

APPLICATION

There are three major areas of application from today's study. *First*, the breadth of a disciple's privileges. Replying to both Philip and Judas, Jesus promises that the one who loves Him will be able to continue to see the Father – more than that, that person will have the Father and the Son dwelling within him or her through the Spirit. This means, therefore, that a disciple now is in a position of even greater privilege than were the disciples themselves when Jesus was with them physically.

Make sure you focus on the intimacy suggested by the words 'in', 'with', 'within' and 'forever'. It will be important, also, to spend plenty of time on the matter of obeying Jesus' word, and the fact that *this* is what indicates a person's genuine love for Jesus. Take care, however, not to encourage salvation by works! Obedience to Jesus is the mark of someone who loves Him, not a condition for belonging to Him.

Secondly, it will be well worth getting straight just who the Spirit is and who He is not! Don't be surprised if there are some pretty strange ideas around. This is one of the key NT passages on the identity of the Holy Spirit, so spend plenty of time thinking through the teaching in these verses. He *is* the Spirit of Jesus, of His truth and of His word. He is *not* a materialistic Spirit who will give disciples the things that Jesus has so far refused to give them. The crowds, at various points in John's narrative, attempted to force their own this-worldly agenda onto Jesus, and we must be aware of the danger of doing the same thing, trying to force our own 'me-centred' agenda onto the Spirit of Jesus. The Spirit has enabled the apostles to record 'all things' and 'everything' that Jesus taught. His words are final and sufficient.

Thirdly, Jesus' answer to Judas should encourage us to ensure that the teaching about the cross is central to our evangelism. For Jesus says that it is as the world sees His loving obedience to the Father (in going to the cross), which he speaks about *before* He dies, that they will come to believe.

THE AIM OF THIS STUDY

To see that, far from being impoverished by the departure of Jesus, those who demonstrate their genuine love of Jesus by obedience will be privileged to have God dwelling in them.

SUGGESTED QUESTIONS

15–21 'SHOW US THE FATHER!' (CONT'D)

- ✤ This passage continues Jesus' reply to Philip's request, 'Lord, show us the Father and that will be enough for us.' What benefits of His 'going' has Jesus already described in verses 9-14?

- ✤ In verses 15–21 Jesus teaches that His departure will lead to the sending of the Spirit. What does He tell us about the Spirit?
  - ↘ How does Jesus' teaching meet Philip's request?

- ✤ Jesus' teaching on the Spirit follows verse 15 and is followed by verse 21. What does this tell us about those to whom the Spirit is given?
  - ↘ What does the Spirit give to Jesus' disciples?
  - ↘ Among the believing people of God, how does the sending of the Spirit of Jesus make possible a spiral of growing love and obedience?
  - ↘ In what ways does this challenge or change your understanding of the Spirit's work?

- ✤ Someone says, 'If only I'd been alive then and been able to meet Jesus! It must have been magnificent for them ... God seems so remote to me.' How would you reply?

22–31 'WHY US AND NOT THE WORLD?'

- ✤ What is it that is troubling Judas?
- ✤ In verses 23–27, what three things does Jesus promise His believing people when He is gone?
- ✤ In verses 28–31 Jesus explains how people will come to believe. Put His explanation into your own words.
- ✤ How do the two parts of Jesus' answer address Judas' question?
  - ↘ When we seek to convince non-Christian friends of the truth of the Christian message, how should we be guided by Jesus' words to Judas?

John 15:1–17
'I am the true vine'

CONTEXT

The words of Jesus in 14:31, 'Come now; let us leave', suggest a break in the discourse. This break marks a slight change in subject matter. In the first part of the discourse Jesus has been answering the disciples' questions about His departure. He has explained that there will be a delay before His kingdom is inaugurated fully and He has taught them what His departure will achieve for them, things that they will experience and enjoy while they wait for His return. But how should they be living, while they wait? This major question is still outstanding. In chapters 15–17 Jesus explains that the most important thing in this life is to remain in Him. His teaching on this has four major parts:

15:1–17   The disciples' relationship to Jesus. Jesus is the true fruit-bearing vine. The disciples must remain in Him through remaining in His word.

15:18– 16:15 The disciples' relationship to the world. The world will hate the disciples, just as it hated Jesus, but they must persevere in His word to the end, just as He did. They will have the help of the Holy Spirit as they wait.

16:16–33   The disciples' relationship to the Father. Jesus' departure is a good thing because it will bring about a permanent relationship with the Father.

17:1–26   Jesus prays that the disciples will be kept to the end.

STRUCTURE

15:1–2   Jesus is the true fruit-bearing vine.

15:3–8   Disciples must remain in the true fruit-bearing vine. The consequences of doing so and also of not doing so.

15:9–17   The vine metaphor explained. The nature of remaining: what it means to remain in Jesus.

OLD TESTAMENT BACKGROUND

The vine: Psalm 80:8–19, Isaiah 5:1–7 and Jeremiah 2:21 are among a number of Old Testament references in which God's chosen people are described as a 'vine'. In every case the people are seen as a fruitless and unfaithful people, and their descriptions are accompanied by warnings of judgment and exclusion from God's kingdom. However, in Psalm 80:17–18 and Isaiah 27:2–6 the writers look forward to a future day when the vine *will* be fruitful. Jesus is claiming to have fulfilled that prophecy.

TEXT NOTES

1–2 JESUS IS THE TRUE FRUIT-BEARING VINE

By introducing Himself as the true vine, Jesus is identifying Himself as the true fruitful Israel (see Old Testament notes). This is a claim of staggering egocentricity. It implies that all other religions are false – only Jesus is the true vine. It suggests that He, at last, will be able to accomplish all that God's people have failed to achieve throughout the Old Testament. And it also suggests that a person can only enjoy the status of being part of God's true fruitful people by being joined to Jesus. Characteristically, Jesus immediately explains (v. 2) that He does not work independently of the Father. As in the Old Testament, the Father is the one who tends the vine, for the Father is passionately concerned for the fruitfulness of His people.

3–8 DISCIPLES MUST REMAIN IN THE TRUE FRUIT-BEARING VINE

The consequences of doing so and also of not doing so.

Jesus discusses the vine and the branches. The branches are identified as 'anyone remaining in Jesus'. Anyone who remains in Jesus will bear fruit. Any branch that is apart from the true vine is unable to bear any fruit at all. This further emphasises the centrality of Jesus and the futility of religion without Jesus. The principle and practice of bearing fruit is what brings the Father glory.

Verse 3. Jesus is the entry point for a person to become part of the vine. Such a person 'joins' the vine by hearing the words that Jesus has spoken (including His words about the cross through which the believer is cleansed).

Verse 4. He continues the metaphor to show that remaining in Him is essential for a person to bear fruit. Jesus, we see, is essential to God's purposes for the fruitfulness of His people.

Verse 5. The principle of this first part is stated in verse 5b: anyone remaining in Jesus is guaranteed to bear much fruit. As for a definition of what this 'fruit' is, it is worth waiting until the second half of the passage, where Jesus explains the metaphor.

Verse 6. Jesus tackles the consequence of 'not remaining'. Fruitless branches are thrown out and burned. These are very strong words; the literal translation from the Greek reads: 'If anyone does not remain in me, was thrown outside like the branch, *and* withers, *and* they gather them, *and* into the fire they throw, *and* they are burned.'

Verse 7. Jesus now focuses on the positive aspect of 'remaining' and 'bearing fruit'. To remain in the vine means continuing in His teaching (cf. 8:31; 10:3). So, both joining the vine and remaining in the vine are dependent upon Jesus' word. Furthermore, bearing fruit is dependent upon His word too, for while the bearing of fruit will be the result of prayer (v. 7b), that prayer will be governed by Jesus' words which must remain in a disciple.

Verse 8. Finally, Jesus explains the purpose of the true vine and its branches. The purpose is to bring glory to the Father – it had always been intended that the people of Israel would do this, but as a nation they failed. Verse 8 begins to give us some idea as to what the 'fruit' ought to be: whatever it is, it will be in line with Jesus' words, it will bring glory to the Father, and it will come as a result of prayer.

Some commentators tie themselves in terrible knots over the issue of whether it is possible for someone who has once been 'joined to the vine' to be cut out of the vine later. Therefore, it is important to note that the vine imagery is not intended to settle disputes about the perseverance of the saints! The obvious purpose of the verses is to insist that true Christians will always produce some measure of fruit. Fruitfulness is an unmistakable mark of true Christianity: from the earliest chapters of John's Gospel the genuine believer has been identified as the one who believes, and *continues to believe*, the words of Jesus. For such a person, says Jesus (vv. 7–8), bearing fruit is guaranteed. But what is this 'fruit'? Jesus answers this vital question as He proceeds to explain the metaphor.

9–17 THE VINE METAPHOR EXPLAINED: THE VINE AT WORK IN THE WORLD

Jesus' explanation of how the vine works, and what the images mean, presents us with a picture of how God's true fruitful people are meant to live. The emphasis is on their loving obedience to His word and work (i.e. His revelation of the Father); this obedience is the indispensable first step to fruitfulness.

9–11 The nature of remaining. The Father has loved Jesus by showing Him all that He does (5:20). Jesus has loved the disciples in the same way, by showing them all things through His words and works (v. 15). Jesus has remained in the Father's love by *loving obedience* to what He was shown – even as far as death. In this respect, the disciples are to model themselves on Jesus, the perfect example of remaining. This kind of obedience leads to joy. Jesus has already taught that holding to His teaching results in freedom (8:31–32); here we see that joy, the true joy that Jesus Himself experienced, can also be ours, as we 'remain in His love' through loving obedience to His command.

12–17 The nature of His command. Jesus has already shown His disciples that obedience to Him means putting self to death in loving service of His people (12:25; 13:12–17; 13:34). Paradoxically, if people obey Jesus' command, He will call them His friends. As people remain in Jesus' love, in *loving obedience* to His command, so they will have the Father's will revealed to them. They will 'know the master's business'. So, on the basis of His word (vv. 14–15) they will be friends and not slaves. Clearly, it is as friends of Jesus, knowing the Father's purposes because Jesus has revealed them to His friends, that they will be able to bear fruit. In verses 16–17 Jesus draws the threads together: the disciples cannot puff themselves up on account of their new-found privileges, because the initiative lies entirely with Jesus (cf. 6:70–71).

Verse 16 enables us to arrive at a better definition of what 'fruit' is. It is possible to argue that fruit is synonymous with Christian behaviour. After all, Christian behaviour is the result of prayer in Jesus' name (v. 16) and it brings glory to the Father (v. 8); it represents obedience to Jesus' commands (v. 10), and it means experiencing His joy (v. 11), loving one another (v. 12), and witnessing to the world (vv. 16, 27). This suggests a broad definition for fruit of anything that is generally godly. However, on examining the suggestion within the context of John, it is hard to avoid the conclusion that the primary meaning of fruit must be what results from evangelism and mission, i.e. new believers.

(Some people like to read into the text, at this point, the idea of the fruit of the Spirit, but there is no indication that John has this idea in mind here. We should stick to the main track, therefore, and *not* be diverted.)

The conclusion above is confirmed by verse 16, where the word for 'appointed you' is a verb used usually to mean appointing someone to a particular task or ministry. Since the context of verse 16 is the 'going' of the disciples, the words 'appointed you' suggest 'mission'. Furthermore, the word 'last', in verse 16 – 'fruit that will last' – is the same word that is translated as 'remain' in the rest of the passage; this implies that the fruit will 'remain in the vine' in obedience, love and so on. Jesus' point is that He is the true vine who has called people and given them the task of bringing others in.

KEY THEMES

It is God's purpose that His people should bear fruit on earth – this is to His glory.

    ✤ Remaining is His work:

        ↘ He initiated our membership by choosing us, loving us and cleansing us by His word.

        ↘ He has shown His love by obeying His Father, dying for His disciples and revealing to them all that God has told Him.

    ✤ The need to remain in Jesus.

        ↘ He is the true fruit-bearing vine promised in the Old Testament. We will only be members of fruit-bearing Israel if we remain in Him.

        ↘ On our own we are helpless and hopeless, fit only for destruction.

        ↘ We must let Jesus' words live in us.

        ↘ We must obey His commands, particularly His command that we should love each other.

    ✤ The consequences of remaining in Him.

        ↘ Those who remain in the vine will bear fruit as they pray according to Jesus' words.

        ↘ The Father will thus be glorified.

APPLICATION

The main impact of this passage should be to make us reassess our relationship with Jesus. Are we taking it seriously?

We learn that God's purpose for His people is that we should bear fruit. It is not His primary purpose that we should have a happy life, or a wealthy trouble-free existence. His concern is that His people should bear fruit and so bring Him glory. Jesus (and His words) alone makes it possible to bear fruit. He assures us that if we remain in Him and He in us we certainly *will* bear fruit, but He warns that the one who does not bear fruit is fit only for destruction. He explains that our remaining is by His choice, through His love, and according to His word dwelling in a person. He teaches that our loving obedience to His word will ensure His continued indwelling.

All this drives us to Jesus, to His word, and to an examination of our own response to Him. As we concentrate on *these* things, fruit certainly *will* follow. Too often we focus on techniques and events, but Jesus teaches that if we focus on Him, and our relationship with Him, evangelistic fruit will come naturally, in answer to our prayer, and in this way we will bring glory to the Father.

The aim of this study

That we should recognise God's ultimate purpose for His people on earth, which is that they should bear fruit and so bring Him glory. (This should lead us to an absolute dependence on Jesus and His words as the only source of true fruitfulness.)

Suggested questions

- ✤ What has been achieved through the answering of the disciples' 'troubled' questions in chapters 13 and 14?

1–2 JESUS IS THE TRUE FRUIT-BEARING VINE

- ✤ The vine is a common Old Testament image for God's people. What is the difference between the image of the vine in Isaiah 5:1–7 and the one in Isaiah 27:2–6?
- ✤ In verses 1–2 Jesus uses the vine imagery to describe Himself, His Father and His people. How does the Old Testament context help to fill out what He is saying?

3–8 DISCIPLES MUST REMAIN IN THE TRUE FRUIT-BEARING VINE

- ✤ What does this passage tell us about how God's purpose for His vine is going to be achieved?
- ✤ What impact do these verses make on your attitude to God's word, and to the different opportunities available to listen to it? Why should we be serious about these opportunities?

9–17 THE VINE METAPHOR EXPLAINED

✤ How do verses 9–11 help us understand what it means to 'remain in Jesus'?

  ↘ How will this affect our attitude to Jesus' words when we study them?

  ↘ How can we practically help one another to 'remain in His love'?

✤ Look at verse 12. Where, earlier in the Gospel, have we come across this command to love one another?

  ↘ How has this teaching affected your life in the last few weeks?

  ↘ Why do you think Jesus mentions it so much?

  ↘ How can we practically help one another to make progress in this area?

  ↘ How is it that Jesus' command leads to friendship and not to slavery?

✤ What is it in verse 16 that shows that the 'fruit' being talked about has to do with the outside world?

✤ What is God's purpose for His people while they remain on earth? What practical steps are you going to take to avoid your church being an 'Isaiah 5' church?

John 15:18–16:4
The disciples' relationship with the world

CONTEXT

In the second part of the Upper Room Discourse, Jesus teaches the disciples that God's purpose for His people as they live now is to be the true fruitful vine. In order to achieve this they will need to persevere as disciples of Jesus.

In 15:1–17 the importance of remaining in Jesus and persevering is the major emphasis. The reason His people need to remain in Him is that this is the only way to bear fruit and to avoid destruction.

The purpose of the next passage, 15:18–16:4, is to warn the disciples (16:1). They have a job to do, as God's fruit-bearing people, in the world, but the world is hostile to Jesus and His teaching. Therefore, remaining in Jesus will mean experiencing the world's hatred. This is inevitable, and cannot be avoided, for God will not give up on the world.

Thus 15:1–17 is primarily about the disciples' relationship with Jesus the vine, and 15:8–16:4 is primarily about the disciples' relationship with the world in which they still live.

STRUCTURE

The world will hate the disciples because of...

15:18–20   ...its hatred of Jesus. Because the disciples belong to Jesus they share in the world's hostility towards Him.

15:21–25   ...its hatred of the Father. This is revealed by the hostility towards Jesus. It is without excuse because the world has seen God's perfect revelation.

15:26–27   ...the Holy Spirit's ongoing testimony to Jesus through the disciples. God has not given up on the world – He will send the Spirit and the disciples into the world to testify to Jesus.

16:1–4   Forewarned is forearmed. The world will persecute God's fruit-bearing people with zealous religious commitment.

TEXT NOTES

17–20 THE WORLD WILL HATE THE DISCIPLES BECAUSE OF ITS HATRED OF JESUS

Jesus warns His disciples that they will be hated by the world, and explains why. It is likely that His command that they should love each other in verse 17 is just as much an introduction to this part as a summary of the previous one. Our love for one another is an indispensable element of our testimony to Jesus as we pursue this goal of fruitfulness in the world (13:34–35; 15:27).

The word used here for 'hate' is a very strong one, meaning 'to detest, abhor, persecute in hatred'; it suggests a fixed ongoing hatred. Verses 19–20 expand on why the world hates the disciples in this way, giving two reasons: the disciples do not belong to the world and, secondly, they do belong to Jesus whom the world hates. In verse 19 Jesus stresses the disciples' separateness from the world by repeating the word 'world' five times (four times in the NIV). The point is that the disciples have been chosen and now belong elsewhere. If a person belongs to Jesus, the true vine, that person has changed sides. Put negatively, he or she no longer belongs to the world; put positively, he or she now belongs to Jesus. So, the primary cause for persecution is the disciples' change of status. The world does 'love' but its love is selfish – it only loves its own. Conversely, the world hates and its hatred is directed primarily at Jesus. The disciples have already seen a mixture of fickle love and hate in the way the world treated Jesus (cf. chs. 5–10).

The world's hostility towards Jesus is underlined in verse 20 where Jesus points to Himself as the model for the disciples. The 'ifs' of verse 20 imply that the hatred is tied to what the disciples have to *say* about Jesus. Obedience to Jesus' teaching (v. 20b) is held up as the positive counterpart to persecution (v. 20a). In general, the world will persecute the disciples for their teaching just as they persecuted Jesus for His. The world may say it likes or respects Jesus, but if it hates His teaching it hates Him. But all is not totally gloomy! Some from the world will obey the disciples' teaching, just as some from the world obeyed Jesus' teaching.

Throughout this first part Jesus has been strengthening the disciples against 'going astray'. If they realise that the world's hostility is directed primarily at Jesus, and that Jesus Himself experienced this hatred, they will be better equipped to persevere and remain in Him.

21–25 THE WORLD WILL HATE THE DISCIPLES BECAUSE OF ITS HATRED OF THE FATHER

Verse 21 summarises the opening statements and introduces the new idea that hostility to Jesus indicates hatred of God. The sentence structure here is made by the two 'If I had not ... but now' statements in verses 22 and 24. They both contain these two points: the guilt of the world and the world's hatred of the Father. In 14:10-11 Jesus had taught that the way He made the Father known was through His words and works. Here, His words and works expose the world's guilt. It is not that if Jesus had not come the world would have been guiltless. Rather, that by coming and speaking and acting Jesus has revealed the Father. Therefore, the world's hatred of Jesus' words and works exposes its central and controlling sin: hatred of the Father (cf. 3:19ff). The disciples should not be surprised at this hatred of the Father – it is written about in scripture. By quoting from Psalm 69:4 Jesus makes the point that if David could be hated for no reason, how much more would God's Messiah (the Son of David) be hated.

Again, the disciples will be far better equipped to keep going and 'not go astray' (16:1), so achieving their purpose of remaining and being fruitful, if they realise these two things: first, that the hatred and persecution are matters of sin for which there is no excuse, and secondly, that while this persecution is conducted *in the name* of the Father, it is nonetheless hatred *of* the Father. Those who persecute will be religious people (16:2) who claim to be acting in worship of God, but here Jesus devastatingly exposes their hearts.

26–27 THE WORLD WILL HATE THE DISCIPLES BECAUSE OF THE HOLY SPIRIT'S ONGOING TESTIMONY TO JESUS THROUGH THE DISCIPLES

The world may hate both Jesus and the Father, but the Father has not given up on the world. After Jesus' departure He will continue to reach out to the world, using two 'agents' to accomplish His purpose: He will send His Spirit and He will send His disciples. The fact that the disciples have been entrusted with this task is the reason why they cannot simply run away from the world that hates them.

So, the ministry of the Spirit and the disciples in the future will ensure that the Father will still be revealed to the world, and that the world's hatred and sin will still be exposed. Note: the Spirit is *not* going to do *new* works of Jesus; He will testify (the same word as is used of John the Baptist), pointing back to the finished works and final words of Jesus. The disciples will follow suit.

16:1–4 FOREWARNED IS FOREARMED: THE WORLD WILL PERSECUTE WITH ZEALOUS RELIGIOUS COMMITMENT

These verses provide us with the explanation of Jesus' purpose in teaching about opposition. His purpose is to 'warn' the disciples (v. 4) and to prevent them from going astray (literally 'stumbling') (v. 1). As to the *nature* of the opposition, this will be exclusion from the recognised religious establishment, and may even lead to martyrdom (v. 2a). The presenting *motive* for this opposition will be religious (v. 2b), but the underlying *reason* for it – and the disciples will now be able to recognise it – will be the world's hatred for both the Father and Jesus (v. 3). So, the world *will* hate the disciples as they testify to the Father and Son. The disciples might reasonably expect opposition from an atheistic world, but to have hostility and hatred coming from the religious establishment is somehow rather more difficult to understand.

Right the way back in the Prologue, we noted that part of John's reason for writing was to assure his readers that the religious establishment's hatred of Jesus was not a legitimate reason for rejecting Him (1:10–12). This passage picks up that theme and explains why members of the religious establishment will always hate true followers of God: though they claim to love His Son, their hatred of His Son's teaching reveals their deep hatred of God.

KEY THEMES

℞ The disciples have been chosen and set apart by Jesus for fruitfulness in the world. They must expect hatred from the world, as they testify to Jesus and His teaching, but they should not stumble on account of it.

↘ The world's hatred is the result of the fact that the disciples do not belong to the world.

↘ It is also the result of the fact that the disciples belong to Jesus and to the Father, whose teaching the world hates and has always hated.

↘ This hatred comes even from the religious establishment. It may lead to the disciples' exclusion from society, and even to death.

↘ It is inescapable because the disciples have a job to do in the world. If they are to testify to Jesus and His teaching, they will have to remain in the world and engage with it.

APPLICATION

To them then: In the first instance this teaching is for the benefit of the eleven apostles in the Upper Room. It gives them the explanation for the Jews' hatred of their message. When, as described later in Acts, they emerge from seclusion and begin to preach and teach about Jesus, they might have easily been unnerved by the absolute rejection of their message by the religious establishment. To John's readers in John's day, secondly, these words of Jesus provide clear reasons for continuing to believe in Him, for persevering as His disciples, and for reaching out to the world in evangelism, rather than withdrawing from the world into a religious ghetto.

To us now: Throughout the history of the church the apostles' teaching has been under attack. Sometimes this attack comes at the hands of the atheistic secular authorities, e.g. the Marxist/ Leninist authorities in the Soviet Bloc. But frequently this opposition has come from zealous religious authorities.

Carson writes: 'The most dangerous oppression comes not from careless pagans but from zealous adherents to religious faith, and from other ideologies. A sermon was preached when Cranmer was burned at the stake. Christians have faced severe persecution performed in the name of Yahweh, in the name of Allah, in the name of Marx – and in the name of Jesus' (p. 531). Today we should not be surprised when so-called Christian leaders vilify those of us who stand up for the orthodox teaching of the apostles on doctrinal and ethical issues. Nonetheless, we must not withdraw into religious ghettos. We too belong not to the world but to Jesus. We too have a task to do – to bear fruit. And we too must keep at it.

THE AIM OF THIS STUDY

To see that the apostles' teaching about Jesus will always attract hostility from the world. We should not cease to persevere in Christ, even when this opposition is highly intense and comes from so-called religious people.

SUGGESTED QUESTIONS

✤ *(Recap on 'Where we are in John'. Suggest using a diagram to illustrate the fact of Jesus' departure and the resulting period of 'waiting' for His return.)*

18–20 THE WORLD WILL HATE JESUS' DISCIPLES BECAUSE
IT HATES JESUS

✤ The word used for 'hate' in verse 18 is a very strong one meaning 'to detest, abhor, persecute in hatred'. What reasons does Jesus give for this hatred?

↘ What do these verses imply about the way the disciples will interact with the world?

↘ Where, in John so far, have we seen an illustration of this truth about the world's hatred of Jesus' disciples? Where do we see it illustrated today?

✤ In 16:1 Jesus tells the disciples *why* He is giving them this piece of teaching. What is His reason? How will His words help us as we face persecution?

21–25 THE WORLD WILL HATE JESUS' DISCIPLES BECAUSE
IT HATES THE FATHER

✤ In verses 22–24 Jesus makes the same point in two similar ways. What is it?

↘ How does the sentence structure of the verses drive home the point?

↘ What purpose is served by the quotation from Psalm 69?

↘ How do these verses help us as we face opposition to Jesus' message from the world?

26–27 THE FATHER CONTINUES TO REACH OUT TO THE WORLD
IN LOVE

✤ The Father reacts to the hatred of the world by sending His Spirit. What has His Spirit come to do? What does this tell us about the Father?

↘ What is the application of these verses to us?

16:1–4 FOREWARNED IS FOREARMED

✤ The aim is to prevent us going astray. In the light of 15:1–17, what is the meaning of 'going astray'?

↘ What is so surprising about who is doing the persecuting? And why they are doing it?

↘ Why might this, especially, make Jesus' disciples go astray?

APPLICATION

꙳ Self-righteous Simon (*Paint a verbal picture of a guy who is being 'persecuted' for reasons other than his testimony to Jesus (i.e. being tactless and obnoxious).*) Why is this guy not facing genuine persecution? (*Answers from the passage!*)

꙳ Monastic Meg (*Paint a verbal picture of a woman who has a constant 'downer' on the world, praises God that 'I'm not like them', but never gets involved with the non-Christian world.*) Why is this woman far away from John 15:18ff?

꙳ Keen Kim (*Paint a verbal picture of a vicar who persecutes a newly-converted Christian because she is adhering to Jesus' teaching about sexual ethics.*) How should this girl react?

John 16:5–33
'I am going to the Father'

CONTEXT

In this second part of the Upper Room Discourse, Jesus has been teaching that God's purpose for His people, as they live in the world now, is that they should persevere in Jesus, God's true fruit-bearing vine. So far we have seen:

15:1–17 Their relationship with Jesus. His people must remain and persevere in Jesus' words so as to bear fruit and avoid destruction.

15:18–16:4 Their relationship with the world. His people will be hated by the world for belonging to Jesus and not to the world. Nonetheless, they must persevere in Him and continue to testify to Him, for the Father has not given up on the world but expects to reach the world through them.

16:5–33 Their relationship with the Father. With this third strand Jesus brings the teaching of the Upper Room Discourse to a close by reminding His disciples that He is going back to the Father (vv. 5, 17, 28). Though they may not immediately understand the implications of His going (via the cross), with hindsight they will understand what His death has achieved, and so their grief will turn to joy. His going is for their good, for it will achieve two wonderful things: the sending of the Spirit, which means that they will not be left alone (this passage, verses 5–15, really belongs with

15:18–16:4); and secondly, a new age of lasting joy, because of knowing the Father, and true peace.

STRUCTURE

16:5–7a   Jesus assures the disciples that His going away really is for their good, despite the world's hatred.

16:7b–15   Jesus' going will lead to the Spirit's coming.

       7b–11   The Spirit will convict the world.

       12–15   The Spirit will lead the apostles into all truth and so bring glory to Jesus.

16:16–28   Jesus' going will bring in a new age of lasting joy.

       16–19   The disciples are confused.

       20–22   His departure will cause them grief but this will turn to lasting, irremovable joy when they realise what the cross has achieved.

       23–28   This joy will be the complete joy of direct access to the Father and full knowledge of the Father because the Father loves them.

16:29–33   Jesus' going will bring true peace.

TEXT NOTES

5–7A JESUS ASSURES THE DISCIPLES THAT HIS GOING AWAY REALLY IS FOR THEIR GOOD, DESPITE THE WORLD'S HATRED

It is important that we remember the context of this passage. Jesus has just explained how He is the true fruit-bearing vine and how His disciples will face the world's hostility as they persevere in Him. The disciples would be understandably perturbed, knowing that Jesus is about to leave. So, Jesus now returns to the issue of His departure. His 'going', and what it means for the disciples, dominates this final part of the teaching in the Upper Room.

Jesus remonstrates with His disciples for not having asked Him where He is going. However, in 13:36 Peter had asked just that question. From verse 6 it seems that Jesus is criticising the disciples for being so self-absorbed in their own loss that they have not yet asked really thoughtful questions about His going and what it means for them. Instead of supplying the answer immediately – it is given in verse 28 – Jesus explains that His departure, with all that it entails in terms of His death and resurrection, is for their own good.

7B–15 JESUS' GOING WILL LEAD TO THE SPIRIT'S COMING

His going is essential to the Spirit's coming. In 15:26–27 Jesus taught the disciples that the Spirit would testify to the Father, and that they were to testify too. These verses explain how the Spirit will enable the disciples to fulfil this task. He has a ministry both to the disciples and to the world.

7b–11 The Spirit will convict the world. Just as Jesus exposes the world's guilt, by showing that what it does is evil, so the Spirit will continue this work. The word translated 'convict' has the sense of shaming the world and convincing it of its own guilt, thus calling it to repentance. It is the same word that Jesus used in 3:20. Our understanding of precisely what Jesus means by 'sin, righteousness and judgment' must therefore be governed by the fact that in each case it is exposure and guilt that is under consideration.

The world is guilty of sin (v. 9) because, as we have seen throughout the Gospel, it does not believe in Jesus. The Spirit's ministry is to bring people to acknowledge this guilt. The world is guilty in regard to righteousness (v. 10): Jesus' ministry has exposed the world's lack of moral purity (3:16ff); by His light He has exposed the world's darkness and hypocrisy (7:7). Now that Jesus is going, the Spirit will continue this ministry in His absence. The world is guilty in regard to judgment (v. 11): Jesus' ministry, climaxing in His death and resurrection, has achieved the condemnation and driving out of Satan (12:31ff). This work is a preview of the Devil's final demise on the Day of Judgment. The Spirit will bring people to a realisation of their position regarding final judgment – some will respond by turning to Jesus; others will remain in the world.

12–15 The Spirit will lead the apostles 'into all truth' and so bring glory to Jesus. Hand in hand with His ministry to the world, the Spirit will guide the apostles into all the truth about Jesus and, therefore, about the Father also. This will enable the disciples both to persevere, since they will have Jesus' words with them, *and* to accomplish the Father's work of bearing fruit (15:8)/doing 'greater things' (14:12)/testifying to the world (15:27), etc. The logic seems to be that it is because the Spirit leads the apostles into all the truth about Jesus that they are able to remain and persevere. As the apostles testify to what they have received from the Spirit about Jesus, so the world will be convicted concerning sin, righteousness and judgment. This is how Jesus is glorified, as the apostles proclaim their message about Jesus. The Spirit's work is to convict, the apostles' work is to testify – and the church's work is to continue that testimony. It is not that there is more new truth for the Spirit to reveal about Jesus; rather, that He has led the apostles into *all* the truth about Jesus. (See also 14:26.)

16–28 JESUS' GOING WILL BRING IN A NEW AGE OF LASTING JOY

16–19 *The disciples are confused.* They are unable to understand what He means by saying that He will leave and then come back to them 'after a little while'. Their confusion is understandable; after all, they were expecting the immediate consummation of all the Old Testament messianic promises.

20–22 *His departure will cause them grief but this will turn to lasting joy.* Again, Jesus explains that His departure (to the cross) will not result in their permanent separation from Him. They will be separated for a short while and in that period they will grieve, but their grief will turn to rejoicing when they realise what His death has achieved. There is considerable discussion in the commentaries about whether 'you will see me' refers to His resurrection appearances, His coming to them in the Spirit, or His second coming. The resurrection appearances must be part of what is in view, but for all the reasons already discussed (see 14:15–27), and in light of the context of verses 5–15, this meaning must then give way to the meaning that He would send the Paraclete to be with them. The main point is that their grief, caused by His imminent departure, will be transformed into lasting joy when they see Him and so realise what His departure has achieved. His return will inaugurate a whole New Age – the Age of the Spirit.

23–28 The joy of direct access to the Father. As if to emphasise that this is a new age, Jesus speaks of a time ('hour') (v. 25) when the disciples will be taught plainly about the Father. This Age of the Spirit will be characterised by the new phenomenon of *direct access*:

Direct access to the Father in prayer. The disciples will no longer have to have go-betweens between themselves and the Father (vv. 23, 26). Jesus drives this point home by insisting that they will not have to pray to Him but that they will be able to go straight to the Father (on the basis of His work on the cross). They will ask 'in His name' (because of what He has done); they will not have to take their requests to Him first, as if He were then to 'ferry' their desires to the Father.

Direct access to the truth about the Father. As with the promise of 15:15, verse 25 suggests that the disciples will know the Father's purposes and will therefore be able to ask in accordance with His desires.

Verse 28 is a very important verse. It answers the question raised by Jesus in verse 5, and so ties together this part of the Discourse. But also, more widely, it summarises the whole mission of Jesus; this is the first really clear statement, in John's Gospel, of what He has come to do. He is telling His disciples that He has achieved what He came to do, and is thereby authenticating all the promises He has made to them, promises that we have read in the preceding verses.

29–33 JESUS' GOING WILL BRING TRUE PEACE

The disciples think they understand, but they don't. Jesus predicts that His imminent departure will result in their being scattered – they will face the hostility of the world. However, they need to realise that His departure accomplishes the conquest of the rebellious world, and that by remaining in Him they will have true and lasting peace.

KEY THEMES

Jesus has come from the Father into the world and is now returning to His Father. The disciples should not grieve, for His departure will bring about a New Age.

✥ In the New Age, His Father will send the Spirit:
  ↘ The Spirit will bring the world to an acknowledgment of personal guilt concerning its failure to respond to Jesus, its moral darkness, and its certain judgment.
  ↘ The Spirit will bring glory to Jesus by guiding the apostles in all the truth about Jesus (and therefore the Father). This will enable the apostles to testify to Jesus.
✥ In the New Age, Christian experience will be marked by these things:
  ↘ There will be lasting joy as Christians see the risen, ascended, triumphant Christ who has conquered the world through His work on the cross.
  ↘ There will be direct access to the Father in prayer. Christians will ask on the basis of Jesus' work on the cross, and their prayers will be answered on the basis of the love that the Father now has for them.

APPLICATION

The Spirit's work in the world. This is the only place in the Bible where the Spirit is described as being at work in the world, i.e. in the lives of people who are in rebellion against their maker. All other references to the Spirit concern His work within the believer. It is important for us to realise that God's work in non-Christians is confined to bringing them to a realisation of their guilt, concerning sin, righteousness and judgment, *in order* that they may repent and believe in Jesus. It is not possible to say that 'the Spirit is at work revealing God in all religions' except to the extent that He convicts the proponents of other religions of the sin of rejecting Christ. Furthermore, the context suggests that the Spirit's work in leading the apostles into all truth is precisely in order that the church (the fruit-bearing vine) may be able to testify to the words and works of Jesus (15:26–27). These verses give us a clear description of God's part and our part in the whole enterprise of bearing fruit: His part is to make Jesus known, through the Spirit's work of convicting the non-Christian and the

Spirit's work of leading the apostles into all truth, and our part is to persevere in that truth in a hostile world.

The nature of genuine Christian experience as we wait for Christ to return. True, lasting and complete joy and peace are experienced by the Christian in the face of deep hostility and opposition from the world. Genuine Christian experience is always rooted in what the cross has achieved and in an ongoing understanding of Christ's word. This will lead to prayer that will be in accordance with His will. This *genuine* experience of 'life' in the Age of the Spirit is far removed from much that is currently taught.

THE AIM OF THIS STUDY

To understand that Jesus' going to the Father is for our good, for the Spirit will be at work convicting the world on the basis of the apostles' message, and believers will experience a genuine, lasting joy grounded in a new relationship with the Father.

SUGGESTED QUESTIONS

- ✤ *(Try to work out how this passage may be divided into different paragraphs, or parts, of teaching material.)* What is Jesus' overall teaching aim in this passage? How does each part contribute to this point?
- ✤ How does the chapter fit into the Upper Room Discourse as a whole?

5–15 JESUS' 'GOING' WILL LEAD TO THE SPIRIT'S COMING

- ✤ Why are the disciples filled with grief?
- ✤ How is it that Jesus' going away will be for the disciples' good?
- ✤ When Jesus has gone the Spirit will be speaking to two groups of people. What are these groups?
  - ↘ What will the Spirit do for each group? *(Work out precisely what it means to 'convict the world of guilt' in each of the areas mentioned – see text notes.)*
  - ↘ What connection do you see between what the Spirit says to one group and what He says to the other?

✣ What impact should there be upon *our* witness as a result of the Spirit's ministry to the world and to the apostles?

16–28 JESUS' GOING WILL BRING A NEW AGE OF LASTING JOY

✣ What is it that the disciples fail to understand in verses 16-19?

✣ In verse 22 Jesus promises that joy will replace their grief. What will be the initial source of that joy? What will bring about the completion of that joy, and the ongoing experience of it?

✣ How would you describe the *source* of genuine Christian experience? And the *nature* of it? Many alternative descriptions, for both the source and the nature of Christian experience, are offered today? How does Jesus' description differ? In the light of 15:18–16:4, why is it the *only* description worth taking seriously?

29–33 JESUS' GOING WILL BRING PEACE IN A TROUBLED WORLD

✣ From these verses, and also from the whole passage, how would you describe 'life' for the Spirit-filled believer now, in this 'in-between' Age of the Spirit?

↘ Among the experiences that are here described as 'normal', are there any that you do not have?

John 17:1–26
Jesus prays for His disciples

CONTEXT

The whole of the section beginning with chapter 11 and ending with chapter 20 deals with Jesus' death and its implications, both present and eternal, for His disciples. In chapters 11–13 Jesus taught that His death would achieve life, because His death would deal with sin and Satan. In chapters 13–17 (the Upper Room Discourse) Jesus explains what His death and departure will mean for His disciples. The Discourse divides into two parts: the first deals with the disciples' questions concerning Jesus' departure (Jesus explains what His departure will achieve); and the second deals with the importance of God's people persevering as disciples of Jesus, as they live now, so that they achieve God's purpose for them of being fruitful.

Jesus' prayer in chapter 17 draws on all the threads of teaching in chapters 11–20. In His prayer Jesus has one major concern: it is that the Father should be glorified through the completion of His eternal plan, the plan to call out a people who 'know and believe' the Father, and also the Son whom He has sent, and who thus have *life*. To this end, Jesus prays first for the completion of His ministry as the Son; secondly, for the keeping of His apostles so that their ministry is achieved; and finally, for the ministry of all who will believe the apostles' message, so that through the church's ministry the 'world' will come to believe.

STRUCTURE

Jesus prays that His Father would accomplish His plan to call out a people ...

17:1–5 ... through the completion of the Son's ministry.

17:6–19 ... through the completion of His apostles' ministry.

> *6–10*   He prays for His apostles, affirming them as being authentic and reliable.
>
> *11–19*   He prays that His apostles may be protected and set apart for the Father's use.

17:20–26 ... through the impact of all believers' ministry.

> *20–23*   He prays that they may all be united in the Father and the Son.
>
> *24–26*   He prays that they may go to dwell with Him in glory for ever.

TEXT NOTES

1–5 JESUS PRAYS THAT HIS FATHER WOULD ACCOMPLISH HIS PLAN ...THROUGH THE COMPLETION OF THE SON'S MINISTRY

Verses 1 and 5. These two verses, opening and closing the first part, contain the same request, that the Father should 'glorify' the Son so that the Father will be glorified. Jesus prays that His Father should acknowledge His work by returning Him to His position of heavenly glory. The prayer of verse 1 could either be taken to refer to the cross, as in the prayer of 12:28, or it could be a prayer for Jesus' exaltation, as in verse 5. The verses in between, verses 2–4, speak of God's purpose in sending His Son.

Verse 2. Jesus refers to the authority over all people that His Father had given Him before time began. The purpose had been that the Son should give eternal life to God's own people. It had been God's eternal plan to call out a people to eternal life through the ministry of His Son on earth. It was to this end that Jesus had come down from heaven. Verse 2 is matched by verse 4.

Verse 3. At the heart of this part, in verse 3, Jesus defines 'eternal life'. Notice that knowing God is eternal life – it is not the *way* to eternal life. Just as being shut out from a relationship with God was central to the Fall, so entering back into a relationship with Him is central to the experience of eternal life now. Thus Jesus' prayer is that God's glory should be manifest through the achieving of His eternal plan, His plan to reverse the effects of the Fall by calling together a people who *know Him* through His Son. This is the complete opposite of the scene in Genesis 3, with Adam and Eve guiltily hiding from their Creator.

Verse 4. We are reminded of *how* this eternal plan is to be put into effect. As in the rest of the Upper Room Discourse, Jesus speaks as if the events of the cross are already completed. The plan will be put into effect through the *going up* of the Son to His Father via the cross.

6–19 JESUS PRAYS THAT HIS FATHER WOULD ACCOMPLISH HIS PLAN ...THROUGH THE COMPLETION OF HIS APOSTLES' MINISTRY

6–10 Jesus prays for His apostles, affirming them as being authentic and reliable. Jesus begins by identifying the subject of His prayer. He is praying particularly for His apostles; not for the world nor even for all believers (v. 20 makes this point again). By defining the apostles from two different (but complementary) angles – God's initiative and humanity's response – Jesus confirms that they are *genuine* followers of His.

God's initiative. The apostles are undeniably God's people, for their status is entirely dependent upon His work in them. They belong to God (vv. 6, 9), they have been given to Jesus by God (vv. 6–10), and God has been fully revealed to them by Jesus.

Humanity's response. The apostles have accepted His words, they know and believe, and they have obeyed by acting on what they have heard.

In other words, Jesus confirms that they *are* the people He spoke about in verses 2–3 – they have been called by God, and they have responded to Jesus – and that their message is therefore trustworthy for others.

11–19 Jesus prays that His apostles may be kept by His Father for their mission. Since He is departing to be with His Father (vv. 11, 13), He prays for His apostles, asking His Father for their protection (vv. 11, 15) and also their unity (v. 11), as they embark on their mission in a hostile world (v. 17). The themes of this part of the prayer are familiar to us, for Jesus is praying about the doctrine and application that He has already taught in the Upper Room Discourse.

Protection. Jesus wants the Father to protect His people. The word translated 'protect' is 'keep'. So far Jesus has kept God's people on earth and guarded them by the power of His name. In biblical thought a 'name' encapsulates a person's whole character, work and action. Jesus, therefore, has kept His apostles through His whole being while He has been on earth (v. 12). He has taught them and enabled them to understand the full measure of God's work for them, thus bringing them 'joy' (v. 13). They are now God's people who 'know ... the only true God, and Jesus Christ, whom [He has] sent' (v. 3), through His word. Because they no longer belong to the world, the world hates them, and yet they need to persevere in the world (v. 14). So Jesus prays that God will continue to keep them, now that He is going (v. 15), in accordance with His name (v. 11).

Unity. There will be more about the nature and source of genuine Christian unity in verses 20–26. Here, Jesus' prayer implies (v. 15) that the evil one will seek to destroy the apostles' unity which has been created through His 'name', i.e. His revelation of the Father through word and work.

Mission. The word 'sanctify' stems from the same root as 'holy' and means 'to set apart or to make holy'. In the Bible as a whole the word 'sanctify' certainly has moral overtones, but it also includes the idea that the holy God makes His people like Himself, in purpose and mission. In this passage it is the latter idea that dominates. The apostles have already been set apart by Jesus through the 'truth' revealed to them through His name. Now Jesus explains that He is setting them apart for the task of going into the world on mission. He is not praying that God should remove His apostles to the monastery, but that He would protect them and their unity while they remain in the world (vv. 11,15).

In this part of the prayer that concerns His apostles, Jesus' desire is that they be enabled to fulfil their mission as they go into the world, taking the word He has taught them. As this prayer is answered, so God's eternal plan will be accomplished.

20–26 JESUS PRAYS THAT HIS FATHER WOULD ACCOMPLISH HIS PLAN ...THROUGH THE IMPACT OF ALL BELIEVERS' MINISTRY

20–23 He prays that they may all be united in the Father and the Son. The prayer extends to encompass all people who belong to Jesus through all time. It covers two areas:

Unity. Jesus' prayer is that His people be united. This unity is defined as being the same as the unity that the Father and the Son share (v. 21). It is not *just* a unity with each other; it is primarily a unity with the Father and the Son. The Father and Son's unity is a unity of purpose and intention, guaranteed by the Son's sacrificial and obedient self-giving. This unity is further defined as coming from 'the glory' that the Father gave the Son (v. 22). The glory that the Father gave the Son is the glory of the gospel message which brings about the reversal of the Fall. And so the basis for His people's unity is to be the gospel of eternal life. This is not some sort of sentimental unity that comes out of abandoning the truth.

Evangelism. The purpose of this unity is evangelistic (v. 21c, 23b). Jesus' desire is that the world should see His people's unity in the truth as it is worked out in relationships within the church, and that people in the world would, on account of this, come to believe the message for themselves.

24–26 He prays that they may go to dwell with Him in glory for ever. Jesus prays that through the glorification of the Father and the Son (vv. 1–5) His people, called together through the witness of His disciples through all generations, may reach the place prepared for them in His Father's house. Jesus' definition of evangelism does not simply stop at a person's conversion; His desire is that that person should dwell with Him in glory forever. This is the reason why He continues to make Himself known to His people, through His Spirit: He wants them to reach heaven.

KEY THEMES

It is Jesus' desire that God should be glorified through the completion of His purpose, that of calling out a people who know the only true God and Jesus Christ whom He has sent. Therefore He prays:

- ✤ that the Father would glorify the Son in order that the Son may finish His work of bringing His people to eternal life.
- ✤ that He would protect His apostles, sent into the world with the message of Jesus' words and works, from Satan's desire to lead them away from God. This protection will be necessary because:
  - ↘ the apostles will be hated by the world.
  - ↘ Jesus, who has been protecting them, is now returning to the Father.
- ✤ that He would unite all who believe in the apostles' message.
  - ↘ They should be united with Jesus and the Father, not just with each other.
  - ↘ The truth of the apostles' message is what will unite them.
  - ↘ The closeness and unity that Jesus and the Father have should be theirs too.
  - ↘ The purpose of this unity among believers is that the world may understand and accept the gospel.

APPLICATION

Jesus' main priority, as He goes towards His death, is that His Father should accomplish His eternal plan, reversing the effects of the Fall and calling together a people who will belong to Him forever. The major impact of this upon us, therefore, should be to challenge our understanding of Jesus' mission and purpose. If this priority is His major concern and chief goal on earth it should be ours too. His prayer for His apostles and for us should focus the challenge for us: is our unity a unity grounded in the apostles' message? Are we 'one' in the Father and the Son, so gripped by, united in and obedient to His gospel purpose that the world around us is being impacted by our witness?

The aim of this study

To see that Jesus' chief desire is the Father's glory. This glory is achieved through the calling together of a people who know the only true God and Jesus Christ whom He has sent, and this calling is effected through the Son's work, the apostles' message, and the believers' united witness.

Suggested questions

1–5 JESUS PRAYS THAT GOD WOULD GLORIFY THE SON FOR HIS OWN GLORY, THROUGH THE CALLING TOGETHER OF A PEOPLE FOR ETERNAL LIFE

↳ Verses 1 and 5 contain Jesus' request as He prays. What is His main desire?

   ↳ What has Jesus done that enables Him to make this request?

   ↳ What do verses 2-4 tell us about the *source* and *nature* of eternal life?

   ↳ In 3:19 Jesus described people as loving darkness. So why is the Father glorified through the calling together of a people who will know Him?

↳ Complete this sentence: '*Jesus' purpose in coming to earth was to ... by ...*.' How does this definition of Jesus' chief concern challenge your priorities and concerns?

6–19 THE COMPLETION OF THE APOSTLES' MINISTRY

↳ In verses 6-11 Jesus identifies those for whom He is praying. Who are they?

↳ He describes them both from God's perspective and from humanity's.

   ↳ What is the divine perspective?

   ↳ What is the human perspective?

↳ Why are these verses here? How do they fit in with verses 1-5?

↳ In verses 12-19 what is the *one* thing uppermost in Jesus' prayer request for His apostles?

   ↳ Jesus gives several reasons for praying this. What are they?

⌐ How have the apostles been 'kept' so far? And how will they be kept when Jesus has gone?

20–26 THE IMPACT OF BELIEVERS' MINISTRY

✤ What two groups of people does Jesus now have in mind as He prays?

✤ What is His desire for those who believe?

  ⌐ What is the *focus* of unity? What is the *source* of this unity. What is its goal?

  ⌐ How does this differ from the way Christian unity is frequently portrayed?

✤ What is Jesus' overriding concern throughout His prayer?

  ⌐ How should His concerns in prayer impact our concerns in prayer?

  ⌐ How do His prayers, for Himself, His apostles, and for us, challenge and change the way we see our own priorities and concerns?

John 18:1–27
'Shall I not drink the cup
the Father has given me?'

CONTEXT

The material of chapters 11–20 may be set, broadly, under two major headings: the theological implications, for Jesus' disciples, of His death; and the developing narrative – the plot to put Jesus to death. In chapters 11–13 the two strands were seen side by side, but during the Upper Room Discourse (chs 13–17) the narrative development was placed on hold as Jesus taught in considerable detail about His death and what it would achieve for the disciples. Now, as Jesus leads His disciples into the olive grove, the narrative is resumed. However, with seventeen chapters of theological explanation and teaching already written, this narrative development should not be read simply as a record of events. As he tells the story John loads the narrative with comments and asides, indicating that he expects the reader to interpret the narrative in line with the theological explanations *already* given in the preceding chapters. The reader must therefore understand the events in the light of the things that John has already spread out for us. This does not mean that we are free to *speculate* in our interpretation of the narrative events; on the contrary, we should understand what is happening to Jesus *in the light* of what we have already been taught.

In 18:1–27 John shows Jesus to be in full control of His arrest, deliberately handing Himself over to His accusers in order to 'drink the cup' of His Father's wrath against human sin. The High Priest's questioning of Jesus is placed after Peter's first denial, with the second and third denials following, a storytelling device that emphasises both Peter's failure and the apparent failure of Jesus' cause. But John wants us to see through this appearance of failure, and he reminds us, before he records the first denial, that Jesus' death is to be on behalf of the people. This reminder shows us the link between the drinking of the cup of God's wrath and substitution. (This idea of a sacrificial substitute, satisfying the wrath of God against the sinner, is technically known as 'propitiation'.)

STRUCTURE

18:1–11   Jesus' death is propitiatory. Divine and in control, Jesus goes to His death in order to drink the cup of His Father's wrath that His Father has given Him.

18:12–27   Jesus' death is substitutionary. Alone and innocent, Jesus goes to His death on behalf of His people.

OLD TESTAMENT BACKGROUND

'... the cup the Father has given me ...': The idea of drinking from a cup given by the Father is one which has both positive and negative connotations from the Old Testament. In the Psalms it is used to refer to God's blessing (Ps. 23:5) and salvation (Ps. 116:13). But there is also a strong emphasis, in the Psalms and elsewhere, on the cup given by God being the cup of His wrath (Isa. 51:17; Jer. 25:15–29; Ps. 75:8). These references stress what is significant about drinking from this cup: it is that the cup contains the full measure of God's wrath, not just a part of it. It is a cup filled to the brim and overflowing, and it must be drained to the dregs. This is what Jesus is referring to, at the time of His arrest, as He sets His face towards His trial and death.

Substitutionary atonement: The matter of dealing with the sin of God's people is so significant that the Old Testament uses several pictures to show us what God will do, how He will take away sin.

Probably the most significant is the idea of a substitute dying in the place of the people, bearing the penalty for their sin (which is death), and in this way removing God's wrath from His people (see Lev. 16). Later, the prophets looked forward to a time when God would finally deal with the people's sins through a 'servant' acting as a substitute (Isa. 53).

TEXT NOTES

1–11 JESUS' DEATH IS PROPITIATORY: HE GOES TO HIS DEATH IN ORDER TO DRINK THE CUP HIS FATHER HAS GIVEN HIM

The main point of this passage comes in verse 11 – Jesus is going to His death in order to drink the cup of His Father's wrath. However, throughout the passage the narrative emphasises Jesus' divinity and His control of events, in order to set this main point in context. Jesus is not 'a pathetic martyr buffeted by the ill winds of a cruel fate' (Carson), but voluntarily and purposefully He heads towards His death in full knowledge of what is about to befall Him. This is the narrative account of the truth expressed in 10:17–18; it emphasises His voluntary obedience (5:19ff) and His willing service of His people (10:11; 13:1–11).

His control. Jesus' control is evident as He takes the initiative, going out of the olive grove to meet the detachment sent to arrest Him (v. 4). Using words reminiscent of chapter 13 (vv. 1,3), where John emphasised Jesus' 'knowledge' of all that was going to happen, John reminds us that Jesus knew what was going to take place. In verses 7–8 He again takes the initiative in giving Himself up for His sheep, asking the soldiers and officials a second time whom they want.

In verse 9 He is seen to be in absolute control of His sheep; the care He takes to save His men from trouble with the authorities exemplifies His far greater care for them, in not letting one of them perish or be snatched out of His hand. He will be laying down His life on their behalf (cf. 10:15,28) in order to achieve this. So what might appear to be an incidental detail turns out to be highly significant: Jesus is authenticating His promise in 6:39, 'I shall lose none of all that He has given me, but raise them up at the last day.'

In verse 11 Jesus' words show that He is determined to do exactly what His Father has commanded Him. Throughout the

Gospel account Jesus has insisted that it is as He goes to His death that His disciples and the world will be given the clearest proof that He is the one He claims to be, the 'I am' (8:28; 13:19; 14:29). This emphasis on His controlled purpose in going towards the cross has the effect of highlighting His perfect obedience to His Father's plan (3:16); it also convinces us of Jesus' love for the Father – 'the world must learn that I love the Father and that I do exactly what my Father has commanded me' (14:31).

His divinity. Jesus' power and authority are displayed, in contrast to the power and authority of the armed soldiers and the officials who come out to arrest Him (v. 3). In verses 5–6 He announces Himself in divine language (cf. Exod. 6:2; Isa. 42:8) and they fall to the ground, powerless. Three times the theologically laden words 'I am He' appear in the narrative. The point being made is that this is the divine Son who is giving Himself up; He *will*, voluntarily, drink the cup that His Father has given Him.

Peter's failure. Peter's failure to understand what is going on throws into relief the main theological point of this passage. Peter has still not learned the lesson of 13:7–8 and 13:37–38; He wants to take dramatic physical action on behalf of Jesus in order to protect Him. But Jesus rebukes him and tells Peter that He *must* drink the cup He has been given. In the light of His coming trial and death, the 'cup' referred to can only be the cup of His Father's wrath. Peter has still not understood that the way Jesus will 'lose none of all that He has given me, but raise them up at the last day' (6:39 and 18:9), is by drinking this cup.

12–27 JESUS' DEATH IS SUBSTITUTIONARY: HE GOES TO HIS DEATH ON BEHALF OF HIS PEOPLE

Here the structure of the narrative, with Peter's denials coming before and after Jesus' first interrogation, emphasise what is apparently the absolute failure of Jesus' mission. But John's 'narrator's comment' in verse 14 enables the reader to make sense of what is going on.

In verses 19–24, Jesus is questioned about His disciples and His teaching. The authorities were concerned both that He was blaspheming (19:7) and that He would gain such a great following that 'the Romans will come and take away both our place [temple] and our nation' (11:48). Ironically, the denials of Peter show this second concern to be utterly unfounded at this point: verses 15–18 and 25–27 show that Jesus has been deserted by His followers. This, in conjunction with the questioning by Annas, presents an apparently failed Jesus. He is being falsely accused and He appears powerless as He stands, bound, in front of those who will resort to physical abuse in the absence of sound argument (vv. 22–23). His disciples won't stand up for Him and His cause appears to be on the rocks. He is innocent, but powerless and isolated.

Before this incident is related, and afterwards too, the narrator shows Peter to be 'warming himself' by the fire and denying Jesus. In 13:37 he had been quick to offer to lay down his life 'on behalf of' Jesus, and in 18:10 he was quick to try to defend Jesus physically. But now he fails completely and denies Him: the cock crows, as Jesus said it would. Note the contrast between Jesus' bold statement, 'I am', and Peter's response to questions, recorded so precisely by John, 'I am not'.

On the morning after the Passover meal, therefore, the reader has a picture of human failure and human inability to stand by Christ. At the same time John shows us that Jesus is alone, innocent, falsely accused, bound and on the way to His death. It appears to be a desperate picture until the theological explanation of verse 14 is put in place.

Verse 14 ties this passage to the previous one. Jesus is advancing towards His death, in full control, in order to drink the cup of His Father's wrath against the sinfulness of the human race. He does this in order to die 'on behalf of' the people. He is the Lamb of God who takes away the sin of the world (1:29,36).

KEY THEMES

✤ Jesus, the Good Shepherd, is advancing towards His death.
　↘ He is in full control of events and knows exactly what is going to happen to Him; He is aware that He is the divine 'I am'.
　↘ He knows He must drink the cup of His Father's wrath against the sin of the world.

⊻ He is in chains and apparently powerless before His guilty accusers.

⊻ He is quite isolated, deserted by His followers and with His mission apparently in tatters.

⊻ He goes to die on behalf of the people, in complete fulfilment of Isaiah 53:1–8; as the Lamb of God He will take away the sin of the world.

APPLICATION

John shapes the narrative in order to show the reader that the death of Jesus is for the express purpose of drinking the cup of His Father's wrath on behalf of the people. The major application must therefore be that we understand this point about penal substitution, that Jesus is suffering the death penalty in the place of others. Jesus is in full control of events, announcing Himself as the divine Son, in divine language (vv. 5, 6, 8), and He is innocent, but He is also deserted, alone and falsely accused: all these things are for the express purpose of His taking God's wrath on Himself, so that His people may be raised up for eternal life.

Our understanding should focus on the authority and power of Jesus, the love of Jesus in handing Himself over, the failure of Peter to understand the nature of Jesus' arrest, Peter's denial of Jesus, the culpability of the Jewish authorities and the apparent failure of Jesus' mission. But John's ultimate concern is that the reader should grasp what all these things add up to – the fact that Jesus is the Lamb of God who is about to take away the sin of the world and that He is now being handed over to die. Our understanding of the points above should enhance our understanding of this core truth. The passage ought to provoke in us a profound sense of awe that God has chosen to give His Son on behalf of the world, and that His Son, fully in control, is going to die, willingly and obediently, as our substitute. He is the Good Shepherd.

THE AIM OF THIS STUDY

To see that Jesus goes to His death completely in control of events; He knows that He is the Son of God who will die on behalf of His people, in order to save them from God's wrath and keep them for eternal life.

SUGGESTED QUESTIONS

✤ What are the main subject divisions?

1-11 JESUS' DEATH IS PROPITIATORY

✤ What do you think is the key point in this passage?

↘ Look up Isaiah 51:17–20 and Jeremiah 25:15–29. What do these verses tell us about the Father's cup? What happens to those who drink it?

✤ The narrative emphasises several points about Jesus, as He goes to drink His Father's cup. In this passage what do Jesus' actions and words remind us of?

✤ How do these reminders – of who Jesus is and what He is doing – reinforce the *main* point that He is going to drink the cup of His Father's wrath?

✤ Why is Peter's action recorded? What does it tell us about how much Peter has understood? (See 13:37)

↘ How does it help to point out what Jesus is doing?

↘ Why is it so important that Jesus' behaviour be correctly understood?

12-27 JESUS' DEATH IS SUBSTITUTIONARY

✤ Imagine this passage was a four-part drama: what would the four parts be and what titles would you give to each scene?

✤ What clues are there to show that the story of Peter's denial has been told in two parts deliberately?

↘ Why do you think John may have separated the denials of Peter?

✤ Contrast the circumstances of Peter and Jesus. Who is talking to whom? What are they saying? Where are they?

✤ What picture of Jesus and His cause are we given in this passage?

✤ What picture are we given of Peter's cause and of Annas' cause?

✤ How does the narrator's comment (in verse 14) help make sense of this passage?

✧ How do the two parts of this passage, verses 1–11 and verses 12–27, relate to one another?

✧ Read Isaiah 53. In what different ways, in today's passage, is Jesus fulfilling this prophecy?

✧ Read John 5:19–20. How does today's passage help to explain the Father–Son relationship? How does this make *you* feel towards Jesus?

✧ How does today's passage fit with John's purpose statement in 20:31?

John 18:28–19:16
'I find no basis for a charge' …
'Crucify Him!'

CONTEXT

In this part of the section running from chapter 11 to chapter 20 the narrative development is dominant, as Jesus is led from Caiaphas to Pilate and on to the cross. But, as the trial develops, it is intended that the reader should understand the narrative according to the theological framework that was put in place by chapters 1–17. John's account of the trial draws on many of the theological ideas built up through the Gospel, but it is the immediate context, verses 1–27 of chapter 18, that gives the prime explanation of events, namely, that Jesus is intent on drinking the cup of His Father's wrath, knowing that He does this on behalf of His people, and that He is being a substitute for them. It is this explanation that we should keep in mind from now on.

Two familiar themes emerge throughout the trial: first, the kingship of Jesus, the innocent suffering servant; and secondly, the exposure of the motives for rejecting this king. During the time that Jesus is within the palace of the Roman governor, much of the dialogue concerns the nature of Jesus' kingdom. In addition, John focuses our attention on this theme by providing reminders, at the beginning of this episode and at the end, that it is now Passover time (18:28 and 19:14; cf. also 18:39). The fact that Jesus' kingdom was not materialistic and earthly has been emphasised repeatedly in the Gospel so far (e.g. 6:15, when it was Passover, verse 4). The most vivid demonstration of this truth, when Jesus rides on a donkey into Jerusalem at Passover time (12:12–16), is followed immediately, in John's narrative, by Jesus' prediction of His death (12:20–33). Using juxtaposition like this, John has shown his readers that Jesus is both God's king and God's innocent Passover Lamb, who has come from God and is going back to God (16:28). The two roles have been presented as inseparable. Now, in the trial before Pilate, the emphasis on Jesus' kingship causes the reader to remember His sacrificial role also.

At the same time, John uses irony to make his second point: that the Jews are guilty. They emerge from the trial with their victim, but they have rejected God's heavenly king and affirmed their allegiance to this world (19:15). This picks up on a theme that runs throughout the Gospel (cf. 8:31–37; 11:48).

STRUCTURE

18:28– 32	The irony of the Jews' situation: in order to eat the earthly Passover the Jews give up the opportunity of eating the heavenly Passover.
18:33– 38	Jesus, the heavenly king, has come to testify to the truth.
18:38b– 19:7	Three times Pilate announces that Jesus is innocent; three times the Jews demand that He should die anyway.
19:8–11	Jesus, the Son of God, subject only to His Father's authority.
19:12– 16	The irony of the Jews' situation: in giving up the heavenly king they affirm their allegiance to an earthly king.

OLD TESTAMENT BACKGROUND

Passover: The Passover was an annual festival instituted by God to ensure that His people remembered His miraculous rescue plan. The death of the Passover Lamb ensured that His people were set free and did not come under the judgment of God. (See 6:41–70.)

Isaiah 53: The prophet looks forward to the coming, from God, of a suffering servant who would die a substitutionary death on behalf of the nations, in order to pay the price for the sin of the world. The servant would be innocent and would be suffering at the hands of God's enemies. In chapters 18 and 19 the two Old Testament ideas of Passover and the substitutionary death of God's suffering servant are brought together in the suffering and death of Jesus.

TEXT NOTES

28–32 THE IRONY OF THE JEWS' SITUATION (1)

In this section John begins to demonstrate the guilt of the Jews. In verse 28 John expands on the fact that it is the morning after the Passover by drawing attention to the Jews' concern about ritual uncleanness. This is heavily ironic since the Passover itself, about which they are so concerned, is about to be rendered redundant by the slaughter of the true Passover Lamb, which they are in the process of engineering. So John is showing us that in order to eat the earthly Passover the Jews are giving up their opportunity to eat the heavenly Passover. This point is evident from the narrative.

The recent appearance of Jesus before Annas (18:19–24) should be kept in mind as we read verse 30. In that 'trial' the authorities had had to resort to physical violence rather than sound argument in order to deal with Jesus who was patently innocent. And now the true motive of the Jews in bringing Jesus before Pilate is seen in verse 31 – they want Him dead! But, as in 18:1–27, John is concerned to help the reader realise that Jesus is not out of control – He is subject to His Father's divine will. Jesus had already taught His disciples that He would die by crucifixion (12:32–33) and it was only the Romans who could kill Jesus in this way.

33–38A JESUS, THE HEAVENLY KING, HAS COME TO TESTIFY TO THE TRUTH

In verses 36–37 Jesus establishes the nature of His kingdom. First, it is not political or regional, but heavenly. By reminding the reader of Jesus' eternal and heavenly kingship (cf. 3:3), John establishes the fact that this substitute, who is intent on drinking the cup of His Father's wrath, is an eternal king; he forces the reader to think beyond merely materialistic images of Jesus and towards eternal issues (cf. John 6; 16:28). In this way the reader is reminded that Jesus has a heavenly agenda, not a materialistic one, and also that Jesus, though a king, can yet still die.

The principal way in which Jesus attracts subjects to His eternal, heavenly kingdom is through testifying to the truth. Truth is what Jesus tells us about God and eternity through His words and works. This is why He has come. And so, while Pilate thinks he is an innocent and objective judge sitting in trial on a local political matter, he is in reality being judged himself. By showing Pilate (and the reader) the nature of His kingdom, Jesus issues him (and us) with a challenge to listen to Him and become part of His kingdom.

18:38B–19:7 THREE TIMES PILATE ANNOUNCES THAT JESUS IS INNOCENT;THREE TIMES THE JEWS DEMAND THAT HE SHOULD DIE ANYWAY

Jesus' innocence. The choreography of Pilate's going in and out of the palace helps to make the point. Three times he comes out and insists that Jesus is innocent of all charges of being an earthly king (18:38; 19:4,6). This is a vitally important point, that the innocence of Jesus should be established. Once He has been identified as the substitute who drinks the cup of God's wrath, and if He really is the Passover Lamb, then it is essential that He be seen to be innocent and perfect, which He is. (For the stipulations regarding the original Passover lambs, see Exod. 12:5.) The mocking and torture described in verses 1–3 further identify Jesus as the true substitute (see Isa. 53:1–12).

The Jews' guilt. By establishing Jesus' innocence Pilate forces the Jews to declare their real motive for wanting Him put to death. They state it plainly in verse 7, bringing out in the open the whole issue of Jesus' kingship. The fact is that the Jews know Jesus' claim to kingship to be a claim to eternal, heavenly status (v. 7), but they are rejecting His rule. They are not on the side of truth, and they do not want a part in His kingdom. This is confirmed by the Jews' deliberate choice of a guilty man (who had committed a political crime) instead of the innocent Jesus (v. 40) and by Pilate's presentation of the innocent Jesus, despised and rejected by men, to the Jews (v. 5). This further emphasises and exposes their guilt: they are not interested in justice, and they will sacrifice all logic to get Jesus killed.

The repeated use of the word 'king' ensures that the reader gets the point, that this is God's king. He is innocent but He is being despised, rejected, oppressed and afflicted by a people intent on rejecting His heavenly rule. The Gentiles are also implicated in this guilt; verses 1–3 show them tormenting the one who is in fact their own king. The whole human race, therefore, is represented in this rejection of God's Messiah.

8–11 JESUS, THE SON OF GOD, SUBJECT ONLY TO HIS FATHER'S AUTHORITY

Jesus' statement in verse 11 makes it plain that He is submitting fully to His Father's eternal plan of rescue. This is no tragic end to an otherwise wonderful life. It is for this very reason that Jesus has come (3:13–16; 12:31ff; 16:28). In view of the recent clamouring of the Jews for His death, the words 'the one who handed me over to you' should be taken as referring to Caiaphas, the representative (as high priest) of the whole Jewish people, who had sent Jesus to Pilate.

12–16 THE IRONY OF THE JEWS' SITUATION (2)

Clamouring for Jesus' death, the Jews are guilty of rejecting God's king. But here the ultimate irony of their position is evident. Their rejection of Jesus, the heavenly king, is achieved at the cost of apparently embracing Roman domination: publicly they state their allegiance to the earthly 'king', Caesar, whose occupying forces they deeply resent. Both Pilate, who rejects the heavenly king out of fear of an earthly king (v. 12), and the Jews are seen to subjugate themselves to an earthly king in preference to submitting to Jesus' kingship. Thus Jesus' teaching about the Jews' true identity in 8:31ff is proven. Meanwhile, God's heavenly king is led away to His death on the morning following the Passover meal.

NB 18:28 and 19:14: 'Problems' with the exact time of these events, in relation to the Passover meal and the Lord's Supper in the other Gospels, are removed when it is realised that the term 'the

Passover' could refer to the combined feast of the supper plus the ensuing Feast of Unleavened Bread, and all that went on in Passover week (see Luke 22:1 and Carson, pp. 589 and 603ff).

KEY THEMES

The two key themes of this passage are the identity of Jesus, and the Jews' response to Him.

✤ The identity of Jesus.

- ↳ He is God's heavenly king whose kingdom is not of this world.
- ↳ His kingdom is established by truth and His subjects enter that kingdom by listening to the truth He teaches about God.
- ↳ He is the innocent Passover Lamb who is despised and rejected by men.
- ↳ He is invested with all the authority of God's king and is subject only to His Father's will.

✤ The Jews' response to God's king.

- ↳ They are so concerned with their religion in this world that they turn their back on God's Passover, His truth and His heavenly king.
- ↳ Their perversion of justice and their insistence that Jesus be killed (the alternative to accepting Him as the Son of God) expose their real position: they are not on the side of truth.
- ↳ They will not accept Jesus as the Son of God and king; they would prefer Caesar's rule.
- ↳ Pilate and the Roman officials are also implicated in the rejection of Jesus, since they have heard His claim to be the king of a heavenly kingdom.

APPLICATION

To them then: The trial *of* Jesus quickly becomes the trial *before* Jesus. As Jesus explains the nature of His kingdom so Pilate and the Jews are put on trial. They are convicted of choosing Jesus' death in order to avoid submitting to Him as king. The implications of this rejection are made clear by the irony of their situation: they have forfeited their part in the heavenly Passover, and they have stated their allegiance to Caesar.

To us now: Throughout the narrative John teaches that the nature of Jesus' kingdom is heavenly and not earthly. Entry into His kingdom is through listening to Him. The kingdom, therefore, is extended by means of teaching His truth, not by building structures and political parties here and now on earth. John narrates the trial in such a way as to force a decision from his readers. It is a decision either to reject Jesus, and so show that one is not on the side of truth and not part of His kingdom, or else to listen to Him and accept Him as king, and so show that one is part of His kingdom. We must realise that rejection of Jesus' kingship does not leave a person in neutral territory. Rejection of Jesus means forfeiting eternal life in heaven, and giving allegiance to earthly masters now.

THE AIM OF THIS STUDY

To see that Jesus is God's heavenly king establishing His kingdom by truth and through His death as the innocent Passover sacrifice. People's reactions to this king expose their ultimate motivation and determine their ultimate destiny.

SUGGESTED QUESTIONS

- ✤ How would you divide and subtitle this passage? How would you explain its structure?

18:38B–19:7 THREE TIMES INNOCENCE IS PROCLAIMED; THREE TIMES DEATH IS DEMANDED

- ✤ How does the narrative emphasise Pilate's verdict on Jesus?
  - ↘ Why is it so important that this point is made at this stage of the Gospel?
  - ↘ What do verses 1–3 add to this point?
- ✤ How does the narrative work to establish the absolute guilt of the Jews?
- ✤ Verse 37b presents us with a choice. What are we being shown here about the implications of not following the truth?

18:33–38 AND 19:8–11 PILATE BEFORE JESUS

   ✤ In 18:33–37 Jesus tells us three things about His kingdom. What are they? How do they help to clarify Jesus' mission in His world?

   ✤ How does Jesus' trial before Pilate in fact put Pilate on trial? And us too?

18:28–32 AND 19:12–16 THE JEWS BEFORE JESUS

   ✤ What has Jesus told us already about the kind of death He is going to die? (See 12:32)

   ✤ What is the irony of the Jews' situation in verses 28–32? and in verses 12–16?

   ✤ In 12:31 Jesus tells us that His death will result in judgment on the world. How has this happened in these verses?

   ✤ What have we learned about Jesus? About the Jews? And about Pilate?

      ↘ What is the challenge and the warning for us, and for our friends who refuse to 'listen to the truth' about Jesus and His kingdom?

      ↘ In what ways does this passage illustrate 1:11 and 1:18?

STUDY 25

John 19:17–42
'It is accomplished!'

CONTEXT

As with the arrest of Jesus and His trial, it is important that John's narrative account of the crucifixion of Jesus be read through the theological framework put in place by the rest of his Gospel. Throughout the Gospel, John has been concerned to emphasise these major themes:

- ✤ Jesus' absolute sovereignty and control in all the events leading up to and including His death (10:17–18).
- ✤ His coming into the world in order to accomplish God's eternal plan of rescue for His people, as revealed in scripture (1:23,41,45; 2:16ff; 5:39,46).
- ✤ His death as the substitutionary Passover Lamb who takes away the sin of the world (1:29; 11:50–52).

It is this theological framework that makes sense of the incidents that John chooses to include in his account. Since his purpose is that his readers should come to believe and have life (20:31), he stresses the fact that God's eternal plan of rescue is being accomplished, even as God's king hangs dying on the cross (19:35,36). So, as we read his account of the crucifixion, we should be aware that the incidents are much more than simply the random observations of an eye-witness.

Each detail of the story is highly significant, picking up on themes previously developed in the Gospel and impressing these themes upon our minds.

Why is it so important for John to demonstrate that Jesus' death is the fulfilment of God's eternal plan, reversing the effects of the Fall and rescuing His people? It is because the fact of God's eternal king *dying on a cross* is so incongruous, so unlikely and so far removed from the Jews' expectations, that we might not believe it to be so. But John's aim is that we should be strenuously encouraged to believe, and to continue to believe, that Jesus has died on our behalf as God's long-awaited Passover Lamb.

Structure

19:16b–22 God's king is crucified.
19:23–37 He dies to fulfil God's plan as revealed in scripture.
19:38–42 God's Passover Lamb is dead.

Old Testament background

They divide my garments ...: Psalm 22 contains an execution scene in which the executioners distribute the victim's clothes (v. 18). But the psalm also contains God's promise that He will vindicate His suffering 'afflicted one' (22:24). In quoting this psalm John is reminding his readers that Jesus' death is part of the whole fulfilment of the Old Testament, and also that God will vindicate His servant.

'*Not one of his bones will be broken*': Throughout the Gospel Jesus has drawn close links between His death and the Passover (e.g. 6:4, 53; 12:1–11). One of the requirements for the Passover Lamb, whose blood marked out the Israelite people for rescue out of Egypt, was that its bones should not be broken (Exod. 12:46; Num. 9:12). In quoting this passage John is confirming the fact, for the last time, that Jesus is the Passover Lamb.

'*They will look on the one they have pierced*': Zechariah 12:10 anticipates a day when all of Jerusalem and the people of God would weep and mourn as they look on the one they have killed. That day would be one in which there would be a fountain of forgiveness for God's people (Zech. 13:1) through the striking of the shepherd of God's sheep (Zech. 13:7ff). In quoting this passage John is reminding his readers that every detail of the crucifixion is happening according to God's explicit will; the horrific event, to which such details belong, is the means by which He is accomplishing His eternal purpose and solving humanity's greatest problem, which is sin.

TEXT NOTES

The main focus in this account is contained in verses 28–30, when Jesus proclaims that His work is accomplished. Before and after this high point John includes a number of other incidents and details. Interestingly, none of these details especially emphasises the physical suffering of Jesus, nor do they play on the emotions of the reader. It is important to ask *why* John has included these particular incidents. It seems that each part of the story underlines the fact that God's purposes are being sovereignly accomplished, despite the supreme effort of both Satan and the people to thwart them. This means that we should read the crucifixion narrative not with a sense of failure and tragedy but, as John insists we should, with a sense of awe and triumph, as we see how God's eternal purpose of rescuing His people, revealed in scripture, is accomplished in history (cf. 17:2–4).

16B–22 GOD'S KING IS CRUCIFIED

Jesus' kingship has been a constant theme throughout the passion narrative. At the crucifixion, with Jesus appearing far from regal, John reminds us once again who He is. The fact that the sign attached to His cross is written in three languages means that the whole world may recognise Him as 'The King of the Jews'. Pilate appears to be taunting the Jews by declaring the pathetic figure of a crucified Jesus to be their king, but notice the sharp irony, for in reality he is proclaiming Jesus' kingship to all nations (cf. 12:21,32). Like Caiaphas before him, Pilate's words cause him to serve God's purpose unwittingly as he confirms Jesus' kingship. And since this incident follows hot on the heels of the trial, the reader is reminded that He is king of an eternal heavenly kingdom (18:33–38).

23–37 JESUS DIES TO FULFIL GOD'S PLAN AS REVEALED IN SCRIPTURE

23–27 His death fulfils the sovereign plan of the Father. Just as the reader needs reminding that this dying figure is king, so the reader also needs to realise that God's sovereign plan is being accomplished. The crucifixion of God's king is not an unforeseen disaster! God foreordained it before the beginning of time and revealed it in the Old Testament. Now, as Jesus dies, apparently helpless, we see that even small details connected with His death were in God's eternal plan (v. 24). The quotation from Psalm 22, in addition, reminds us that God will vindicate His king (see Old Testament notes).

We do not know precisely why verses 25–27 are here. It may be that John wants to show the reader that the Son of Man, who came from heaven, returns to heaven with no human obligation unfulfilled. In accomplishing the mission His Father has given Him He does not violate the law in any respect. Instead, even as He hangs dying, Jesus ensures that His mother is cared for. This poignant exchange also shows the reader that John definitely was there. His account is that of an eye-witness, so that credibility combines with the impact of scripture being fulfilled. John is letting the reader know that God's eternal plan was being fulfilled and that he was there to witness it. It definitely did happen!

28–30 'It is accomplished!' The three words 'completed' (v. 28), 'fulfilled' (v. 28) and 'finished' (v. 30) all come from the same Greek verb, *tele-- o*. It is the same word that Jesus used in His prayer in 17:4 and it would probably be better translated as 'accomplished'. The plan and purpose of God in sending His Son to earth, to die on behalf of sinful men, has now been accomplished (v. 30).

In verse 28 it is hard to know exactly which of a number of possible scriptures Jesus is fulfilling (Ps. 22:15 is most likely), but John wants us to know that Jesus, in full obedience to His Father, is accomplishing God's eternal plan of redemption as revealed in scripture. John is eager to show us that Jesus' death, far from being an isolated event, *is the climax* towards which the whole of the Old Testament – all God's revelation and activity – had been moving. This is the key event in God's eternal plan, His plan of calling together a people who would 'know Him' in eternal life.

Even in death Jesus is seen to be in charge; John records that He 'gave up' His life – no-one took it from Him.

31–37 He is His people's Saviour accomplishing His people's rescue. The main point of this passage is contained in verses 36–37: Jesus is God's perfect Passover Lamb, without blemish and without broken bones. John makes the point by recalling the Exodus and Numbers requirements for the Passover Lamb – that the bones should not be broken – and by quoting from Zechariah 12:10 (see Old Testament notes). By emphasising that he saw the incident with the spear (v. 35) and that his testimony can be relied upon, John shows the reader that the scripture really has been fulfilled, and the fountain of forgiveness has been opened.

Verse 35 identifies for us the main application of this passage: addressing the reader directly, '... so that you also may believe', John makes clear his intention in recording these specific events of the crucifixion, which is that his reader should believe, and continue to believe, that Jesus is the long-awaited Passover Lamb.

38–42 GOD'S PASSOVER LAMB IS DEAD

The witness theme of verses 31–37 is continued here as John makes it plain that Jesus really is dead. This is most important, for the fact of Jesus' physical death is central both to His being the true Passover Lamb (the lamb *must* die) and to the possibility that He should be physically raised – there will be more on this in chapter 20. The fact that it is Joseph and Nicodemus who retrieve the body of Jesus gives us hope that at least some of the Jewish establishment will turn to Him, even after the widespread rejection of chapters 5–10.

NB Some commentators have devoted paragraphs to the hidden symbolism of the dividing of the clothes, the provision for Mary, and the blood and water flowing from Jesus' side. As with other events in the Gospel (e.g. 2:1–11), it is important that we should be disciplined in our interpretation and stick to the 'main road', noting the controls on interpretation that John gives us. The primary control for this passage is verse 35 (see above) where John urges us to believe, on the basis of his having witnessed the fulfilment of scripture. However tempting it is to do so, we must not speculate!

KEY THEMES

☙ God's eternal, sovereign rescue plan is accomplished through Jesus' death on the cross.

  ↘ Jesus dies and yet He is God's king – no-one, at the time, can see this.

  ↘ In everything that happens, the Old Testament is being fulfilled, even at those moments when it seems that Jesus is not in control and that His enemies are triumphing over Him.

  ↘ His death is not a failure but the point at which He accomplishes what He had come to do, dying in the place of God's people as the Passover Lamb, achieving their rescue and opening for them a fountain of forgiveness.

  ↘ God's people need to know this and to continue believing it.

APPLICATION

Verse 35 gives us John's intended application, as valid for the whole Gospel as it is for this passage. Each of the details is recorded here for the express purpose of urging the reader to believe, and go on believing. We need to recognise these things:

☙ Jesus, though weak and dying, is in reality God's king, accomplishing God's eternal purpose of rescuing His people from God's wrath.

☙ God is therefore sovereign through all time: thousands of years in advance He had planned Jesus' suffering, even to the most minute details.

☙ Jesus is the Passover Lamb. Because His death has opened the fountain of forgiveness, there need be no fear of judgment, no earning of forgiveness ... but rather praise and worship of God's king who has been lifted up.

THE AIM OF THIS STUDY

To see and believe that Jesus' death, far from being a tragic failure, accomplishes God's eternal plan of rescue for His people.

Study 25

Suggested Questions

↬ How would you subdivide and title the passage?

↬ What is the main, central point of this passage?

↬ How does the structure of the passage work to make this point?

16b–22 GOD'S KING IS CRUCIFIED

↬ What different facts are highlighted for us, as John records the details of this episode?

  ↘ Why might any of these facts be in doubt?

  ↘ How do Jesus' comments to Pilate, in the trial, make sense of what is going on?

23–37 JESUS DIES TO FULFIL GOD'S ETERNAL PLAN OF RESCUE

↬ Throughout the Gospel, God's control over His Son's death has been emphasised. How do the details in this passage add to this emphasis?

↬ Look carefully at verses 28–30. The words 'completed', 'fulfilled' and 'finished' are all translations of the same verb meaning 'to accomplish'. What is it that has been 'accomplished'?

  ↘ The same word is used in 17:4. How does this help our understanding of verses 28–30?

↬ On either side of the cry of victory in verse 30 are two statements that scripture has been fulfilled. Look up Psalm 22:18. Psalm 22 is a psalm about God's servant who suffers at the hands of His enemies and is ultimately vindicated. What is John's point in drawing this to our attention in verse 24?

  ↘ What does this tell us about God's sovereign planning and the nature of His purposes?

↬ Look up Exodus 12:46 and Numbers 9:12. What do these verses tell us about the Passover Lamb? Look up Zechariah 12:10–13:1. What do these verses tell us about the Great Day that the Jews were looking forward to?

  ↘ What, therefore, is the *theological point* that John is making about the death of Jesus?

  ↘ Why is verse 35 so important?

  ↘ How will it affect the way we apply these verses?

🖖 How do the two fulfilments of scripture on either side of the cry of victory affect the way we understand that cry?

38–42 GOD'S PASSOVER LAMB IS DEAD

🖖 What does this part of the crucifixion narrative add to the whole?

🖖 How would this passage help you answer someone who said that the death of Jesus was just the tragic end to an otherwise wonderful and fruitful life?

🖖 John tells us, in verse 35, the reason why he has included these details in his Gospel. How has his account of the crucifixion enabled you to believe, and go on believing, the Gospel?

John 20:1–31
'We have seen the Lord!'

CONTEXT

The resurrection appearance of Jesus is the sign that closes this section of John's Gospel. It is paired with the resurrection of Lazarus (ch. 11), the sign that opened the section. Jesus' words in this chapter (vv. 17, 21–23, 27–29) encourage the reader to look back and combine the sign with the explanatory words in chapters 12–19. The major theme of the section has been eternal life, and this has been achieved by the death of Jesus. John has recorded how Jesus explained this achievement, and also explained what this eternal life would be like now for those who belong to Him and wait for His return.

The achievement of Jesus' death. As a result of His death, judgment will come on the world in rebellion against Him, Satan will be driven out, and all kinds of people will be drawn to Himself (12:31–32). It will make it possible for Jesus to prepare a place for His people in heaven (14:1ff), and it will also enable His people, here on earth, to know the Father (17:3). His death will effect the 'washing' of His people, after which the Spirit will be sent from the Father to His people, in order to bring them eternal life (3:5; 14:15–21). The Spirit will remind the apostles of everything that Jesus has said to them, so that their message will be both accurate

233

and sufficient for the bringing of eternal life to others (14:26). No further revelation is required.

The experience of eternal life. For those who belong to Jesus this will mean an intimate personal relationship with the Father and the Son through the Spirit, a relationship that will call for their loving obedience to God as they await Jesus' return (14:15ff). Living this life will also call for perseverance, as they face suffering at the hands of a world that hates Jesus' people (15:18ff). But Jesus' people will most certainly experience joy and peace as they engage in active mission to the world, living as His messengers (16:22,33).

But chapter 20 contains more than the end of the story. In chapter 19, at the crucifixion, the voice of the eye-witness was plainly heard – eye-witnesses first appeared in chapter 1, verses 34,46,50 – and now, in chapter 20, it dominates the narrative, announcing a conclusion in verses 30–31. The emphasis on eye-witnesses, combined with the emphasis on the achievements of Jesus' death and resurrection, has the effect of urging the reader to come to a decision. It has been shown that Jesus really has achieved all that He promised, and that the apostles really have seen 'heaven opened and angels ascending and descending on the Son of Man'! Jesus is the true Israel, God's true Son, who has come from the Father. Therefore, all the blessings promised in the Gospel are available to those who will listen and believe.

STRUCTURE

20:1–9   Peter and John see the empty tomb and John believes.

20:10–18 Mary Magdalene sees Jesus and He sends her to tell the apostles that He has accomplished His mission of bringing eternal life.

20:19–23 The apostles see Jesus and He assures them of His forgiveness and sends them into the world with the assurance that their message is the message of life.

20:24–29 Thomas sees Jesus and believes. Jesus states that seeing is no longer necessary for belief, for the apostles' message is sufficient for belief.

20:30–31 Summary.

Study 26

Old Testament background

Jesus had to rise from the dead: There are specific references in the Old Testament stating that God's Messiah would live forever (e.g. Ps. 16:10; Isa. 9:6–7). Furthermore, Isaiah 53:10ff implies that the Suffering Servant will rise from the dead. John has shown us in his Gospel that Jesus combined both these Old Testament types, which is why he says confidently that Jesus *had* to rise from the dead (v. 9).

Text notes

1–9 PETER AND JOHN SEE AND JOHN BELIEVES

In Jewish law the witness of two men establishes credible evidence (Deut. 19:15). Peter and John provide such credibility concerning the empty tomb; John's record of what they saw is highly detailed, suggesting authenticity. So the two witnesses establish that the tomb was empty. This evidence on its own does not prove the resurrection. However, when taken with the rest of the chapter it confirms that the body seen by Mary Magdalene and the disciples was the same physical Jesus who had been dead and buried. This is important proof that the resurrection of Jesus was a physical, bodily resurrection, not just some kind of 'spiritual experience' or 'imagining' that the disciples were caught up in.

The theme of 'witness leading to belief' appears twice in this chapter (vv. 8–9 and verses 29–30), making a pair of brackets; it also makes a link between this chapter and chapter 1:19–51. The comment in verses 8–9 suggests that the empty tomb alone was enough to convince them of what they should have known from the Old Testament (see Old Testament notes).

10–18 MARY MAGDALENE SEES JESUS AND HE SENDS HER TO TELL THE APOSTLES THAT HE HAS ACCOMPLISHED HIS MISSION OF BRINGING ETERNAL LIFE

The most significant point of this passage is in verse 17. Mary is told to go and pass on the message to Jesus' apostles that He is returning to His Father. When she sees them she reports that she has seen the Lord and then passes on this message. The full significance of the message can only be understood in the light of all that has been said throughout the Gospel about Jesus' coming to earth and returning to His Father. Each time this theme appears – see 3:13–16; 13:3; 16:28; 17:4–5 – it presents a summary of God's purpose in sending His Son, that His Son should accomplish His eternal plan and rescue His people; the theme also includes God's vindication and glorification of Jesus. Jesus' message about returning to His Father would have reminded the disciples that His death and resurrection (His 'going') was for the purpose of obtaining forgiveness for His people; *this* was how the gate of heaven was to be opened, *this* was how a place would be prepared for them in heaven.

By emphasising the words 'your Father ... your God' Jesus points to the new relationship that now exists; through His wrath-bearing death He has made it possible for His people to have the same access to God that He Himself has (cf. 14:20,23; 16:25–27). Mary Magdalene's report of her encounter with Jesus, if this was all we had, would have carried sufficient theological content to convince the apostles; Jesus' words to her allude to all that He had said to them in the Upper Room Discourse, and so they realise who He is and what He has done.

19–23 THE APOSTLES SEE JESUS AND HE ASSURES THEM OF HIS FORGIVENESS AND SENDS THEM INTO THE WORLD WITH THE ASSURANCE THAT THEIR MESSAGE IS THE MESSAGE OF LIFE

Jesus shows the disciples His hands and side (v. 20) in order to remind them of the events of the cross: 'the risen Lord is none other than the crucified sacrifice' (Carson). This gesture, together with His words, helps them recall His teaching in chapters 13–17. There are two main themes:

Assurance. With the greeting 'Peace be with you', and by breathing on the apostles, Jesus reminds His disciples of all that His death has achieved for them. As the 'Lamb of God who takes away the sin of the world', He has washed them clean through His wrath-bearing death, and now He is able to impart to them God's Holy Spirit (see Context for notes on the achievement of His death). Previously, God could not indwell sinful individuals, but now that sin has been dealt with, God can 'make His home' with His people (14:23). The greeting 'Peace be with you' is an everyday greeting, but by repeating it Jesus reminds His disciples of His promise of peace in a world that hates Him, and them too. Through His death and resurrection He has now obtained forgiveness for them; He has 'overcome the world' and secured their place in heaven. As they remain in Him, they *will* now experience the peace He had promised them, with His Holy Spirit dwelling within them.

NB Some people have used verse 22 to support their theology of a two-stage Spirit baptism. Carson has useful comments that show the flaws in this argument (pp. 650ff). His conclusion is that 'Jesus' "exhalation" and command "Receive the Holy Spirit" are best understood as a kind of acted parable pointing forward to the full enduement still to come...', and that, like the foot-washing which anticipated the spiritual washing achieved through the cross, Jesus' action here is symbolic.

Commission. The words of the commission in verses 21–23 remind the apostles, next, of all that Jesus had said about His people's responsibility to bear fruit (see notes on 15:9–17). This fruit, together with the 'greater works' (14:12), was seen to be the spreading of His message of forgiveness to a world in rebellion against Him, through the teaching of His powerful, Spirit-inspired, word. This could only be accomplished with the empowering and enabling of the indwelling Spirit, who would not only enable them to testify, but also guarantee the accuracy of their teaching. In verses 21–23 the risen Lord commissions His apostles, who will receive His Spirit, to set about the task of bringing this accurate message of forgiveness to the world (cf. 17:18ff).

Verse 20 gives further evidence that this is the physically risen Jesus, but in view of His greeting, "Peace be with you", it appears to be here to remind us that Jesus is the Passover Lamb who has been pierced.

24–29 THOMAS SEES JESUS AND BELIEVES. JESUS STATES THAT SEEING IS NO LONGER NECESSARY FOR BELIEF, FOR THE APOSTLES' MESSAGE IS SUFFICIENT FOR BELIEF

The response of Thomas in verse 28 is the climax of the Gospel! At the same time, it provides a model response for the reader to follow. Initially, Thomas refuses to believe the apostles' witness – in this sense he is *not* a model believer. However, Thomas' doubt turns to belief that Jesus *is* Lord and God (cf. 1:1–18). This is what the reader *should* make of the resurrection.

Jesus' promise in verse 29 takes further what has already been taught about the nature of belief. Throughout the Gospel, John has been encouraging the reader to make a right response to the miraculous signs by focusing on them and accepting Jesus' words about them (cf. 2:23–25; 4:48; 6:26): the result of this right response is eternal life. Now Jesus restates this fact: real favour with God (being blessed) does not depend upon being able to see Him, but on trusting the words of the apostles. Further signs or revelation are unnecessary, for these words alone are sufficient to bring someone to eternal life (vv. 23,31).

30–31 SUMMARY

The commentaries discuss whether John's purpose is evangelism of the unbeliever or edification of the believer. Such a distinction is out of line with Jesus' teaching within the Gospel. He has said that His gospel message brings eternal life to the unbeliever (i.e. it is the means of entry into life, see 5:24) and also that it sustains the believer in eternal life (i.e. *continuing* to listen to His words is essential to remaining in Him and to persevering as a believer; see 10:27 and 15:7). Therefore, to separate the two purposes is to create a division that the Bible knows nothing of.

KEY THEMES

- ✤ Jesus' resurrection is attested by the empty tomb, by three appearances in front of multiple witnesses, and by the conversion of Thomas.
- ✤ The words of the risen Jesus show that God's eternal plan of rescue has been achieved:
  - ↘ He is the Son who has come from the Father and is returning to the Father.
  - ↘ Through His death as the Passover Lamb He has satisfied His Father's wrath.
  - ↘ Having 'washed' His apostles He can send them His Holy Spirit.

↘ Then He commissions them to take His message of peace to the world.

↘ He is Lord and God!

↯ The right response is to believe the apostles' words about Jesus. They are sufficient to bring life. Demands for further evidence are discouraged.

APPLICATION

Evidence for the resurrection. John provides us with sufficient well-documented and carefully observed detail to show that the resurrection of Jesus was a physical, bodily reality.

Accomplishment of God's eternal plan. Jesus' words to Mary Magdalene and the disciples resonate with His teaching in the Upper Room, and take us back to the lessons learned there. His words assure us that He had come from God, that He has now obtained the forgiveness of sin, that this drinking of the cup of the Father's wrath has enabled Him to send His Spirit to His 'washed' people, and that therefore His commission to His apostles, that they should take to the world the Spirit-taught message about the finished work of Jesus, will result in the True Vine bearing much fruit.

The nature of belief. Jesus' words to Thomas teach us that true belief and true favour with God come not from physical sight but from faith in the apostles' words about Him. These words are sufficient for belief and no further proofs or revelation are necessary.

THE AIM OF THIS STUDY

To believe the apostles' witness that Jesus has risen, and so to believe His words that God has accomplished His eternal plan to rescue the world and bring life through His Son.

SUGGESTED QUESTIONS

1–9 THE EYE-WITNESS EVIDENCE

↯ Make the case for the bodily resurrection of Jesus from today's passage.

↘ How does 19:38–42 help to strengthen your case?

10–18 MARY MAGDALENE SEES JESUS AND IS GIVEN THE MESSAGE ABOUT HIS ACCOMPLISHMENT

- ✤ John tells us the purpose of the signs in verse 31. What is it?
  - ↘ We have already seen that this resurrection sign has been paired with Lazarus' resurrection in chapter 11. What has been the main point of chapters 11–20?
- ✤ In verse 17 Jesus gives Mary a message for the disciples. Where have we heard this idea before? How does it sum up Jesus' mission?
  - ↘ How do the pronouns ('my', 'your') of verse 17 help to make the point?
- ✤ How would this verse help someone who feels that God is distant and remote, far removed from his or her daily life? How would it help the person for whom following Jesus has become a matter of daily ritual and duties, such as attending meetings and having quiet times?

19–23 THE APOSTLES SEE JESUS AND ARE COMMISSIONED TO TAKE OUT THE MESSAGE OF PEACE

- ✤ How does Jesus' explanation of His 'going', in chapters 13–17, inform our understanding of Jesus' words and actions in this passage?
  - ↘ In what way does this passage give us final confirmation that the apostles' message is accurate, and that it is sufficient for bringing life to all who listen?

24–31 THOMAS SEES JESUS AND BELIEVES

- ✤ In what ways is Thomas a 'model believer'? In what ways is he not?
  - ↘ How would this paragraph encourage the person who feels himself or herself to be a 'second-class' Christian because he or she has not had exciting visions and dreams of Jesus?
  - ↘ How does this passage challenge the person who considers himself or herself to be somehow superior because he or she claims to have had additional revelation from Jesus?

30–31 JOHN'S PURPOSE

- ✤ How has John's purpose, stated in verses 30–31, been achieved through his recording of the sign of Jesus' resurrection?

John 21:1–25
'Feed my sheep!'

CONTEXT

Any number of interpretations have been read into the account of the miraculous catch of fish – some more speculative than others! However, if we stick with the pattern that John has already established in the rest of the Gospel, many of the supposed difficulties are ironed out. With all the other signs in the Gospel, John has provided an interpretation of the sign in the discourse that follows; this sign is also followed by a discourse. The subject of the discourse between Jesus and Peter concerns the feeding of Jesus' 'sheep', His future disciples. Jesus has just fed His disciples with fish from the miraculous catch of fish. Thus the subject matter of the final chapter is all centred around this event of the feeding of Jesus' apostles. Jesus feeds His apostles and reinstates Peter – as a representative of all the apostles – so that he and they may feed His people.

This sign, at the end of John's Gospel, ties in tightly with the purpose statement in 20:31. By recording Jesus' feeding of the apostles and Peter's reinstatement, John is once again providing substantial evidence for the reader as to why he should take this written account seriously. Here is the risen Jesus recommissioning His apostles for their task of testifying to Him. Jesus' emphasis on the authenticity of the apostles' commission has been one of the major thrusts of the Gospel, and now, as he ends his account, John selects one final sign and discourse to show the reader that this commission still stands. In the light of the apostles' wholesale desertion of Jesus, the reader might be tempted to doubt the apostles' words. However, the apostles are now fed miraculously by the risen Christ and are given the task of feeding the risen Christ's people.

Furthermore, given that this sign is 'unpaired', there is the suggestion that Jesus' work is to continue in the age between His 'going' and His return: as the apostles proclaim His word, His 'lambs' *will* be fed. This was one of the major emphases of the Upper Room Discourse.

STRUCTURE

21:1–14   Jesus feeds His apostles.
21:15–25   Jesus calls His apostles to feed His sheep.

TEXT NOTES

1–14 JESUS FEEDS HIS APOSTLES

Perhaps the most common of the many interpretations given to the story of the miraculous catch of fish is that Jesus is giving the disciples a symbolic anticipation of the great harvest of 'fish' that they are going to gather in, on His behalf, as He turns them into 'fishers of men'. This gives rise to the classic three-point talk on this passage: 'Fish, Feed, Follow'! The trouble with such an interpretation is that there has been no prior reference to fish in the Gospel – apart from chapter 6, the feeding of the five thousand with bread and fish. New disciples have been symbolically alluded to as fruit on a vine (15:16), or as sheep (10:16), but never as fish! John could easily have included Jesus' words to Peter and Andrew recorded in Matthew's Gospel (4:19), but he didn't. Therefore, it seems much safer to understand this sign according to the explanation given in the following discourse, in which Jesus commissions Peter to feed His sheep. (In this way we will be abiding by the pattern of sign-plus- explanation that John has maintained from chapter 2 onwards.)

In the light of this, the sign shows the disciples failing to catch fish, but Jesus miraculously providing for them. When they land they find that He has already got a fire going with fish cooking on it; He invites them to breakfast and feeds them, first with these fish and then with fish from the miraculous catch.

Throughout the Gospel, Jesus has been concerned with the feeding of His people. The Good Shepherd has promised both to keep and to feed His sheep, as they listen to His words (10:27–28). It has been established that these words are Jesus' teaching about His words and works on earth (14:8–21). And the accuracy of these words has been guaranteed through the promised sending of the Spirit to the apostles (14:25ff; 16:12–15; 20:22–23). Now, in this final sign of the Gospel, we see the risen Christ miraculously feeding His apostles, and so assuring them that they are now equipped to go out and feed His people.

So, this open-ended finish to the Gospel shows that Jesus' concern, in the post-resurrection era, will be with the feeding of His people through what He has fed His apostles. It is a summary statement of much of the Gospel and a final authentication that the apostles' witness is genuine.

This interpretation of the sign doesn't rule out the possibility that John intended the miraculous catch of fish to recall the feeding of the five thousand in chapter 6. Both the geographical setting and much of the language in the narrative recalls the memory of that sign. If this is John's intention, then that sign and its following discourse will bring back, for the reader, the message that is to be the apostles' food, namely, that Jesus is 'the bread of life' and that 'if a man eats of this bread, he will live for ever'. Many of the major themes of the Gospel are thus recalled: the nature of Jesus' heavenly kingdom, in contrast to the world's desire for a material kingdom, the necessity of Jesus' death as the Passover Lamb, the importance of belief, and the inevitability of division.

15–25 JESUS CALLS HIS APOSTLES TO FEED HIS SHEEP

This passage has three main emphases:

15–17 Peter is reinstated as an under-shepherd. The repetition of the question 'Do you love me?' deliberately recalls Peter's three denials. The fact that Peter was 'hurt' (v. 17) at the repetition adds weight to the link with his past failure. But now his failure in the high priest's courtyard is put behind him and Jesus graciously calls him back into service. This reinstatement is done in public, in front of the other disciples. And Peter is taught that loving Jesus involves feeding His people. The repetition of '*my* sheep' emphasises that the sheep that are to be fed belong to Him, and from the rest of the Gospel the reader knows that feeding these sheep will involve teaching them about Jesus' words and works. Prior to the death of Jesus, Peter had no understanding and no message for Jesus' sheep, now he is beginning to understand and he has the message of forgiveness and eternal life to bring to God's people, as he teaches them about the words and works of Christ. Once again the implication is that the reader can trust the apostles who have been given this specific commission to feed Jesus' people.

18–22 Peter is told that for him feeding Jesus' sheep will mean following Jesus to the point of death. Ironically, the contrast that was drawn between Peter and Christ in chapter 18 is now replaced by a comparison, as Peter is commissioned to shepherd the sheep of the Good Shepherd. He is told that the manner of his death will be similar to that of Christ's death. The purpose of this part, about the manner of Peter's death, is probably to add further weight to the reinstatement of Peter, as an apostle whose witness could be trusted. Nevertheless, the irony of the situation is clear. So too are the lessons about discipleship. Before the crucifixion Peter had bragged that he would lay down his life on Jesus' behalf; now, after the crucifixion, Peter is called to do just that, to lay down his life on behalf of the risen Christ and so glorify God. Now that he has been served, Peter is ready to serve. It is a call to the type of discipleship that Jesus talked about in 12:25–26.

This part of Peter's reinstatement recalls Jesus' original call to His disciples, back in 1:43. The open-ended nature of the chapter, with just one sign and no 'pair' to close the section, suggests that, from now on, this is to be the pattern of discipleship and service to which all readers of the Gospel are called. The risen Jesus still calls for this kind of fruitful service from His disciples; if they are prepared to lose their lives and follow Jesus, they will be honoured by the Father (12:25–26).

23–25 John does not die but lives to record Jesus' words and works, feeding His sheep in a different way. John's inclusion of a reference to himself makes it clear that not all Jesus' apostles will be called to lay down their lives. Some, like John, have been commissioned to feed Jesus' sheep by recording, for them, His words and works (vv. 24–25). Nonetheless, all disciples are to be ready to follow Jesus to the point of death if that is the path chosen for them.

KEY THEMES

- ✤ The miraculous catch of fish is a sign that indicates the risen Christ's intention of feeding His apostles so that they may feed His people.
  - ↘ Miraculously, He feeds His apostles.
  - ↘ He reinstates and recommissions His apostles to feed His people.
  - ↘ His people can trust His apostles' words about Him.
- ✤ At the same time, the risen Christ indicates that His apostles will face different ends.
  - ↘ As Jesus' disciples follow Him, the task of feeding His people is to be continued even to the point of death.
  - ↘ In this life His people are called to walk different paths. Peter glorifies God by following Christ and feeding His people to the point where he must die a martyr's death, but the beloved disciple does not die in a noteworthy way. Dying and not dying are equal. We serve and love best by walking the path He has allocated to us.

APPLICATION

The sign and the discourse establish that Jesus' key priority, now, is the feeding of His sheep through the words of the apostles. He commissioned His disciples to engage in this task and to follow Him in it even to the point of death. There are two levels of application:

First, if Jesus' priority, for the period between His resurrection and His return, is that His people should be fed, through hearing His apostles' teaching, we should make it *our* priority to feed on that teaching ourselves. The authenticity of this teaching is guaranteed for us, not least by the recommissioning of Peter and the recognition of John's role in recording the Gospel: we can trust the apostles' record of Jesus' words. We should make sure, therefore, that we belong to the kind of church where we can feed on His word ourselves, and also serve others by helping them to feed on His word. Only then will God's work be done (14:8–14).

Secondly, if Jesus' priority is the feeding of His sheep – those who know His voice and follow Him – we should make it *our* priority to ensure that His sheep are fed. Whatever our role within His people, we should be clear that His chief concern, now, is that His word should go out to His people. If we are teachers ourselves, we can be encouraged by the reinstatement of Peter after such a great fall; at the same time we need to remember that the people we teach are *His*, not ours to rule over. All God's people have a role to play in the spreading of His word to those who have not yet heard His voice; each of us have gifts, given by Him, to use in advancing the ministry of gospel proclamation. As His people pursue this ministry, so the True Vine will bear 'much fruit'.

THE AIM OF THIS STUDY

To recognise that the apostles' testimony to Jesus is trustworthy, and also that Jesus' priority for His disciples is that they should be fed, so that they in turn may take on the responsibility of feeding His people, whatever this may cost.

SUGGESTED QUESTIONS

1–14 JESUS FEEDS HIS APOSTLES

    ✠ In his Gospel so far, how has John presented the signs?
- How have we been able to understand the significance of other signs?
- What, therefore, will help us interpret this sign?
- What are the details of this sign?

15–25 JESUS CALLS HIS APOSTLES TO FEED HIS SHEEP

✤ How do Jesus' instructions to Peter in verses 15–19 elaborate on what He has already told the apostles in the Upper Room Discourse?

  ↘ What did Jesus teach the apostles, in the Upper Room, about the ministry of 'feeding His people'?

✤ Why might Peter have felt unable to carry out this task, following Jesus' death?

  ↘ For Peter, what will be the cost of carrying out this instruction?

✤ How does the mention of the beloved disciple and his ministry (v. 24) tie in with the instructions to Peter?

✤ How does the discourse help us understand what Jesus is doing when He feeds the apostles?

✤ What is the irony in verses 18–19.

  ↘ What do verses 18–24 add to the recommissioning of the apostles?

APPLICATION

✤ How does this passage help you to trust the words of the apostles more fully?

✤ If the feeding of His people through His apostles' words was such a major priority for Jesus, what implications does this have for us, as we too live in the period between His departure and His return?

✤ How will this (your answer to the question above) affect your own Christian growth?

  ↘ When thinking about which church family to join, how will this affect your choice?

  ↘ How will this affect the way you use the gifts and the time that God has given you?

Group Preparation
Questions

The following pages contain some introductory notes and then sets of preparation questions for each study, so that group members may be helped to get the most out of their time together. Also included are study tips and a list of recommended books.

Prep. questions. One of the lessons that we hope members will learn, during the year of studying John's Gospel, is the value of studying the passage before coming to the group study. This may be new to them but, in our experience, when people do prepare like this it transforms the midweek meeting! For each study, therefore, there are a few questions to help people get to the heart of the passage. Usually the last question will ask them to think through the implications of the passage for us today. These final questions call for hard thinking, so that the study of God's word does indeed result in the changed lives of His people.

Study tips. As members study John's Gospel we hope that they will learn much about how to study the Bible more effectively. We have therefore included a number of study tips which we hope will give them a head start when approaching a passage, and also build up their confidence for studying the Bible in future.

Recommended books. A list of titles that have encouraged and built up Christians over many years. Reading Christian books will complement the *Read Mark Learn* studies, as members grow in their knowledge and love of God, and discover for themselves what it means to 'have life in His name'.

INTRODUCTION

A Gospel overview

The best way to get started in John's Gospel is to read it! Set aside some time when you can read the whole book at one sitting. Read fairly rapidly, trying to get a feel for the book as a whole: the main themes, the structure, the language. The point of this exercise is to take in the big picture, so don't worry about understanding all the details at this stage. At the end note down your first impressions. (If you struggle to make mental notes, jot down a few very brief comments with references as you read, but don't lose your momentum.)

JOHN'S PURPOSE

...these are written that you may believe that Jesus is the Christ, the Son of God, and that by believing, you may have life in His name. (20:31)

This is an important verse, towards the end of the Gospel, which tells us what was John's intention in writing. If you have the opportunity to read through the Gospel again, keep these questions in mind:

- ✤ What does John say about Jesus being the Christ, the Son of God?
- ✤ What does it mean to 'have life' in His name?
- ✤ What does a right response of belief in Him look like?

John 1:1–18
God on earth!

PREP. QUESTIONS

↳ List all of the attributes and activities of the Word.

_____

↳ Read verses 10–13 and describe, in your own words:
  ↘ the bad news

  ↘ the good news

↳ What is John the Baptist's role?

↳ How can I be sure of what God is like?

STUDY TIP: OBSERVATION

One of the essential skills of Bible Study is that of observation – looking carefully at a passage to see what it really says. The following questions may seem obvious, but they are worth asking:

+ What are the main events in the passage?
- Do I understand the words?
- Am I reading what the passage says or what I want it to say? It is easy to have presuppositions about what a passage is saying.
- Are there any surprises? This is a good question to ask, to avoid being swayed by presuppositions.

John 1:19–51
'We have found the Messiah!'

PREP. QUESTIONS

✥ Summarise, in a couple of sentences, the action in this passage.

✥ How does the Baptist fulfil his role as described in 1:6–8?

✥ This passage shows Jesus fulfilling many Old Testament promises. List those you can spot and suggest why they are important.

✥ For the background to verse 51, look up Genesis 28:10–19. Note God's promise and Jacob's response. What do you think Jesus is saying to his disciples?

✥ What should be our reaction to this passage?

Study Tip: Knowing when to cross-reference

Some cross-references provide the key to understanding a passage; others are just confusing. As a rule:

- ✤ Look up passages to which the author points you – either by means of a direct quote, or by placing a clue in the text (e.g. 'It was Passover').
- ✤ The Old Testament context is always relevant and important; New Testament authors knew the Old Testament well.
- ✤ Don't compare details in different Gospels. The four Gospels were written by different authors, each with a different purpose.

John 2:1–25
God's King is here. Glory! Judgment!

PREP. QUESTIONS

✣ Contrast the different aspects of Jesus' character that we see in this passage.

✣ What phrase does John use to describe the miracle in verses 1–11? What does this phrase suggest?

✣ Read Psalm 69:9 (picked up in v. 17) in its context. How is David's experience fulfilled by Jesus?

✣ What different responses to Jesus do we see in this passage?

✣ What questions are raised by verses 23–25?

John 2:23–3:36
Entry into the kingdom of God

PREP. QUESTIONS

✤ How does the beginning of chapter 3 follow on from the end of chapter 2?

✤ What are the requirements for entering the kingdom of God? How does Ezekiel 36:24–29 explain them?

✤ How does the story of the bronze snake (Numbers 21:4–9) relate to the gaining of eternal life (vv. 14,15)?

✤ What do verses 19–21 tell us about why people do or do not believe?

✤ These verses contain some tough teaching. List the different reasons given in verses 22–36 as to why we should accept it.

STUDY TIP: CONTEXT

We rarely open books in the middle and expect to understand whatever we find, yet people often do this with the Bible. Context is crucial to the meaning of any text and the text of the Bible is no exception. We need to keep in mind three kinds of context:

- ✤ *The immediate context,* provided by the verses before and after the ones we are studying. This is largely a matter of good observation.
- ✤ *The wider context,* provided by the book we are studying or – in most books – by the section of the book our passage is in.
- ✤ *The whole Bible context.* In this sense, the Bible is one book with one story. Where does this passage fit into the grand sweep of salvation history? Does it have Old Testament background? Not the easiest kind of context to work out, but essential.

STUDY 5

John 4:1–54
The Saviour of the world!

PREP. QUESTIONS

✤ What issues from chapter 3 are still in evidence in chapter 4?

✤ What new issues appear in chapter 4? How does John emphasise their significance?

✤ Look up Ezekiel 37:15–28. How does this prophecy throw light on chapter 4?

✤ How does the second sign summarise the main points on which John has been focusing since 2:1?

✤ In chapter 4 what are the chief lessons for:
↘ the disciples?

↘ us?

John 5:1–47
He came to His own(1)

PREP. QUESTIONS

✤ What is the structure of chapter 5? How do the different parts relate to one another?

✤ Why do the Jews turn against Jesus? How do Jesus' words in verses 19–30 (in verse 19 especially) answer the Jews' concerns and objections?

✤ How do verses 31–47 add to what Jesus has said in the first part of this chapter?

✤ How does this passage challenge the world's and our views of Jesus?

STUDY TIP: THINKING ABOUT STRUCTURE

It is important not to think of the Gospels as scrapbooks, random collections of memories about Jesus' life and teaching. All the Gospel writers deliberately structured their accounts in order to aid our understanding. With any passage, therefore, it is a useful exercise to do the following:

- ✤ Divide the passage into its natural sections.
- ✤ Give each section a title.
- ✤ Think how the sections fit together to make the main point.

John 6:1–40
He came to His own (2)

PREP. QUESTIONS

✤ What themes from earlier chapters do we see in this passage?

✤ Identify the Jews' motives and their attitudes to Jesus throughout the passage.

✤ How do Jesus' words in verses 35–40 relate to the earlier parts of the chapter?

✤ What warnings and encouragements do we find in this passage?

STUDY 8

John 6:41–71
He came to His own (3)

PREP. QUESTIONS

❧ What is the immediate context of this discussion between Jesus and the Jews?

❧ What new explanation about the 'bread from heaven' do we learn from this passage? How is this related to the forthcoming Passover feast? (See Exod. 12:1–30.)

❧ Jesus describes, in different ways, how someone may have eternal life? What are these descriptions, and how are they related?

❧ What is the shock of verses 60–71? What else do we learn from these verses?

❧ What does this passage teach us about genuine discipleship?

John 7:1–52
His own did not receive Him

PREP. QUESTIONS

✢ List the different reactions to Jesus to be found in chapter 7.

✢ How are Jesus' words in verse 7 demonstrated in verses 11–31?

✢ What do we learn about Jesus' mission in this chapter?

✢ How should this passage inform our evangelism?

GROUP PREPARATION QUESTIONS

STUDY TIP: LOOK FOR THE MAIN POINT

It is important, when studying a passage, to look for the author's main point (or points). As John writes he includes specific lessons he wants us to pick up, and we should be alert to recognise them. Although passages may contain much detail, we should remember that the details will be used to teach the main point. If we leave a study having looked only at details, we will have missed that main point and so missed the main purpose of studying the passage.

John 8:12–59
Children born of natural descent

(Vv. 1–11 are left out because they were almost certainly not part of John's original Gospel. See the note in the NIV version.)

PREP. QUESTIONS

✤ What themes from earlier chapters are seen again in verses 12–30?

✤ How might verse 31 affect the way we read the rest of the chapter?

✤ List the distinctive characteristics of the two families that Jesus describes in verses 31–59.

✤ In what ways does Jesus shock the Jews in verses 31–59? How do these things challenge us?

John 9:1–41
Born of God

PREP. QUESTIONS

✎ Contrast the attitudes of the man born blind and the Jews after the miracle.

✎ How does John intend us to understand the chapter in view of these verses:
↘ verse 3?

↘ verse 39?

✎ How should this chapter affect
↘ our evangelism?

↘ our attitude to our own salvation?

STUDY TIP: APPLICATION IS VITAL

The result of any Bible study should be a change in our lives. God gives us many warnings about the folly and danger of not doing what His word says, e.g. Matthew 7:26–27, James 1: 22–24.

- ✣ Don't let any personal or group study time go by without allowing time to consider the implications, and the application, of the passage. (We need to help one another with this.)
- ✣ Come to the study having put time into the prep. questions on application. Don't be satisfied with the first thought that comes to mind.
- ✣ After the group study spend time on your own, thinking through how the passage should affect you personally.

John 10:1–42
The Good Shepherd

PREP. QUESTIONS

✤ How do verses 1–6 follow on from chapter 9?

✤ Read Ezekiel 34. Trace the parallels with this chapter.

✤ What do we learn about Jesus as 'The Good Shepherd'?

✤ In what ways do the Jews continue to show a wrong response to Jesus?

✤ Identify the two-way relationship between Jesus and His followers.

John 11:1–54
'I am the resurrection and the life'

PREP. QUESTIONS

✤ What pointers are we given to help us understand the raising of Lazarus?

✤ What can we learn from Jesus' reaction to Lazarus and the mourners?

✤ From what we have seen in John so far, explain the reaction of the Sanhedrin in verse 48.

✤ What significance is to be found in Caiaphas' comment and 'prophecy'?

✤ How can we effectively explain the truths of this passage to our friends and colleagues?

STUDY TIP: STUDYING NARRATIVE PASSAGES

Much of the Bible (and of John) is composed of narrative. If handled poorly, narrative passages can be a minefield because of the tendency to align ourselves with particular characters and decide to do what they do. On the other hand, there is so much for us to learn from these passages, especially about the character and actions of God, that we should resist the temptation to skip over them simply because they do not contain specific instruction.

- ✤ First, look to see if any explanation is provided in the surrounding passages.
- ✤ Learn to distinguish what is descriptive (telling us what happened) from what is prescriptive (giving instruction).
- ✤ Lessons *can* be learned from narrative passages, but we must understand them in their wider contexts. Often it is the 'big picture' that will show us if there is an example to follow or to avoid.
- ✤ Look for *principles* to apply, rather than actions to mirror.

John 11:55–12:50
Death in this world – life in eternity

PREP. QUESTIONS

✤ How does this passage divide up? Give each part a title.

✤ Read Zechariah 9:9–13. How do these verses shed light on the significance of Jesus' arrival in Jerusalem?

✤ What do we learn about
  ↘ the reasons for Jesus' death?

  ↘ the achievements of His death?

✤ From the whole passage, identify a right and a wrong response to Jesus. Where do we fall short? How should we change?

John 13:1–30
The cross is central!

PREP. QUESTIONS

✤ What are the two main elements in this passage?

✤ Bearing in mind the main lessons of 12:23–36, what indications are there that there is more to this incident than just washing feet?

✤ In what ways does Peter misunderstand Jesus' teaching?

✤ How should we understand Judas' betrayal of Jesus in the light of this passage?

✤ Explain the place of the cross in your life. How does this passage challenge that view?

John 13:31–14:4
'Lord, where are you going?'

PREP. QUESTIONS

✤ How does this passage relate to the previous passage?

✤ How do verses 31–32 clash with our thinking?

✤ What will it mean for Christians to love one another as Jesus commands?

✤ How does Jesus answer Peter's question (v. 36) and the disciples' anxiety?

✤ Note down three major lessons we should learn from this passage.

STUDY 17

John 14:5–14
'How can we know? ... Show us!'

PREP. QUESTIONS

✣ John 14.6 is very well-known. How do our studies in John's Gospel so far explain Jesus' answer to Thomas' question?

✣ How do verses 9–11 address Philip's request in verse 8? Summarise Jesus' answer.

✣ What are the 'greater things' that Jesus promises we will do? (NB 'greater works' is a better translation than 'greater things.')

   ↘ What were the 'greater things' (same phrase) in 5:20?

   ↘ How are they linked to the Father's 'work' (v. 10)?

✣ What are the implications of this passage for
   ↘ the sincere Muslim/Jew/Hindu, etc.?

   ↘ the Christian who wants to know God better?

STUDY TIP: THE BIBLE IS RIGHT!

When faced with difficult verses or passages it is easy to treat the Bible as a confused ancient text and to think it's up to us to make the best of it. Remember that the Bible is God's perfect word, and that if we don't understand it, the problem is with us, rather than the text. Work at it and pray for understanding!

John 14:15–31
'Show us ...why us and not the world?'

PREP. QUESTIONS

✥ The disciples are still troubled about Jesus leaving them (v. 27). What insight and reassurance does He give them about His departure

↘ in verses 15–21?

↘ in verses 22–31?

✥ What is the role of the Spirit according to Jesus? Does this differ from contemporary teaching on His role? How?

✥ What do we learn from this passage about what it means to be a believer?

John 15:1–17
'I am the true vine'

PREP. QUESTIONS

✤ How do the following Old Testament passages help us to see the significance of Jesus' words in verse 1?
   ↘ Isaiah 5:1–7 and Jeremiah 2:21

   ↘ Isaiah 27:2–6

✤ What do we discover, in verses 3–8, about the consequences of remaining or not remaining in the true vine?

✤ What does it mean, to remain in Jesus, according to verses 9–17?

✤ How is our responsibility to 'remain' related to Jesus' prior actions?

John 15:18–16:4
The disciples' relationship with the world

PREP. QUESTIONS

✤ What different reasons does Jesus give for the world hating (or persecuting) the disciples? What are the underlying motives?

✤ What form of persecution are you most likely to face?

✤ Bearing in mind this persecution, how should the disciples, and we, be helped by Jesus' teaching
  ↘ in this passage?

  ↘ in the Upper Room Discourse so far?

Study Tip: Good application

The application of a passage is vital (see earlier tip in Study 11), but it is more than a matter of bolting on a plan of action (usually involving more prayer, evangelism, or Bible study). Keep these points in mind:

- ✤ The most significant application usually comes from the wider context. In John, this means that we must always keep 20:31 in our sights.
- ✤ Often, it is our thinking and attitudes that are wrong (with regard to God, ourselves and salvation) and these will only change over time. Right thinking will then lead to the right kind of action. (See James 3:13.)
- ✤ We naturally think individually, but the Bible is usually addressed to God's *people*. We need to help one another to live obediently. If you do make 'plans' at the end of a study, pray for God's help and discuss how you are getting on the following week.

John 16:5–33
'I am going to the Father'

PREP. QUESTIONS

❧ What does Jesus tell us about the work of the Spirit? What have we heard before and what is new?

❧ How does this differ from common views (or our views) of the Spirit's work?

❧ What reasons does Jesus give, in verses 16–28, for the disciples' rejoicing? What privileges of the Christian life are described here?

❧ To what extent do we appreciate and take advantage of these privileges?

John 17:1–26
Jesus prays for His disciples

PREP. QUESTIONS

✤ What does Jesus specifically pray for in verses 1–5? How is this related to His words in verses 2–4?

✤ What do we learn about the disciples in verses 6–11? Why is this important, in view of verse 18?

✤ How is this related to Jesus' prayer for them?

✤ For what (specifically) does Jesus pray for all future believers, and why?

✤ What should we learn from Jesus' priorities in prayer?

John 18:1–27
'Shall I not drink the cup the Father has given me?'

PREP. QUESTIONS

🕭 What is the main point that John emphasises in verses 1–11?

🕭 Look up Isaiah 51:17, Jeremiah 25:15 and Psalm 75:4–8. What is Jesus saying in verse 11?

🕭 Contrast Jesus with Peter in verses 12–27.

🕭 Why does John include verse 14? How might this verse influence the way we read the rest of the passage?

🕭 What reasons does this passage give us to be thankful?

STUDY TIP: JOHN 18 ONWARDS...

After all the *explanatory theology* of the Upper Room Discourse, we move back into the *unfolding narrative* (these are the two main elements of chapters 11–20). In the narrative, however, John gives us clues which indicate how we are to interpret events, in the light of the theology already given. So we must resist the temptation to speculate in our interpretation and instead be alert to pick up the words and phrases that John uses.

John 18:28–19:16
'I find no basis for a charge'
...'Crucify Him!'

PREP. QUESTIONS

✤ Divide the action in this passage into scenes.

✤ What does Jesus' trial teach us about
   ↘ who He is and what He has come to do?

   ↘ a right response to Him?

✤ In what ways are the Jews themselves 'tried and found guilty' in this passage?

✤ How, today, could we be found similarly guilty?

John 19:17–42
'It is accomplished!'

PREP. QUESTIONS

✤ This passage refers to several Old Testament passages. What is *the context* of each of the following verses? (First, read the two psalms and summarise each in a sentence.)

↘ Psalm 22:18

↘ Psalm 69:21

↘ Exodus 12:46; Numbers 9:12

↘ Zechariah 12:10 (NB 13:1)

✤ Divide the passage into parts and give a title to each part.

✤ What main point is John making, and how does each part of the passage tie in with it?

✤ What are the implications of this passage for the Christian?

Study Tip: The Bible provides its own interpretation

Evangelical (Bible-believing) Christians are often accused of taking one particular interpretation and ignoring other possibilities. But the Bible does not simply relate events and then leave us to interpret those events for ourselves. Rather, it gives us both the events and their interpretation. The importance of understanding the biblical interpretation, rather than one that suits us, cannot be overstated and is a good reason to work hard at the text.

John 20:1–31
'We have seen the Lord!'

PREP. QUESTIONS

✤ Look carefully through the passage and find all the evidence for the physical resurrection of Jesus.

✤ What do we learn about the significance of Jesus' resurrection? What previous lessons from John's Gospel are confirmed here?

✤ How should we react to this passage? How should we not? How do we?

John 21:1–25
'Feed my sheep!'

PREP. QUESTIONS

✎ The account of the miraculous catch of fish seems to have two functions. How is it related
  ↘ to the previous chapter?

  ↘ to Jesus' conversation with Peter?

✎ What are Jesus' priorities for His people? How do chapters 13–17 help us to understand them more fully?

✎ What part is to be played by
  ↘ Peter?

  ↘ John?

  ↘ us?

PREP. QUESTIONS

By now, you will be familiar with John's purpose statement (20:31) *... these are written that you may believe that Jesus is the Christ, the Son of God, and that by believing you may have life in his name.*

֍ What have you learned about
↘ who Jesus is?

↘ what it means to have life in His name?

֍ How have you been encouraged to believe?

֍ Having studied John's Gospel, what new reasons do you have to be thankful?

Commentaries on John's Gospel
D.A. Carson, *The Gospel According to John* (Inter-Varsity Press, 1991)
A.J. Kostenberger, *John (Baker Exegetical commentary on the New Testament)* (Fleming H. Revell, 2004)

Other good books to read
A great way to grow spiritually and develop your mind is to read excellent Christian books. But which ones? Here are some books that have helped many people to grow as disciples of Jesus.

UNDERSTANDING THE BIBLE
Nigel Beynon and Andrew Sach, *Dig Deeper* (Inter-Varsity Press, 2004)
Vaughan Roberts, *God's Big Picture (Tracing the story-line of the Bible)* (Inter-Varsity Press, 2003)

BASIC DOCTRINE
J.I. Packer, *Knowing God* (Hodder & Stoughton, 1973)
John Piper, *The Pleasures of God* (Mentor/Christian Focus, 2001)
Mark Meynell, *Cross-examined: The Life-changing Power of the Death of Jesus* (Inter-Varsity Press, 2005)
John Stott, *The Cross of Christ* (Inter-Varsity Press, 2006)
John Frame, *Salvation belongs to the Lord* (P & R Publishing, 2006)
Graham Beynon, *Experiencing the Spirit: New Testament Essentials for Every Christian* (Inter-Varsity Press, 2006)
David Jackman, *A Spirit of Truth* (Christian Focus, 2006)

CHRISTIAN LIVING
Christopher Ash, *Married for God* (Inter-Varsity Press, 2007)
Jerry Bridges, *Pursuit of Holiness* (Navpress, 1985)
John Chapman, *Know and Tell the Gospel* (Matthias Media, 1998)
Mark Dever, *The Gospel and Personal Evangelism* (Crossway, 2007)
Joshua Harris, *Stop Dating the Church* (Multnomah Press, 2004)
Kris Lungaard, *The Enemy Within* (P & R Publishing, 1998)

EVANGELISTIC (Books to give away)

Mike Cain, *Real Life Jesus* (Inter-Varsity Press, 2008) - based on John's Gospel

Vaughan Roberts, *Turning Points* (Authentic Lifestyle, 1999)

Rico Tice and Barry Cooper, *Christianity Explored* (The Good Book Company, 2005)

CHRISTIAN BIOGRAPHY

Don Cormack, *Killing Fields, Living Fields* (Monarch Books, 2001)

John Piper, *Tested by Fire* (Inter-Varsity Press, 2001)

J.C. Ryle, *Five English Reformers* (Banner of Truth, 1960)

TRAINING DAYS AND RESOURCES

St Helen's Church can assist with local churches running training days for small group Bible study leaders. For details please contact:

RML Administrator
St Helen's Church Office
Great St Helen's
London EC3A 6AT
Tel: 020 7283 2231
e-mail: st-helens@st-helens.org.uk

Audio training resources for leading small group Bible studies are available from the St Helen's Media website at www.st-helens-media.net

On John's gospel there is an *Overview of John's Gospel* by William Taylor as well as a series by Dick Lucas on chapters 1-10 entitled *God Made Known* with both available on Audio CD and MP3 CD.

READ / MARK / LEARN

ROMANS

A SMALL GROUP BIBLE STUDY

ST HELEN"S
BISHOPGATE

Read / Mark / Learn is a small group Bible study series that is designed to equip people to study God's Word for themselves – and in studying it, know God's purpose for their lives.

Each book studies whole books of the Bible and so enables people to understand scripture in context. In an era that claims that the Bible can say what you want it to say it is important to re-establish the truth that you just can't – if you explain the scripture with honesty, fairness and in context.

Each study establishes

+ the context, aim and structure of the passage
+ links with the Old Testament
+ lessons from each part of the passage – highlighting key issues
+ practical applications and suggestions

Each section also includes conversational discussion starters and suggested questions for leading a Bible study. There is also a section for photocopying for group members to pre-prepare for each study

'We found these notes supremely beneficial for clarifying the message of Romans, providing quality training for Bible study leaders and planting deep missionary convictions in young Christians.'

Richard Coekin, Senior Minister, the CO-MISSION Initiative

'This is an exciting commentary on Romans, because it is the result of careful reflection on the meaning of the text and its theological implications, though very much designed to answer the questions of ordinary people. Those who want to use the material in a study group will find plenty of resources for engaging with the text, and a set of questions that will set everybody thinking about the true meaning of each passage.'

David Peterson, former Principal, Oak Hill Theological College, London

'Read / Mark / Learn has taught hundreds of us over the years to know our Bibles and our God better.'

Hugh Palmer, All Souls Church, Langham Place, London

ISBN 978-1-84550-362-8

PARTNERSHIP
PHILIPPIANS WILLIAM TAYLOR

CONCISE, PORTABLE SPIRITUAL FOOD

PARTNERSHIP

Concise, portable spiritual food - Philippians

WILLIAM TAYLOR

The church at Philippi is considered to be one of the model churches of the New Testament.

But if this were a report at a shareholders' meeting we might be asking ourselves whether the Chairman has really got this right? Is something being hidden? It seems too good to be true! Can a church really be that good?

But there's no doubting that Paul has the right church. Perched on the edge of Southern Greece, Philippi was the first city to hear the Christian message in Europe - we have much to learn from the church that grew there. This fresh and lively study book is ideally suited to the more interactive way we learn in today's church.

> 'Who should this book be given to? Give it to a new Christian, and they will delight to find they really can understand a whole book of the Bible. Give it to a growing Christian, and they will have a model of how the Bible should be handled. Give it to an experienced Christian, and they will be reminded of how refreshing Bible Study can be. Most of all, give to a preacher and we'll all be a good deal better off!'

Evangelicals Now

> 'This book on Philippians exude the warmth of the letter itself. It engage with our lives and is insightfully applied. William is a man who recognises the eternal significance of pastoral leadership; it is his compassionate pastoral care, so evident at St Helen's, which reflects itself in his preaching and in this book.'

David Cook, Principal, Sydney Missionary Bible College

> '... a lively, brilliant and courageous exposition of Paul's Letter to the Philippians. I am delighted to recommend this gem of a book about a gem of a New Testament church. It is the work of a first class preacher of God's Word and deserves to be very widely read.'

Rev Dr. Mark Stibbe, St. Andrews, Chorleywood, England

William Taylor is the minister of St. Helen's, Bishopsgate, London

ISBN 978-1-84550-231-7

SPIRIT OF TRUTH

Unlocking the Bible's Teaching on the Holy Spirit

DAVID JACKMAN

THE SPIRIT OF TRUTH:

Unlocking the Bible's Teaching on the Holy Spirit

DAVID JACKMAN

The Holy Spirit has worked in the lives of believers since creation.

As Christ's replacement in the life of the church, the Holy Spirit has been even busier! He has been bringing people to repentance, comforting the broken-hearted, guiding the faithful and helping Christians to pray. The story of the church is his story too. Despite this pivotal role there is much debate in the church over the nature of his activity in our lives. Differing interpretations have resulted in divisions in the church.

This book clarifies the Holy Spirit's character and work, enabling the person leading a bible study or preaching to teach authoritatively about him: maintaining a healthy, vibrant church that honours God in unity - in spirit and truth.

The Church can only carry out the cultural and evangelistic mandates given to it if we listen to the Holy Spirit and work with him. Communities and nations can only be changed if people listen to his calling through the church.

David Jackman has produced a work that will be of immense help to Christians who seek to gain more of an understanding of how the Holy Spirit moves in our lives.

'In a topic usually known more for its disagreements, Jackman steers a sure-footed course through the main lines of thought about the Holy Spirit. Every Christian should be a theologian of the Holy Spirit and this book will greatly help us in this goal. It carries us along, with skillful and pastoral insight, to a greater appreciation for the third Person of the Trinity.'

Derek W. H. Thomas,
Reformed Theological Seminary, Jackson, Mississippi, USA

David Jackman is the President of the Proclamation Trust and was the founder-director of the Cornhill Training Course.

ISBN 978-1-84550-057-3

THE
PLEASURES
GOD OF

Revised and expanded edition

Voted one of the
century's top 100 books
by World Magazine

JOHN PIPER

THE PLEASURES OF GOD

JOHN PIPER

God is happiest being in the universe. To know him in his pleasures is to see him as he truly he is. This the proposition put forward by John Piper.

The things that make God glad are the measures of his greatness. John here studies 10 ways which God reveals gives him pleasure.

'...ranks as one of the top three books written this century on the being of God.'
L R Shelton Jr.

'This is a unique and precious book.'
J.I. Packer

'Again John Piper has provided a rich feast for the serious believer.'
John MacArthur

'I encourage you to read The Pleasures of God twice.'
Erwin Lutzer

'It is theology of the best and deepest sort.'
The Late Jame M. Boice

'This rich and profound book is for anyone who has grown weary of shallow, cotton candy ideas of God.'
The Christian Courier

'I have never felt more compelling responsibility that I felt from reading these chapters. The book is a gold mine. Don't just glance at it. Read, reflect and be enriched.'
Fellowship Today

Senior pastor of Behtlehem Baptist Church, Minneapolis, Minnesota, John Piper is the author of many books and a respected conference speaker. He holds degrees from Wheaton College, Fuller Seminary and the University of Munich (Doctor of Theology). He is married to Noel and they have four sons and a daughter.

ISBN 978-1-85792-700-9

St HELEN"S
MEDIA

St Helen's Bishopsgate in London is committed to serving the wider church by providing gospel-centred resources in both written and spoken format. The St Helen's Media website has a wide range of sermons available (on CD and for MP3 download) by Dick Lucas, William Taylor and many others. Books published by St Helen's include bible study resources on Romans in the *Read, Mark, Learn* series, *Dig Deeper (Tools to unearth the Bible's treasure)*, *Partnership* by William Taylor and *Just Love* by Ben Cooper.

Christian Focus Publications

publishes books for all ages

Our mission statement –

STAYING FAITHFUL

In dependence upon God we seek to help make His infallible Word, the Bible, relevant. Our aim is to ensure that the Lord Jesus Christ is presented as the only hope to obtain forgiveness of sin, live a useful life and look forward to heaven with Him.

REACHING OUT

Christ's last command requires us to reach out to our world with His gospel. We seek to help fulfil that by publishing books that point people towards Jesus and help them develop a Christ-like maturity. We aim to equip all levels of readers for life, work, ministry and mission.

Books in our adult range are published in three imprints.

Christian Focus contains popular works including biographies, commentaries, basic doctrine and Christian living. Our children's books are also published in this imprint.

Mentor focuses on books written at a level suitable for Bible College and seminary students, pastors, and other serious readers. The imprint includes commentaries, doctrinal studies, examination of current issues and church history.

Christian Heritage contains classic writings from the past.

Christian Focus Publications Ltd,
Geanies House, Fearn, Ross-shire,
IV20 1TW, Scotland, United Kingdom
info@christianfocus.com
www.christianfocus.com